ON LITERATURE

UMBERTO ECO

ON LITERATURE

Translated from the Italian
by Martin McLaughlin

HARCOURT, INC.

Orlando   Austin   New York   San Diego   Toronto   London

www.HarcourtBooks.com

This is a translation of *Sulla Letteratura*.

Library of Congress Cataloging-in-Publication Data
Eco, Umberto.
[Sulla letteratura. English]
On literature / Umberto Eco; translated from the Italian by
Martin McLaughlin.—1st U.S. ed.
p. cm.
Includes bibliographical references.
ISBN 0-15-100812-4
1. Literature—History and criticism. I. Title.
PN85.E4313 2004
809—dc22   2004010664
ISBN 0-15-100812-4

Text set in AGaramond
Designed by Cathy Riggs

Printed in the United States of America

First U.S. edition
A C E G I K J H F D B

CONTENTS

INTRODUCTION

This book gathers together a series of occasional writings, though all of them are concerned with the problem of literature. They are occasional in the sense that they were stimulated by the title of a conference, symposium, congress, or volume to which I had been invited to contribute. Sometimes being constrained by a theme (even though one clearly goes to conferences whose theme is closely linked to one's own interests) helps to develop a new thought, or simply to restate old ones.

All the pieces have been rewritten for this volume, sometimes abbreviated, sometimes expanded, sometimes trimmed of references that were too closely tied to the occasion. But I have not tried to hide this very quality, their occasional character.

The reader will be able to spot the return, in different essays, and perhaps even at some years' distance, of the same example or theme. This seems natural to me, since each one of us carries our own baggage of illustrative literary "places." And repetition (so long as it does not actually disturb the reader) serves to highlight these.

Some of these writings are also, or, rather, especially, auto-biographical or autocritical, in the sense that I speak of my own activity not as a theorist but as a practicing writer. As a general rule I do not like to confuse the two roles, but sometimes it is necessary, in order to explain what one means by literature, to turn to one's own experience—at least in informal occasions like the majority of those in this book. Moreover, the genre of "statement of poetics" is one that is authorized by a venerable tradition.

On Literature

ON SOME FUNCTIONS OF LITERATURE

Legend has it, and if it is not true it is still a good story, that Stalin once asked how many divisions the Pope had. Subsequent events have proved to us that while divisions are indeed important in certain circumstances, they are not everything. There are non-material forces, which cannot be measured precisely, but which nonetheless carry *weight*.

We are surrounded by intangible powers, and not just those spiritual values explored by the world's great religions. The power of square roots is also an intangible power: their rigid laws have survived for centuries, outliving not just Stalin's decrees but even the Pope's. And among these powers I would include that of the literary tradition; that is to say, the power of that network of texts which humanity has produced and still produces not for practical ends (such as records, commentaries on laws and scientific formulae, minutes of meetings or train schedules) but, rather, for its own sake, for humanity's own enjoyment—and which are read for pleasure, spiritual edification, broadening of knowledge, or maybe just to pass the time, without anyone forcing us to read them (apart from when we are obliged to do so at school or in the university).

True, literary objects are only partly intangible, since they usually come to us on paper. But at one stage they came to us through the voice of someone who was calling on an oral tradition, or written on stone, while today we are talking about the future of e-books, which apparently will allow us to read a collection of jokes or Dante's *Divine Comedy* on a liquid-crystal screen. Let me say at once that I do not intend to dwell this evening on the vexed question of the electronic book. I belong, of course, to those who prefer to read a novel or poem in the paper medium of books, whose dog-eared and crumpled pages I will even remember, though I am told that there is now a generation of digital hackers who, not having ever read a book in their lives, have now enjoyed *Don Quixote* for the first time thanks to the e-book. A clear gain for their minds but at a terrible cost for their eyesight. If future generations come to have a good (psychological and physical) relationship with the e-book, the power of *Don Quixote* will remain intact.

What use is this intangible power we call literature? The obvious reply is the one I have already made, namely, that it is consumed for its own sake and therefore does not have to serve any purpose. But such a disembodied view of the pleasure of literature risks reducing it to the status of jogging or doing crossword puzzles—both of which primarily serve some purpose, the former the health of the body, the latter the expansion of one's vocabulary. What I intend to discuss is therefore a series of roles that literature plays in both our individual and our social lives.

Above all, literature keeps language alive as our collective heritage. By definition language goes its own way; no decree from on high, emanating either from politicians or from the academy, can stop its progress and divert it toward situations that they claim are for the best. The Fascists tried to make Italians say *mescita* instead of *bar, coda di gallo* instead of *cocktail, rete* instead of *goal, auto pubblica* instead of *taxi,* and our language paid no attention. Then it suggested a lexical monstrosity, an unacceptable archaism like *autista* instead of *chauffeur,* and the language accepted it. Maybe because it avoided a sound unknown to Italian. It kept *taxi,* but gradually, at least in the spoken language, turned this into *tassì.*

Language goes where it wants to but is sensitive to the suggestions of literature. Without Dante there would have been no unified Italian language. When, in his *De Vulgari Eloquentia* (*On Vernacular Eloquence*), Dante analyzes and condemns the various Italian dialects and decides to forge a new "illustrious vernacular," nobody would have put money on such an act of arrogance, and yet with *The Divine Comedy* he won his bet. It is true that Dante's vernacular took several centuries to become the language spoken by all of us, but if it has succeeded it is because the community of those who believed in literature continued to be inspired by Dante's model. And if that model had not existed, then the idea of political unity might not have made any headway. Perhaps that is why Bossi does not speak an "illustrious vernacular."

Twenty years of Fascist talk of "Rome's fated hills" and "ineluctable destinies," of "unavoidable events" and "plows tracing furrows in the ground," have in the end left no trace in contemporary Italian, whereas traces have been left by certain virtuoso experiments of futurist prose, which were unacceptable at the time. And while I often hear people complain about the victory of a middle Italian that has been popularized by television, let us not forget that the appeal to a middle Italian, in its noblest form, came through the plain and perfectly acceptable prose of Manzoni, and later of Svevo or Moravia.

By helping to create language, literature creates a sense of identity and community. I spoke initially of Dante, but we might also think of what Greek civilization would have been like without Homer, German identity without Luther's translation of the Bible, the Russian language without Pushkin, or Indian civilization without its foundation epics.

And literature keeps the individual's language alive as well. These days many lament the birth of a new "telegraphese," which is being foisted on us through e-mail and mobile-phone text messages, where one can even say "I love you" with short-message symbols; but let us not forget that the youngsters who send messages in this new form of shorthand are, at least in part, the same young people who crowd those new cathedrals of the book, the multistory bookstores, and who, even when they flick through a book without buying it, come into contact with cultivated and elaborate literary styles to which their parents, and certainly their grandparents, had never been exposed.

Although there are more of them compared with the readers of previous generations, these young people clearly are a minority of the six billion inhabitants of this planet; nor am I idealistic enough to believe that literature can offer relief to the vast number of people who lack basic food and medicine. But I would like to make one point: the wretches who roam around aimlessly in gangs and kill people by throwing stones from a highway bridge or setting fire to a child—whoever these people are—turn out this way not because they have been corrupted by computer "new-speak" (they don't even have access to a computer) but rather because they are excluded from the universe of literature and from those places where, through education and discussion, they might be reached by a glimmer from the world of values that stems from and sends us back again to books.

Reading works of literature forces on us an exercise of fidelity and respect, albeit within a certain freedom of interpretation. There is a dangerous critical heresy, typical of our time, according to which we can do anything we like with a work of literature, reading into it whatever our most uncontrolled impulses dictate to us. This is not true. Literary works encourage freedom of interpretation, because they offer us a discourse that has many layers of reading and place before us the ambiguities of language and of real life. But in order to play this game, which allows every generation to read literary works in a different way, we must be moved by a profound respect for what I have called elsewhere the intention of the text.

On one hand the world seems to be a "closed" book, allowing of only one reading. If, for example, there is a law governing planetary gravitation, then it is either the right one or the wrong one. Compared with that, the universe of a book seems to us to be an open universe. But let us try to approach a narrative work with common sense and compare the assumptions we can make about it with those we can make about the world. As far as the world is concerned, we find that the laws of universal gravitation are those established by Newton, or that it is true that Napoléon died on Saint Helena on 5 May 1821. And yet, if we keep an open mind, we will always be prepared to revise our convictions the day science formulates the great laws of the cosmos differently, or a historian discovers unpublished documents proving that Napoléon died on a Bonapartist ship as he attempted to escape. On the other hand, as far as the world of books is concerned, propositions like "Sherlock Holmes was a bachelor," "Little Red Riding-Hood is eaten by the wolf and then freed by the woodcutter," or "Anna Karenina commits suicide" will remain true for eternity, and no one will ever be able to refute them. There are people who deny that Jesus was the son of God, others who doubt his historical existence, others who claim he is the Way, the Truth, and the Life, and still others who believe that the Messiah is yet to come, and however we might think about such questions, we treat these opinions with respect. But there is little respect for those who claim that Hamlet married Ophelia, or that Superman is not Clark Kent.

Literary texts explicitly provide us with much that we will never cast doubt on, but also, unlike the real world, they flag with supreme authority what we are to take as important in them, and what we must *not* take as a point of departure for freewheeling interpretations.

At the end of chapter 35 of *The Red and the Black,* Julien Sorel goes to the church and shoots at Madame de Rênal. After observing that Julien's arm was trembling, Stendhal tells us that the protagonist fires a first shot and misses his target. Then he fires again, and the woman falls. We might claim that his trembling arm and the fact that his first shot missed prove that Julien did not go to the church with firm homicidal intentions, but, rather, was drawn there by a passionate, if vaguely intentioned, impulse. Another interpretation can be placed beside this one, namely, that Julien had originally intended to kill, but that he was a coward. The text allows for both interpretations.

Some people have wondered where the first bullet went—an intriguing question for Stendhal aficionados. Just as devotees of Joyce go to Dublin to seek out the chemist shop where Bloom bought a lemon-shaped bar of soap (and in order to satisfy these literary pilgrims, that chemist's, which really does exist, has begun to produce that kind of soap again), in the same way one can imagine Stendhal fans trying to find both Verrières and the church in the real world, and then scrutinizing every pillar to find the bullet hole. This would be a rather amusing instance of a literary devotee's obsession. But let us suppose that a critic wanted to base his entire interpretation of the novel on the fate of that missing bullet. In times like ours this is not impossible. There are people who have based their entire reading of Poe's "Purloined Letter" on the position of the letter with regard to the mantelpiece. But while Poe makes the position of the letter explicitly relevant, Stendhal tells us that nothing more is known about that first bullet and thus excludes it from the realm of fictitious speculation. If we wish to remain faithful to Stendhal's text, that bullet is lost forever, and where it ended up is ultimately irrelevant in the context of the narrative. On the other hand, what remains unsaid in Stendhal's *Armance* regarding the protagonist's potential impotence pushes the reader toward frenetic hypotheses in order to complete what the story does not tell us explicitly. Similarly, in Manzoni's *I promessi sposi* (*The Betrothed*) a phrase like "the unfortunate woman responded" does not tell us the lengths to which Gertrude has gone in her sin with Egidio, but the dark halo of hypotheses stirred up in the reader is part of the fascination of this highly chaste and elliptical passage.

At the beginning of *The Three Musketeers* it is said that D'Artagnan arrived at Meung on a fourteen-year-old nag on the first Monday of April, 1625. If you have a good program on your computer, you can immediately establish that that Monday was the 7th of April. A juicy tidbit of trivia for devotees of Dumas. Can one base an overinterpretation of the novel on this detail? I would say no, because the text does not make that detail relevant. Over the course of the novel it becomes clear that D'Artagnan's arrival on a Monday was not particularly important—whereas the fact that it was in April is quite relevant (one must remember that in order to hide the fact that his splendid shoulder strap was embroidered only on the front, Porthos was wearing a long cloak of crimson velvet, which the season did not justify—so much so that the musketeer had to pretend that he had a cold).

All this may seem quite obvious to many people, but such obvious (if often forgotten) points remind us that the world of literature inspires the certainty that there are some unquestionable assumptions, and that literature therefore offers us a model, however fictitious, of truth. This literal truth impinges on what are often called hermeneutic truths: because whenever someone tries to tell us that D'Artagnan was motivated by a homosexual passion for Porthos, that Manzoni's Innominato was driven to evil by an overwhelming Oedipus complex, that the Nun of Monza was corrupted by Communism, as certain politicians today might wish to suggest, or that Panurge acts the way he does out of hatred for nascent capitalism, we can always reply that it is not possible to find in the texts referred to any statement, suggestion, or insinuation that allows us to go along with such interpretative drift. The world of literature is a universe in which it is possible to establish whether a reader has a sense of reality or is the victim of his own hallucinations.

Characters migrate. We can make true statements about literary characters because what happens to them is recorded in a text, and a text is like a musical score. It is true that Anna Karenina commits suicide in the same sense that it is true that Beethoven's Fifth Symphony is in C minor (and not in F major, like the Sixth) and begins with "G, G, G, E-flat." But certain literary characters—not all of them by any means—leave the text that gave birth to them and migrate to a zone in the universe we find very difficult to delimit. Narrative characters migrate, when they are lucky, from text to text, and it is not that those who do not migrate are ontologically different from their more fortunate brethren; it is just that they have not had the luck to do so, and we do not encounter them again.

Both mythical characters and those from "secular" narratives have migrated from text to text (and through adaptations into different mediums, from book to film or to ballet, or from oral tradition to book): Ulysses, Jason, King Arthur or Parsifal, Alice, Pinocchio, D'Artagnan. Now, when we talk about such characters are we referring to a particular score? Let's take the case of Little Red Riding-Hood. The most famous scores, Perrault's and the Grimms', display profound differences. In the former the little girl is eaten by the wolf and the story finishes there, inspiring severe moralistic reflections on the risks of not being careful. In the latter the huntsman arrives, kills the wolf, and restores the child and her grandmother to life. Happy ending.

Now let us imagine a mother telling the tale to her children and stopping when the wolf devours Little Red Riding-Hood. The children would protest and demand the "true" story, in which Little Red Riding-Hood comes back to life, and it would be pointless for the mother to claim that she was a strict textual philologist. Children know the "true" story, in which Little Red Riding-Hood really does revive, and this story is closer to the Grimms' version than to Perrault's. Yet it does not coincide exactly with the Grimms' score, because it omits a whole series of minor details—on which the Grimms and Perrault disagree in any case (for instance, what kind of gifts Little Red Riding-Hood is bringing to her grandmother)—details children are more than willing to compromise on, because they concern a character who is much more schematic, more fluctuating in the tradition, and who appears in various scores, many of them oral.

Thus Little Red Riding-Hood, D'Artagnan, Ulysses, or Madame Bovary become individuals with a life apart from their original scores, and even those who have never read the archetypal score can claim to make true statements about them. Even before reading *Oedipus Rex* I had learned that Oedipus marries Jocasta. However fluctuating, these scores are not unverifiable: anyone who claimed that Madame Bovary reconciles with Charles and lives happily ever after with him in the end would meet with the disapproval of people of sound common sense, who share a set of assumptions regarding Emma's character.

Where exactly are these fluctuating individuals? That depends on the format of our ontology, whether it also has room for square roots, the Etruscan language, and two different ideas on the Most Holy Trinity—the Roman one, which holds that the Holy Spirit proceeds from the Father *and* the Son ("ex Patre Filio*que* procedit"), and the Byzantine one, which has it that the Spirit proceeds only from the Father. But this region has a very imprecise status and contains entities of varying substance, for even the Patriarch of Constantinople (who is ready to fight the Pope over the "Filio*que*" question) would agree with the Pope (at least I hope he would) in saying that it is true that Sherlock Holmes lives on Baker Street, and that Clark Kent is the same person as Superman.

Nevertheless, it has been written in countless novels or poems that—I'm inventing examples at random here—Hasdrubal kills Corinna or Theophrastus is madly in love with Theodolinda, and yet no one believes that true statements can be made on these matters, because these ill-starred characters have never left their native text or managed to become part of our collective memory. Why is the fact that Hamlet does not marry Ophelia any more true than the fact that Theophrastus married Theodolinda? What is that part of our world where Hamlet and Ophelia live but not poor old Theophrastus?

Certain characters have become somehow true for the collective imagination because over the course of centuries we have made emotional investments in them. We all make emotional investments in any number of fantasies, which we dwell on either with open eyes or half-awake. We can be moved by thinking about the death of someone we love, or experience physical reactions when imagining ourselves having an erotic relationship with that person. Similarly, we can be moved by Emma Bovary's fate through a process of identification or projection, or, as happened to several generations, be drawn toward suicide by the misfortunes of young Werther or Jacopo Ortis. However, if someone were to ask us if the person whose death we imagined was really dead, we would reply no, that it was a totally private fantasy of our own. Whereas if someone asks us whether Werther really did kill himself, we reply yes, and the fantasy we are talking about here is not private, it is a real fact on which the entire community of readers agrees. So much so that anyone who killed himself just because he had imagined (being well aware that this was simply the product of his imagination) that his loved one was dead would be judged by us to be mad, while somehow or other we try to justify someone killing himself because of Werther's suicide, knowing full well that the latter was a fictional character.

We will have to find a space in the universe where these characters live and shape our behavior to such an extent that we choose them as role models for our life, and for the life of others, so that we are clear about what we mean when we say that someone has an Oedipus complex or a Gargantuan appetite, that someone behaves quixotically, is as jealous as Othello, doubts like

Hamlet, is an incurable Don Juan, or is a Scrooge. And in literature this happens not only with characters but also with situations and objects. Why do the women who come and go, talking of Michelangelo, Montale's sharp shards of bottles stuck in the wall in the dazzling sun, Gozzano's good things of bad taste, Eliot's fear that is shown us in a handful of dust, Leopardi's hedge, Petrarch's clear cool waters, Dante's bestial meal, become obsessive metaphors, ready to tell us over and over again who we are, what we want, where we are going, or what we are not and what we don't want?

These literary entities are here among us. They were not there from the beginning of time as (perhaps) square roots and Pythagoras's theorem were, but now that they have been created by literature and nourished by our emotional investment in them, they do exist and we have to come to terms with them. Let us even say, to avoid ontological and metaphysical discussions, that they exist like a cultural habitus, a social disposition. But even the universal taboo of incest is a cultural habitus, an idea, a disposition, and yet it has had the power to shape the destinies of human societies.

However, as some people today claim, even the most enduring literary characters risk becoming evanescent, mobile, and shifting, losing that fixity which forced us to acknowledge their destinies. We have now entered the era of electronic hypertext, which allows us not only to travel through a textual labyrinth (be it an entire encyclopedia or the complete works of Shakespeare) without necessarily "unraveling" all the information it contains but to penetrate it like a knitting needle going into a ball of wool. Thanks to hypertext, the phenomenon of free creative writing has become a reality. On the Internet you can find programs that let you write stories as a group, joining in narratives whose denouement one can change ad infinitum. And if you can do this with a text that you are jointly creating with a group of virtual friends, why not do the same with already existing literary texts, buying programs that allow you to change the great narratives that have obsessed us for millennia?

Just imagine that you are avidly reading *War and Peace,* wondering whether Natasha will finally give in to Anatoly's blandishments, whether that wonderful Prince Andrej will really die, whether Pierre will have the courage to shoot Napoléon, and now at last you can re-create your own Tolstoy, conferring a long, happy life on Andrej, and making Pierre the liberator of Europe. You could even reconcile Emma Bovary with poor Charles and make her a happy and fulfilled mother, or decide that Little Red Riding-Hood goes into the woods and meets Pinocchio, or rather, that she gets kidnapped by her stepmother, given the name Cinderella, and made to work for Scarlett O'Hara; or that she meets a magic helper named Vladimir J. Propp in the woods, who gives her a magic ring that allows her to discover, at the foot of the Thugs' sacred banyan tree, the Aleph, that point from which the whole universe can be seen. Anna Karenina doesn't die beneath the train because Russian narrow-gauge railways, under Putin's government, are less efficient than their submarines, while away in the distance, on the other side of Alice's looking-glass, is Jorge Luis Borges reminding Funes the Memorious not to forget to return *War and Peace* to the Library of Babel . . .

Would this be so bad? No, in fact, it has already been done by literature, from Mallarmé's notion of *Le Livre* to the surrealists' exquisite corpses to Queneau's *One Hundred Million Million Poems* and the unbound books of the second avant-garde. And then there are the jam sessions of jazz music. Yet the fact that the jam session exists, where every evening a variation on a particular musical theme is played, does not prevent or discourage us from going to concert halls, where every evening Chopin's Sonata in B-flat Minor, op. 35, will finish in the same way.

Some say that by playing with hypertexts we escape two forms of oppression: having to follow sequences already decided on by others, and being condemned to the social division between those who write and those who read. This seems silly to me, but certainly playing creatively with hypertexts—changing old stories and helping create new ones—can be an enthralling activity, a fine exercise to be practiced at school, a new form of writing very much akin to the jam session. I believe it can be good and even educational to try to modify stories that already exist, just as it would be interesting to transcribe Chopin for the mandolin: it would help to sharpen the musical brain, and to understand why the timbre of the piano was such an integral element of the Sonata in B-flat Minor. It can be educational for one's visual taste and for the exploration of forms to experiment with collages by putting together fragments of *The Marriage of the Virgin,* of *Les Demoiselles d'Avignon* and the latest Pokémon story. This is essentially what great artists have always done.

But these games cannot replace the true educational function of literature, an educational function that is not simply limited to the transmission of moral ideas, whether good or bad, or to the formation of an aesthetic sense.

Jurij Lotman, in his *Culture and Explosion,* takes up Chekhov's famous advice, namely, that if a story or play mentions or shows a shotgun hanging on the wall, then before the end that gun has to go off. Lotman suggests that the real question is not whether the gun will actually be fired or not. The very fact that we do not know whether it will be fired confers significance on the plot. Reading a story means being seized by a tension, a thrill. Discovering at the end whether the gun has gone off or not involves more than a simple piece of information. It is the discovery that things happen, and have always happened, in a particular way, no matter what the reader wants. The reader must accept this frustration, and through it sense the power of Destiny. If you could decide on characters' destinies it would be like going to the desk of a travel agent who says: "So where do you want to find the whale, in Samoa or in the Aleutian Islands? And when? And

do you want to be the one who kills it or let Queequeg do it?"
Whereas the real lesson of *Moby-Dick* is that the whale goes wherever it wants.

Think of Victor Hugo's description of the battle of Waterloo
in *Les Misérables.* Unlike Stendhal's description of the battle
through the eyes of Fabrizio del Dongo, who is in the midst of it
and does not know what is going on, Hugo describes it through
the eyes of God, seeing it from above. He is aware that if Napoléon
had known that there was a steep descent beyond the crest of the
Mont-Saint-Jean plateau (but his guide had not told him so),
General Milhaud's cuirassiers would not have perished at the feet
of the English army; and that if the little shepherd guiding Bülow
had suggested a different route, the Prussian army would not have
arrived in time to decide the outcome of the battle.

With a hypertextual structure we could rewrite the battle of
Waterloo, making Grouchy's French arrive instead of Blücher's
Germans. There are war games that allow you to do such things,
and I'm sure they are great fun. But the tragic grandeur of those
pages by Hugo resides in the notion that things go the way they
do, and often in spite of what we want. The beauty of *War and
Peace* lies in the fact that Prince Andrej's agony ends with his
death, however sorry it makes us. The painful wonder that every
reading of the great tragedies evokes in us comes from the fact
that their heroes, who could have escaped an atrocious fate,
through weakness or blindness fail to realize where they are heading, and plunge into an abyss they have often dug with their own
hands. In any case, that is the sense conveyed by Hugo when,
after showing us other opportunities Napoléon could have seized
at Waterloo, he writes, "Was it possible for Napoléon to win that
battle? We reply no. Why? Because of Wellington? Because of
Blücher? No. Because of God."

This is what all the great narratives tell us, even if they replace God with notions of fate or the inexorable laws of life. The
function of "unchangeable" stories is precisely this: against all our

desires to change destiny, they make tangible the impossibility of changing it. And in so doing, no matter what story they are telling, they are also telling our own story, and that is why we read them and love them. We need their severe, "repressive" lesson. Hypertextual narrative has much to teach us about freedom and creativity. That is all well and good, but it is not everything. Stories that are "already made" also teach us how to die.

I believe that one of the principal functions of literature lies in these lessons about fate and death. Perhaps there are others, but for the moment none spring to mind.

Lecture given at the Literature Festival, Mantua, September 2000.

A READING OF THE *PARADISO*

"As a result, the *Paradiso* is not read or appreciated very much. Its monotony is particularly tedious: it reads like a series of questions and answers between teacher and pupil." Thus Francesco De Sanctis in his *History of Italian Literature* (1871). He articulates a reservation many of us had in school, unless we had an outstanding teacher. Whatever the case, if we look through some more recent histories of Italian literature, we find that Romantic criticism downgraded the *Paradiso*—a disapproval that also carried weight into the next century.

Since I want to maintain that the *Paradiso* is the finest of the three canticas of *The Divine Comedy*, let us go back to De Sanctis, a man of his time certainly, but also a reader of exceptional sensibilities, to see how his reading of the *Paradiso* is a masterpiece of inner torment (on the one hand I say one thing, on the other another), a revealing mixture of enthusiasm and misgivings.

De Sanctis, a very acute reader, immediately realizes that in the *Paradiso* Dante speaks of ineffable things, of a spiritual realm, and wonders how the realm of the spirit "can be represented." Consequently, he says, in order to make the *Paradiso* artistic Dante has imagined a human paradise, one that is accessible to the senses and the imagination. That is why he tries to find in light the link with our human potential for comprehension. And here De Sanctis becomes an enthusiastic reader of this poetry where there are no qualitative differences, only changes in luminous intensity, and he cites "the throngs of splendours" (*Par.* 23.82), the clouds "like diamonds whereon the sun did strike" (*Par.* 2.33), the blessed appearing "like a swarm of bees delving into flowers" (*Par.* 31.7), "rivers from which living flames leap out, lights in the shape of a river that glows tawny with brightness" (*Par.* 30.61–64), the blessed disappearing "like something heavy into deep water" (*Par.* 3.123). And he observes that when Saint Peter denounces Pope Boniface VIII, recalling Rome in terms that smack more of the *Inferno*: "he [Boniface] has made a sewer of my burial-place, a sewer of blood and stench" (*Par.* 27.25–26), all the heavenly host expresses its contempt by simply turning red in color.

But is a change in color an adequate expression of human passions? Here De Sanctis finds himself a prisoner of his own poetics: "In that whirlwind of movement, the individual disappears. [. . .] There is no change in features, just one face, as it were. [. . .] This disappearance of forms and of individuality itself would reduce the *Paradiso* to just one note, if the earth did not come into it, and with the earth other forms and other passions. [. . .] The songs of the souls are devoid of content, mere voices not words, music not poetry. [. . .] It is all just one wave of light. [. . .] Individuality disappears in the sea of being." If poetry is the expression of human passions, and if human passion can only be carnal, this is an unacceptable flaw. How can this compare with Paolo and Francesca kissing each other "on the mouth, all trembling"? Or with the horror of Ugolino's "bestial meal," or the sinner who makes the foul gesture toward God?

The contradiction in which De Sanctis is caught rests on two misunderstandings: first, that this attempt to represent the divine merely through intensity of light and color is Dante's original but almost impossible attempt to humanize what human beings cannot conceive; and second, that poetry exists only in representations of the carnal passions and those of the heart, and that poetry of pure understanding cannot exist, because in that case it would be music. (And at this point, we might well pause to mock not good old De Sanctis but the "Desanctism" of those fools who assert that Bach's music is not real poetry, but that Chopin's comes a bit closer, lucky for him, and that the Well-Tempered Clavier and the Goldberg Variations don't speak to us of earthly love, but the Raindrop Prelude makes us think of George Sand and the shadow of consumption hanging over her, and this, for God's sake, is true poetry because it makes us cry.)

Let us begin with the first point. Cinema and role-playing games encourage us to think of the Middle Ages as a series of "dark" centuries; I don't mean this in an ideological sense (which is not important in the cinema anyhow) but rather in terms of nocturnal colors and brooding shadows. Nothing could be more false. For while the people of the Middle Ages certainly did live in dark forests, castle halls, and narrow rooms barely lit by the fire in the hearth, apart from the fact that they were people who went to bed early, and were more used to the day than to the night (so beloved by the Romantics), the medieval period represents itself in ringing tones.

The Middle Ages identified beauty with light and color (as well as with proportion), and this color was always a simple harmony of reds, blues, gold, silver, white, and green, without shading or chiaroscuro, where splendor is generated by the harmony of the whole rather than being determined by light enveloping things from the outside, or making color drip beyond the confines of the figures. In medieval miniatures light seems to radiate outward from the objects.

For Isidore of Seville, marble is beautiful because of its whiteness, metals for the light they reflect, and the air itself is beautiful and bears its name because *aer-aeris* derives from the splendor of *aurum,* i.e., gold (and that is why when air is struck by light, it seems to shine like gold). Precious gems are beautiful because of their color, since color is nothing other than sunlight imprisoned and purified matter. Eyes are beautiful if luminous, and the most beautiful eyes are sea green eyes. One of the prime qualities of a beautiful body is rose-colored skin. In poets this sense of flashing color is ever present: the grass is green, blood is red, milk is white. For Guido Guinizelli a beautiful woman has a "face of snowy whiteness colored with carmine," Petrarch writes of "clear, cool and sweet waters," and Hildegard of Bingen's mystic visions show us glowing flames and compose even the beauty of the first fallen angel from gems shining like a starry sky, so that the countless number of sparks, shining in the bright light of all his ornaments, fills the world with light. In order to allow the divine to penetrate its otherwise dark naves, the Gothic church is cut through with blades of light from its windows, and it is to make room for these corridors of light that the space increases thanks to the side windows and rose windows, so that the walls almost disappear in a play of buttresses and climbing arches. The whole church is built on this system of light bursting through a fretwork of structures.

Huizinga reminds us of Froissart the chronicler's enthusiasm for ships with flags and ensigns fluttering in the wind, and gaily colored escutcheons flashing in the sun, the play of the sun's rays on helmets, breastplates, lance tips, the pennants and banners of knights marching; and in coats of arms, the combinations of pale yellow and blue, orange and white, orange and pink, pink and white, black and white; and a young damsel in purple silk on a white horse with a saddlecloth of blue silk, led by three men clothed in vermilion and capes of green silk.

At the root of this passion for light there were theological influences of distant Platonic and Neoplatonic origin (the Supreme Good as the sun of ideas, the simple beauty of a color given by a shape that dominates the darkness of matter, the vision of God as Light, Fire, or Luminous Fountain). Theologians make light a metaphysical principle, and in these centuries the study of optics develops, under Arab influence, which leads in turn to ideas about the marvels of the rainbow and the miracles of mirrors (in Dante's third cantica the mirrors often appear to be liquid and mysterious).

Dante did not, therefore, invent his poetics of light by playing on a subject matter that was recalcitrant to poetry. He found it all around him, and he reformulated it, as only he could, for a reading public who felt light and color as passions. In rereading one of the best essays I know on Dante's *Paradiso,* Giovanni Getto's "Aspetti della poesia di Dante" (Aspects of Dante's Poetry, 1947), one can see that there is not a single image of Paradise that does not stem from a tradition that was part of the medieval reader's heritage, I won't say of ideas, but of daily fantasies and feelings. It is from the biblical tradition and the church fathers that these radiances come, these vortices of flames, these lamps, these suns, these brilliances and brightnesses emerging "like a horizon clearing" (*Par.* 14.69), these candid roses and ruby flowers. As Getto says, "Dante found before him a terminology, or, rather, a whole language already established to express the reality of the life of the spirit, the mysterious experience of the soul in its catharsis, the life of grace as stupendous joy, a prelude to a joyous, sacred eternity." For medieval man, reading about this light and luminosity was equivalent to when we dream about the sinuous gracefulness of a movie star, the elegant lines of a car, the love of lost lovers, brief encounters, or the magic of old films and love songs, and they read it all with a deeply passionate intensity that is unknown to us. This is anything but doctrinal poetry and debates between teacher and pupil!

We now come to the second misunderstanding: that there cannot be poetry of pure intellect, capable of thrilling us not just at the kiss of Paolo and Francesca but at the architecture of the heavens, at the nature of the Trinity, at the definition of faith as the substance of things hoped for and the evidence of things unseen. It is this appeal to a poetry of understanding that can make the *Paradiso* fascinating even for the modern reader who has lost the reference points familiar to his medieval counterpart. Because in the meantime this reader has known the poetry of John Donne, T. S. Eliot, Valéry, or Borges, and knows that poetry can also be a metaphysical passion.

Speaking of Borges, from whom did he get the idea of the Aleph, that fateful single point which showed the populous sea, dawn and dusk, the multitudes of the Americas, a silver cobweb in the center of a black pyramid, a broken labyrinth that was London, an inner courtyard in Calle Soler with the same tiles he had seen thirty years previously in the entryway of a house in Calle Frey Bentos, bunches of grapes, snow, tobacco, veins of metal, steam coming off waters, convex equatorial deserts, an unforgettable woman in Inverness, an exemplar of the first translation of Pliny in a house in Adrogué, and simultaneously every letter on every page, a sunset at Querétaro that seemed to reflect the color of a rose in Bengal, a terraqueous globe placed between two mirrors that multiplied it endlessly in a study in Alkmaar, a beach on the Caspian Sea at dawn, a pack of tarot cards in a shopwindow at Mirzapur, pistons, herds of bison, tides, all the ants that live on the earth, a Persian astrolabe, and the shocking remains of what had once been the delicious Beatriz Viterbo? The first Aleph appears in the final canto of the *Paradiso,* where Dante sees (and, as far as he can, makes us see) "bound with love in a single volume whatever is spread throughout the universe, substances and accidents and their behavior, almost fused together . . ." (*Par.* 33.88–89). In describing "the universal form of this bond," with "mind suspended and inadequate language," in "that clear subsistence," Dante sees three circles of three colors, and not, like Borges, the shocking remains of Beatriz Viterbo, because his Beatrice, who had turned into shocking remains some time previously, has come back again as light—and so Dante's Aleph is more passionately rich in hope than the one in Borges's hallucination, which is clearly informed by the understanding that he would not be allowed to see the Empyrean, and that all he had left was Buenos Aires.

It is in the light of this centuries-old tradition of metaphysical poetry that the *Paradiso* can best be read and appreciated today. But I would like to add one further point, to strike the imagination of young readers, or of those who are not particularly interested in God or intelligence. Dante's *Paradiso* is the apotheosis of the virtual world, of nonmaterial things, of pure software, without the weight of earthly or infernal hardware, whose traces remain in the *Purgatorio.* The *Paradiso* is more than modern; it can become, for the reader who has forgotten history, a tremendously real element of the future. It represents the triumph of pure energy, which the labyrinth of the Web promises but will never be able to give us; it is an exaltation of floods and bodies without organs, an epic made of novas and white dwarf stars, an endless big bang, a story whose plot covers the distance of light-years, and, if you really want familiar examples, a triumphant space odyssey, with a very happy ending. You can read the *Paradiso* in this way too; it can never do you any harm, and it will be better than a disco with strobe lights or ecstasy. After all, with regard to ecstasy, Dante's third cantica keeps its promises and actually delivers it.

Written as an article for *la Repubblica* on 6 September 2000, in a series of pieces to celebrate the seventh centenary of *The Divine Comedy.*

ON THE STYLE OF
THE COMMUNIST MANIFESTO

It is difficult to imagine that a few fine pages can single-handedly change the world. After all, Dante's entire oeuvre was not enough to restore a Holy Roman Empire to the Italian city-states. But, in commemorating *The Communist Manifesto* of 1848, a text that certainly has exercised a major influence on the history of two centuries, I believe one must reread it from the point of view of its literary quality, or at least—even if one does not read it in the original German—of its extraordinary rhetorical skill and the structure of its arguments.

In 1971 a short book by a Venezuelan author was published: Ludovico Silva's *Marx's Literary Style.* (An Italian translation was published in 1973.) I think it is no longer available, but it would be worthwhile reprinting it. In this book Silva retraces the development of Marx's literary education (few know that he had also written poetry, albeit awful poetry, according to those who have read it), and goes on to analyze in detail Marx's entire oeuvre. Curiously, he devotes only a few lines to the *Manifesto,* perhaps because it was not a strictly personal work. This is a pity, for it is an astonishing text that skillfully alternates apocalyptic and ironic tones, powerful slogans and clear explanations, and (if capitalist society really does want to seek revenge for the upheavals these few pages have caused it) even today it should be read like a sacred text in advertising agencies.

It starts with a powerful drumroll, like Beethoven's Fifth: "A specter is haunting Europe" (and let us not forget that we are still close to the pre-Romantic and Romantic flowering of the gothic novel, and specters are to be taken seriously). This is followed immediately by a bird's-eye history of class struggle from ancient Rome to the birth and development of the bourgeoisie, and the pages dedicated to the conquests achieved by this new, "revolutionary" class constitute a foundation epic that is still valid today, for supporters of free-market enterprise. One sees (I really do mean "one sees," in an almost cinematographic way) this unstoppable force, which, urged on by the need for new markets for its goods, pervades the whole world on land and sea (and, as far as I am concerned, here the Jewish, Messianic Marx is thinking of the opening of Genesis), overturns and transforms distant countries because the low prices of products are its heavy artillery, which allows it to batter down any Chinese wall and force surrender on even the barbarians who are most hardened in their hatred for the foreigner; it sets up and develops cities as a symbol and as the foundation of its own power; and it becomes multinational, globalized, and even invents a literature that is no longer national but international.*

---

*Obviously, when I wrote this article, the term "globalization" already existed, and I did not use the expression by chance. But today, now that all of us have become sensitive to this problem, it really is worth going back and rereading these pages. It is astonishing how the *Manifesto* witnessed the birth, 150 years ahead of its time, of the era of globalization, and the alternative forces it would unleash. It almost suggests that globalization is not an accident that happens during the course of capitalist expansion (just because the Wall has come down and the Internet has arrived) but rather the inevitable pattern that the emergent class could not fail to follow, even though at the time, through the expansion of markets, the most convenient (though also the most bloody) means to this end was called colonization. It is also worth dwelling again (and this is advisable not just for the bourgeoisie but for all classes) on the warning that every force opposing the march of globalization is initially divided and confused, tends toward mere Luddism, and can be used by its enemy to fight its own battles.

At the end of this eulogy (which is convincing and borders on sincere admiration), suddenly we find a dramatic reversal: the wizard discovers that he is unable to control the subterranean powers he has conjured up, the victor is suffocated by his own overproduction and is forced to bring forth from his loins the digger of his own grave—the proletariat.

This new force now enters the scene: at first divided and confused, it is forged in the destruction of machinery and then used by the bourgeoisie as shock troops forced to fight its enemy's enemies (the absolute monarchies, the landed property holders, the petite bourgeoisie), until gradually it absorbs the artisans, shopkeepers, and peasant landowners who once were its adversaries but have now been turned into proletarians by the bourgeoisie. The upheaval becomes struggle as workers organize thanks to another power that the bourgeoisie developed for its own profit: communications. And here the *Manifesto* cites the example of the railways, but the authors are also thinking of new mass media (and let's not forget that in *The Holy Family* Marx and Engels were able to use the television of that age—namely, the serial novel—as a model of the collective imagination, and they criticized its ideology by using the very language and situations the serials had made popular).

At this point the Communists come onstage. Before saying in a programmatic way what they are and what they want, the *Manifesto* (in a superb rhetorical move) puts itself in the position of the bourgeois who fears them, and advances some terrified questions: Do you want to abolish property? Do you want common access to women? Do you want to destroy religion, the nation, the family?

Here things become more subtle, because the *Manifesto* seems to reply to all these questions in a reassuring way, as though to mollify its adversaries—then, in a sudden move, it hits them in the solar plexus, winning the cheers of the proletarian public . . . Do we want to abolish property? Of course not. But property relations have always been subject to change: did not the French Revolution abolish feudal property in favor of bourgeois property? Do we want to abolish private property? What a crazy idea; there is no chance of that, because it is the property of a tenth of the population, which works against the other nine-tenths. Are you reproaching us for wanting to abolish "your" property? Well, yes, that is exactly what we want to do.

Common access to women? Come on, we prefer to relieve women from their role as instruments of production. Do you see us having common access to women? Possessing women in common was invented by you, since apart from using your own wives you take advantage of workers' wives, and as your ultimate sport you practice the art of seducing your peers' wives. Destroy the nation? But how can you take from the workers something they have never possessed? On the contrary, we want to turn ourselves into a nation and triumph . . .

And so on up to the masterpiece of reticence that is the reply to the question of religion. We can intuit that the reply is "We want to destroy this religion," but the text does not say so: just when it broaches such a delicate topic, it glides over it and lets us infer that all transformations come at a price, but for goodness' sake, let's not take up such delicate issues immediately.

There then follows the most doctrinal part, the movement's program, the critique of different kinds of socialism, but by this stage the reader is already seduced by the preceding pages. And just in case the programmatic part is too difficult, here we find a final sting in the tail, two breathtaking slogans, easy, memorable and destined (it seems to me) to have an extraordinary future: "Workers have nothing to lose but their chains," and "Workers of the world, unite!"

Even apart from its genuinely poetic capacity to invent memorable metaphors, the *Manifesto* remains a masterpiece of political (but not only political) oratory, and it ought to be studied at school along with Cicero's *Invectives against Catiline* and Mark Antony's speech over Julius Caesar's body in Shakespeare, especially as it is not impossible, given Marx's familiarity with classical culture, that he had in mind these very texts when writing it.

Article published in *L'Espresso,* 8 January 1998, for the 150th anniversary of *The Communist Manifesto.*

THE MISTS OF THE VALOIS

I discovered *Sylvie* when I was twenty, almost by chance, and I
read it knowing very little about Nerval. I read the story in a state
of total innocence, and I was bowled over. Later I discovered that
it had made the same impression on Proust as it did on me. I do
not remember how I articulated this impression in the vocabulary I had then, especially as now I can only express it in Proust's
words from the few pages he devotes to Nerval in *Contre Sainte-
Beuve* (*Against Sainte-Beuve*).

    Sylvie is certainly not, as Barrès (and a certain strand of "reac-
tionary" criticism) insisted, a typically French, neoclassical idyll;
it does not express a rootedness in the French soil (if anything, by
the end the protagonist feels uprooted). *Sylvie* speaks to us of
something that has unreal colors, the kind of thing we sometimes
see when asleep and whose contours we would like to pin down,
and which we inevitably lose when we awake. *Sylvie* is the dream
of a dream, and its oneiric quality is such that "we are constantly
compelled to go back to the preceding pages, to see where we
are. . . ." The colors in *Sylvie* are not those of a classic watercolor:
Sylvie is of "a purple color, a pink-purple color like purple-violet

satin, at the opposite pole from the watercolor tones of 'moderate France.'" It is a model not of "gracefulness full of restraint" but, rather, of a "morbid obsession." The atmosphere of *Sylvie* is "bluish and purple," although this atmosphere is found not in the words but in the spaces between one word and another: "like the mists in a morning at Chantilly."*

Perhaps at twenty I could not have put it like this: but I emerged from the story as though my eyes were glazed, not quite as happens in dreams, but, rather, as though I were on that morning threshold when you slowly awaken from a dream, you confuse the first conscious reflections with the last glimmers of the dream, and you cannot make out (or have not yet crossed) the border between dream and reality. Without having read Proust at that time, I knew I had felt the mist-effect.

I have reread this story very many times in the course of the last forty-five years, and on each occasion I would try to explain to myself or to others why it had this effect on me. Each time I thought I had discovered the reason, and yet each time I started to reread it I would find myself as at the beginning, still a victim of the mist-effect.

In what follows I will try to explain why and how the text manages to produce its mist-effects. But whoever wants to follow me must not be afraid of losing the magic of *Sylvie* by knowing too much about it. On the contrary, the more the reader knows about it, the more able will s/he be to reread it with renewed astonishment.†

---

*Marcel Proust, "Gérard de Nerval," in *Against Sainte-Beuve,* trans. John Sturrock (Harmondsworth: 1994), 24–33.

†A piece of advice I must give to the reader is to read (or reread) the text of *Sylvie* before tackling this essay. Before moving on to critical reflection it is important to discover or rediscover the pleasure of an "innocent" reading. Moreover, seeing that I will often refer to the various chapters, and that we have just said, in Proust's words, that "we are constantly compelled to go back to the preceding pages, to see where we are," it is indispensable to experience personally this to-ing and fro-ing.

LABRUNIE AND NERVAL

I must begin with a very important distinction. I want to eliminate from the outset an unwelcome character—namely, the empirical author. The empirical author of this story was called Gérard Labrunie, and he wrote under the nom de plume of Gérard de Nerval.

If we try to read *Sylvie* thinking about Labrunie, we are immediately on the wrong track. For instance, one then has to try, as many critics have done, to see how and to what extent the facts narrated in *Sylvie* refer to Labrunie's life. Thus it is that editions and translations of *Sylvie* are generally accompanied by biographical notes debating whether Aurélie was the actress Jenny Colon (incidentally, whoever looks at her portrait, reproduced in various editions, becomes seriously disillusioned), whether there really was an archery company at Loisy (or whether it was not rather at Creil), whether Labrunie really had received an inheritance from his uncle, or whether the character of Adrienne was based on Sophie Dawes, Baroness of Feuchères. Many solid academic reputations have been built on the basis of such meticulous research, all very useful for writing a biography of Gérard Labrunie but not for understanding *Sylvie*.

Gérard Labrunie committed suicide after passing through several psychiatric clinics, and we know from one of his letters that he had written *Sylvie* in a state of hyperexcitement, in pencil and on tiny sheets of paper. But if Labrunie was mad, Nerval was not; that is to say, there was no madness in that Model Author we manage to discern only through a reading of *Sylvie*. This text tells the story of a protagonist who borders on madness, but it is not the work of someone who is unwell: whoever wrote it (and this person is the one that I shall from now on call Nerval), it is constructed with astonishing care, with a play of internal textual symmetries, oppositions, and echoes.

If Nerval is not a character who is extraneous to the story, how does he appear in it? First and foremost as narrative strategy.

Story and Plot

In order to understand Nerval's narrative strategy and how he manages to create in the reader the mist-effects I spoke of, I refer you to Table A.* Along the horizontal axis I have plotted the sequence of chapters in the tale, while on the left, vertical axis, I have reconstructed the temporal sequence of the events mentioned in the story. Thus, along the vertical axis I have plotted the *fabula* or story, and along the horizontal axis the development of the plot.

The plot is the way in which the story is constructed and gradually revealed to us: a young man comes out of a theater and decides to go to the ball at Loisy, during his journey there he recalls a previous journey, arrives at the ball, sees Sylvie again, spends a day with her, goes back to Paris, has an affair with the actress, and finally (Sylvie is by now married in Dammartin) decides to tell his own story. Seeing that the plot begins on the evening when the protagonist was coming out of a theater (conventionally represented as $Time^1$), the development is represented by the black line that proceeds from that evening, through successive moments in time ($Time^1$—$Time^{14}$), to the end of the story.

But in the course of these events previous times are recalled, represented by the arrows pointing upward to times preceding $Time^1$. The unbroken vertical lines represent the protagonist's reconstructions, the dotted lines represent references to the past that occur, sometimes fleetingly, in the course of the dialogues

---

*A similar table appeared in *Six Walks in the Fictional Woods,* page 40. Table A and Table B are taken from the Einaudi translation of *Sylvie,* by kind permission of the publisher.

TABLE A

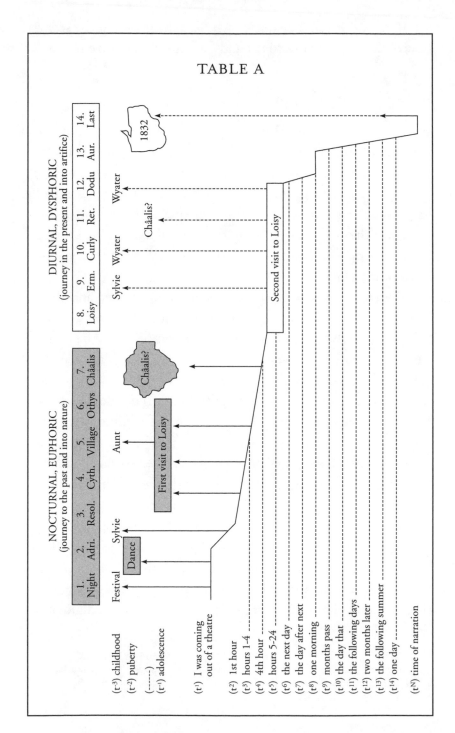

between the various characters. For instance, between 1 A.M. and 4 A.M. the protagonist recalls his previous journey to Loisy (in *Time¹*), which on the plot level takes up three chapters, whereas in chapters 9 and 10 there are fleeting evocations of episodes in Sylvie's life as a young girl and the "wyater" event, in *Time⁻³*.

Thanks to these flashbacks one can reconstruct the story *by fits and starts,* or, rather, the temporal sequence of all the events the plot mentions: initially, when the protagonist was small, he loved Sylvie; then, when slightly older, he meets Adrienne at a ball; later he goes back to Loisy; finally, one evening, when the boy has become a man, he decides to go back there, and so on.

The plot is just that, we have it before our eyes as we read. The story, on the other hand, is not so obvious, and it is in the attempt to reconstruct the story that some mist-effects are created, since we never quite catch precisely what time the narrating voice is referring to. I do not claim to dissolve the mist-effects with my table, but rather to explain how they come about. And the story is reconstructed in a hypothetical way, in the sense that it is *probable* that the events evoked correspond to experiences lived through initially at age ten or eleven, then between fourteen and sixteen, and finally between sixteen and eighteen (but one could even count this differently: the protagonist might have been extremely precocious, or a very late bloomer).

The extent to which the reconstruction (and it is only a probable one) must be based on the text and not on elements of Labrunie's biography is confirmed by the experience of some commentators who try to place the evening at the theater in 1836, since the moral and political climate evoked seems to fit the one obtaining at that time, and the club mentioned is apparently the Café de Valois, which was subsequently closed at the end of 1836, along with other gaming houses. If we collapse the protagonist onto Labrunie, a rather grotesque series of problems ensues. How old was the young man, then, in 1836, and how old was he when he saw Adrienne at the ball? Since Labrunie (born in 1808) stopped living with his uncle at Mortefontaine in 1814 (at age six), when did he go to the ball? If he started at the Collège Charlemagne in 1820, at the age of twelve, is that when he goes back in the summer to Loisy and sees Adrienne? But in that case is he twenty-eight that evening at the theater? And if, as many accept, the visit to Sylvie's aunt at Othys happens three years before, is it not a rather big boy of twenty-five who plays with Sylvie, dressing up as gamekeepers, and is treated by her aunt as a nice little blond lad? A big boy who has received an inheritance of thirty thousand francs in the meantime (1834), and who has already traveled to Italy—a genuine initiation rite—and in 1827 has already translated Goethe's *Faust*? As you see, there is no solution here, and so one must reject such biographical calculations.

JE-RARD AND NERVAL

The story begins: "Je sortais d'un théâtre." We have here two entities (an "I" and a theater) and one verb in the imperfect.

Since it is not Labrunie (whom we have abandoned to his sad fate), who is the "Je" who is speaking? In a first-person narrative the person who says "I" is the protagonist of the story, and not necessarily the author. Therefore (having excluded Labrunie), *Sylvie* is written by Nerval, who brings onto the scene an "I" who tells us something. We thus have the narration of a narration. To eliminate any doubt, let us decide that the "I" who was coming out of a theater at the beginning is a character we will call "Je-rard."

But *when* does Jerard speak? He speaks in what we will call the Time of Narrative Enunciation (or $Time^N$); that is to say, at the point when he begins writing and recalling his past by telling us that one day (*Time^1*, the Beginning of the Plot) he was coming out of a theater. If you like, given that the story was published in 1853, we could think that $Time^N$ is that year, but this would be pure convention, just to allow us to attempt a backward calculation. Since we do not know how many years pass between

Time^{14} and *Time*^{N} (but it must be many, because at *Time*^{N} he already remembers that Sylvie has two children who are old enough to be archers), the evening at the theater could be placed either five or ten years previously; it does not matter, so long as one imagines that at *Time*$^{-3}$ Jerard and Sylvie were still children.

So the Jerard speaking at *Time*^{N} tells us about a self of many years previously, who in turn was recalling events concerning Jerard the child and adolescent. Nothing strange here: we too can say, "When I [I^1, who am speaking now] was eighteen [I^2, then], I could not get over the fact that I at sixteen [I^3] had been involved in an unhappy love affair." But this does not mean that I^1 still feels the adolescent passion of I^3, nor that he can explain the melancholy memories of I^2. At most he can recall them indulgently and tenderly, thus revealing himself to be different from who he had once been. In a certain sense this is what Jerard does, except that, realizing that he is so different each time, he can never tell us with which of his past I's he identifies, and he ends up so confused about his own identity that in the course of the story he never names himself once, except in the first paragraph of chapter 13, when he refers to himself as "an unknown admirer." Thus even that first-person pronoun, apparently so clearly defined, always denotes an Other.

Yet it is not only that there are so many Jerards, it is also the fact that sometimes the narrator is not Jerard but Nerval, who, as it were, creeps into the tale. Note that I said "into the tale," not into the story or plot. Story and plot coincide, but only because they are communicated to us through a *discourse*. To make the point more clearly, when I translated *Sylvie* I changed its original discourse in French into a discourse in Italian, while trying to keep the same story and plot. A film director could "translate" the plot of *Sylvie* into a film, allowing the spectator to reconstruct the story through a series of fade-outs and flashbacks (though I would not like to say with what degree of success), but he certainly could not translate the discourse like I did, since he would have to change words into images, and there is a difference between writing "as pale as the night" and showing the image of a pale woman.

Nerval never appears in story or plot, but he does in the discourse, and not only (as would happen with any author) as the mechanism that selects the words and articulates them in phrases and sentences. He comes in surreptitiously, as a "voice" speaking to us his model readers.

Who is it that says (in the second paragraph of Chapter 3), "Let us go back to reality"? Is it Jerard talking to himself after wondering whether Adrienne and Aurélie were the same person? Is it Nerval encouraging his character or us readers who have been caught up in that enchantment to go back to reality? Later on, between one and four in the morning, while Jerard is traveling toward Loisy, the text says: "While the carriage is climbing up the hills, let us piece together the memories of the time when I used to come here so often." Is this Jerard in $Time^3$ talking, in a kind of interior monologue that is happening at the present time of the first verb? Or is it Jerard in $Time^N$, saying "while *that character* is climbing uphill in the carriage, let us abandon him for a moment and try to go back to a previous period"? And is that "let us piece together" an exhortation by Jerard to himself, or by Nerval to his readers, inviting us to participate in the course of his writing?

Who is it that says at the beginning of chapter 14, "Such are the chimeras which bewitch us and lead us astray at the dawn of our lives"? It could be Jerard in $Time^N$, participant in and victim of his own past illusions, but it will be noted that that observation justifies *the order in which the events have been narrated,* with a direct address to the readers ("but many hearts will understand me"). The person who is speaking—therefore—does not seem to be Jerard, but the author of the book we are reading.

Much has been written on this interplay of voices, but everything remains unresolved. It is Nerval himself who has decided to remain unresolved, and he tells us so not only to join us in our sense of bewilderment (and to understand it) but also to compound it. Over the course of fourteen chapters we never know whether the person who is speaking is saying things or is *representing* someone else who is saying things—nor is it ever entirely clear whether this someone is experiencing these things or simply recalling them.

LEAVING THE THEATER?

Right from the first sentence of the story, the theme of the theater literally takes center stage, and it will be present until the end of the tale. Nerval was a man of the theater, Labrunie had really fallen in love with an actress, Jerard loves a woman he has seen on the stage, and he haunts various stages until near the end of the story. But the theater reappears in *Sylvie* at every moment: the dance on the lawn with Adrienne is a theatrical event, as are the flower festival at Loisy (and the basket from which the swan rises is a theatrical machine), the mise-en-scène that Jerard and Sylvie devise at her aunt's house, and the sacred drama at Châalis.

In addition, many have noted that Nerval uses a kind of theatrical lighting for the most crucial scenes. The actress appears at first illuminated by the footlights on the stage, then by the light of the auditorium chandelier, but theatrical lighting techniques are also put into play at the first dance on the lawn, where the sun's last rays arrive through the foliage of the trees, which act as a curtain; and while Adrienne sings, she is picked out as it were by the light of the moon (and she emerges from what today we would call a spotlight with a graceful bow, worthy of an actress saying farewell to her audience). At the beginning of chapter 4, in "The Journey to Cythera" (which above all is a verbal representation of a visual one, inspired as it is by one of Watteau's paintings), the scene is again illuminated from above by the vermilion rays of the evening. Finally, when Jerard enters the ball at Loisy in chapter 8, we witness a masterpiece of stage direction, which gradually leaves the bases of the lime trees in shade and tinges their summits in a bluish light until, in this struggle between artificial light and the dawning day, the stage is slowly pervaded by the pale light of day.

We must therefore not allow ourselves to be deceived by a "crude" reading of *Sylvie* and say that—as Jerard is torn between the dream of an illusion and the desire to find reality—the story plays on a clear and precise contrast between the theater and reality. First and foremost, every time Jerard leaves one theater he enters another. He begins, already in the second chapter, with a celebration of the sole truth of illusion, which intoxicates him. In chapter 3 he seems to begin a journey toward reality, since the Sylvie he wants to reach does "exist," but again he finds her to be no longer a creature of nature but one steeped in culture, who sings with musical "phrasing" (and who by now uses her aunt's wedding clothes to go to a masked ball, and is prepared, like a consummate actress, to imitate Adrienne and sing once more the song she sang at Châalis, with Jerard acting as director). And consequently Jerard himself behaves like a theatrical character (in chapter 11) when he makes the final attempt to conquer her, adopting a pose out of classical tragedy.

Thus the theater is sometimes the place of all-conquering and redeeming illusion, sometimes the place of disillusion and disappointment. What the story questions (creating in the process another mist-effect) is not the opposition between illusion and reality but the fracture that cuts through the two worlds and mixes them up.

SYMMETRIES OF PLOT

If we go back to Table A, we see that the fourteen chapters into which the plot is organized can be divided into two halves, one largely nocturnal, the other prevalently diurnal. The nocturnal sequence concerns a world lovingly evoked in memory and in dreams: everything in it is experienced in a euphoric tone, in the enchantment of nature, and characters move slowly through space, which is described with a full range of cheerful details. In the diurnal sequence, on the other hand, Jerard finds a Valois that is mere artifice, made up of fake ruins, where the same stages of the preceding journey are revisited in a state of dysphoria, without dwelling on the landscape and focusing solely on epiphanies of disappointment.

From the fourth to the sixth chapter, after the festival, which had been an opportunity for fairy tale–like surprises such as the appearance of the swan, and the encounter with Sylvie, who by now seems to embody the gracefulness of the two exorcised ghosts, Jerard makes his way through the forest at night (with the help of a moon that is also theatrical as it lights up the sandstone rocks): in the distance pools dot the misty plain, the air is perfumed, and gradually elegant medieval ruins can be seen on the horizon. The village is jolly, Sylvie's bedroom is virginal as she works at her lace cushion, and the journey to her aunt's house is a feast of flowers, amid buttercups and great tits, periwinkles and foxgloves, and the hedges and streams that the two young people happily leap over. The river Thève gradually becomes smaller as they approach its source, and comes to rest in the fields, forming a little lake between irises and gladioli. There is little more to say about the eighteenth-century idyll at Othys, where the past smells so good.

In the second journey (chapters 8–11), Jerard arrives when the festival is over, the flowers in Sylvie's hair and on her bodice are fading, the Thève shows pools of stagnant water, and the perfume of the hayricks no longer inebriates the way it once did. If in the first journey to Othys the two youngsters leaped over hedges and streams, now they do not even think of crossing the fields.

Without describing the journey, Jerard goes to his uncle's house and finds it abandoned, the dog dead, and the garden overgrown with weeds. He takes the road for Ermenonville, but oddly the birds are silent and the place-names on the signposts have faded. What he does see are the artificial reconstructions of the Temple of Philosophy, but by now these too are in ruins; the laurels have disappeared, and on the (artificial) lake, beneath Gabrielle's tower, "the scum bubbles up and the insects drone." The air is mephitic, the sandstone is dusty, everything is sad and solitary. When Jerard arrives at Sylvie's bedroom, canaries have replaced the linnets, the furniture is modern and affected, Sylvie herself no longer makes her bobbins resound but works a "mechanism," and her aunt is dead. The walk to Châalis will be not a mad dash through the meadows but a slow journey with the help of a little donkey, in the course of which they will no longer gather flowers but instead will compete in terms of culture, in an atmosphere of mutual mistrust. Near Saint-S*** they have to watch where they put their feet because treacherous streams meander through the grass.

When finally, in chapter 14, Jerard returns to those very same places, he will no longer find the woods that once were there, Châalis is being restored, the pools that have been dug up show in vain the stagnant water "that the swans now shun," there is no longer a direct road to Ermenonville, and the space has become even more of a senseless labyrinth.

The search for inverted symmetries could be carried farther, and it has been by many, so much so that what emerges are relations of almost diametrical opposition between the various chapters (that is to say, between the first and the last chapter, the second and the thirteenth, etc., even though the correspondences do not follow this rule precisely). Here are the most glaring examples:

EUPHORIC	DYSPHORIC
1. Archery as mythical evocation	14. Archery as children's game
2. Adrienne's graceful farewell, as she heads for the monastic life	13. Aurélie's graceful farewell, woman of the world

EUPHORIC	DYSPHORIC
2. The kiss as mystic experience	8. The kiss is merely affectionate
2. All thought they were in paradise	4. This is simply an old genteel festival
2. Jerard is the only boy at the dance	4. Each boy has a girl partner
3. Broken clock: promise of time to be recovered	12. Broken clock: memory of lost time
5 Solitary, enchanted walk	9. Solitary, depressed walk
6. Uplifting walk and visit to her aunt	10. The aunt is dead, embarrassed departure for Châalis
7. Apparition of Adrienne singing	11. Vague recollection of Adrienne; Sylvie sings

In fact, the disturbing Châalis chapter breaks the symmetry and separates the first six chapters from the remaining seven. On the one hand we have in this seventh chapter a reversal of the ball in chapter 4: this is an aristocratic celebration as opposed to the people's festival on the island (there are no young people except on the stage: Jerard and Sylvie's brother creep in only as intruders), it is set in a closed space as opposed to the open space of Cythera, Adrienne's apocalyptic song contrasts with the sweet song she sang while still an adolescent, and finally, this is a funereal celebration as opposed to a *Pervigilium Veneris,* the return of his obsession with Adrienne as opposed to the reconciliation and conquest of Sylvie . . .

The chapter contains themes from the other chapters as well, but they are dreamily unresolved and neutralized. It cites without any obvious reason the archery contest, the clock, a kind of dance-spectacle, a crown that is a halo of gilt cardboard, and above all a swan. Many critics imply that the swan is not just an emblem, a coat of arms engraved or sculpted (as the heraldic term "éployé" would suggest), but a real swan crucified on the door. This seems excessive, even though in a dream everything is possible, but whatever it is, this swan is halfway between the living, triumphant swan of chapter 4, and the one that is now absent in chapter 14.

There has been talk of "degradation rituals," but one does not need to uncover all the symmetries in order to detect them. The correspondences work almost unbeknownst to the reader; each return of a motif that has already been sounded causes a sense of déjà vu, but we notice only that something that we thought we had been given has been taken from us.

GOING ROUND AND ROUND

Mist-effects, labyrinth-effects: Poulet has spoken of "metamorphoses of the circle." Perhaps critics have seen more circles than there really are in *Sylvie,* like the magic circle of the stage, the concentric circles of the dance on the lawn (the dance on the "pelouse" framed by the trees, the one that involved the circle of young girls and finally, in the whirlwind of the dance, as though in a close-up, the long gold circles of the girl's hair), and in the second festival at Loisy the three circles of the pool, the island, and the temple. But sometimes I feel as if they have underestimated the circles.

For instance, in chapter 9, during the visit to his dead uncle's house, the word *"jardin"* is repeated three times in the same paragraph. This is not stylistic slackness: there are three gardens, belonging to three different epochs, but arranged concentrically, if not in terms of spatial perspective at least in a temporal one. It is as if Jerard's eye saw first his uncle's garden, in the distance the circle of his childhood, and farther away again the circle of History (the garden as the eternal place of archaeological finds). In a sense this triple garden becomes as it were the miniature model of the whole story, but seen from its final point. From a place re-visited in a state of disillusionment (by now the garden is just a mass of weeds), there emerges in the mists of memory first the trace, still well-defined though partially canceled out, of the child's enchanted universe; and then in the distance, when the garden is the object no longer of Jerard's eye but of his memory, amid the fragments lined up in his study, one hears the echo of those Roman and Druidic times that had already been summoned up at the beginning of the story.

Finally, it is a circular movement that Jerard carries out in each of his visits to Loisy: first of all leaving from Paris, only to return in the space of a day, then leaving from the village, only to return after crossing pools, woods, and moors.

This circling-round is worthy of an effort that almost amounts to a land survey, but I believe it is worth doing. I decided to draw a map of the places (Table B), more to help myself when translating *Sylvie*. Even though I kept my eye on several maps of the Valois,* I did not go in for the excessive nuances of meridians and parallels, and I tried to give an approximate visualization of the mutual relationships between villages and forests. However that may be, it should be borne in mind that from Luzarches to Ermenonville is about twenty kilometers as the crow flies, from Ermenonville to Loisy three kilometers, and two from Loisy to

---

*In a fit of obsessive precision I actually visited the places. Naturally the roads are no longer the same, but the forests and many pools are still there (those near Commelle are particularly evocative, with the swans and Queen Blanche's castle). You can follow the Thève in its meandering route, the structure of Ermenonville is still more or less what it once was, with the road passing above La Launette and the four dovecotes, Châalis is still touchingly dilapidated, and at Loisy they show you what was presumably Sylvie's house. The greatest danger for the sentimental Nervalian is to come across, somewhere between Orry and Morte-fontaine, the Parc Astérix, and to find, in the desert, a reconstruction of the Wild West and the Sahara, with Indians and dromedaries (France's Disneyland is not far off). Forget about the road to Flanders, because Gonesse is close to Charles de Gaulle airport, stuck between high-rise blocks and refineries. But after Louvres you can start to go back to your memories again, and the mists are still what they once were, even though the distant landscape has to be seen from a motorway.

Mortefontaine. We are told in chapter 13 that the dance in front of the castle with Adrienne took place near Orry. But I have identified the place of the first and second dance at Loisy as the pools immediately north of Mortefontaine, where the Thève now rises (but at that time apparently it rose between Loisy and Othys).

If you read while also looking at the map, the space comes to look like a bit of chewing gum, changing shape every time you chew it over. It seems impossible that the post carriage takes the route it does to drop Jerard near Loisy, but who knows what the roads were like then? The route chosen by Sylvie's brother on the night at Châalis totally throws commentators with a passion for checking topography, and they solve the problems by noting that the boy was tipsy. Did one really have to go through Orry and run parallel to Halatte Forest to get from Loisy to Châalis? Or were the two youths not coming from Loisy? Sometimes it seems that Nerval is reconstructing his own Valois but that he cannot avoid interference from Labrunie's. The text says that Jerard's uncle stayed at Montagny, while we know that Labrunie's uncle stayed at Mortefontaine. Now if we reread carefully, following the table, we see that—if Jerard's uncle stayed at Montagny—this does not work out, and we are forced to conclude that he stayed at Mortefontaine, or, rather, that—in the Valois of the story—Montagny occupies the exact spot where Mortefontaine is.

Jerard, in chapter 5, says that after the dance he goes with Sylvie and her brother to Loisy, and then "returns" to Montagny. It is obvious that he can return only to Mortefontaine, all the more so since he goes up through a little wood between Loisy and Saint-S*** (which in reality is Saint-Sulpice, a stone's throw from Loisy), goes along the edge of Ermenonville forest, clearly to the southwest, and after sleeping sees nearby the walls of the convent of Saint-S***, and in the distance La Butte aux Gens d'Armes, the ruins of the abbey of Thiers, the castle of Pontarmé,

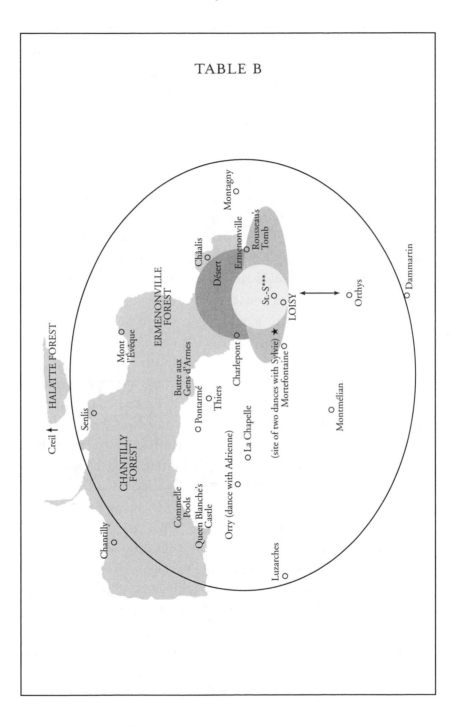

TABLE B

all of which are places to the northwest of Loisy, where he returns to. He cannot have taken the road for Montagny, which is too far to the east.

At the beginning of chapter 9 Jerard goes from the spot where the dance had taken place to Montagny, then goes back on the road to Loisy, finds everyone asleep, heads toward Ermenonville, leaves the "Desert" on the left, reaches Rousseau's tomb, and then goes back to Loisy. If he really went to Montagny he would be taking a very long route by crossing the Ermenonville area, and it would be crazy to return to Loisy—crossing back through the Ermenonville area—only then to decide to go up once more toward Ermenonville, and finally return again to Loisy.

In biographical terms this might mean that Nerval had decided to move his uncle's house to Montagny, and then was not able to maintain the fiction, and kept on thinking (along with Labrunie) of Mortefontaine. But this question must be of only minimal importance to us, unless we are seized by the desire go and take the walk again. The text is there only to make us travel in a Valois where memory is confused with dreams, and its function is to make us lose our bearings.

If that is the case, why make such efforts to reconstruct the map? I think most readers give up, as I did for many years, because it is enough for them to be seized by the fascination of the names. Proust already pointed out how much power names have in this story, and concluded that whoever has read *Sylvie* cannot fail to feel a thrill when they happen to read the name of Pontarmé on a train schedule. However, he also pointed out that other place-names, equally famous in the history of literature, do not cause the same turmoil in us. Why do the toponyms that appear in this tale become embedded in our mind (or heart) like a musical sequence, a Proustian "petite phrase"?

The answer seems obvious to me: because they keep returning. Readers rarely draw maps for themselves, but they sense (in their ears) that with every "return" to the Valois, Jerard goes back to the same places, almost in the same order, as if the same motif started up after every stanza. In music this form is called a rondo, and the term *"rondeau"* comes from *"ronde,"* which means a round dance. So readers perceive aurally a circular structure, and in some sense *they see it*, yet they see it only in a confused way, as if it were a spiral movement, or a successive shifting of circumferences.

For this reason it is worth reconstructing the map, to understand visually what the text makes us feel aurally. You will see on my little table, starting from Loisy, three nonconcentric, differently shaded circles. They trace the three main walks—not the real journey, but the presumed area of the trip. The lightest circle refers to Jerard's nocturnal walk in chapter 5 (from Loisy to Montagny—or, rather, Mortefontaine—but changing direction to skirt the Ermenonville forest, going past Saint-S***, and returning at last to Loisy, while Pontarmé, Thiers, or La Butte can be seen in the distance); the slightly shaded circle represents Jerard's walk in chapter 9 (from the dance area to his uncle's house—which must be at Mortefontaine—then to Loisy and finally to Ermenonville as far as Rousseau's tomb, and returning once more to Loisy); the darkest circle follows Jerard's and Sylvie's walk to Châalis in chapters 10 and 11 (from Loisy, through the forest of Ermenonville as far as Châalis, then back to Loisy via Charlepont). The journey to Othys is a round trip to the eighteenth century and back.

Finally, the biggest circle, which covers the entire area in Table B, corresponds to the wanderings with Aurélie in chapter 13. Jerard tries desperately to find everything and loses the central core of his first wanderings. He will never find it again. In the end, since Sylvie by now lives in Dammartin, the returns mentioned in chapter 14 never go beyond the margins of this circumference. Jerard, Sylvie, everyone, they are all now excluded from the magic circle at the start, which Jerard can see only at a great distance, from a hotel window.

In any case, what strikes us visually (as we previously had been struck aurally, albeit in the guise of echoes answering each other from a distance) is that in every journey Jerard simply goes around in a circle (not as in the perfect circle of the first dance with Adrienne, but like a crazed moth fluttering inside a lamp-shade on a chandelier) and never rediscovers what he had left there on the previous occasion. So much so that one has to agree with Poulet, who saw in this circular structure a temporal meta-phor: it is not so much Jerard who goes around in circles in space; it is time, his own past dancing in a circle around him.

THE IMPERFECT

Let us go back to the first sentence in the story: "Je sortais d'un théâtre." We have considered the implications of that "Je" and of that "théâtre," now let us consider the "sortais." The verb is in the imperfect.

The imperfect is a tense of duration and is often iterative. It always expresses an action not fully completed, and all we need is a tiny contextual hint to establish whether the action is also itera-tive, that is to say, is carried out several times. The fact is that Jerard came out of that theater every evening, and had been doing so for a year.*

I apologize for the apparent tautology, but the imperfect is so called because it is in fact im-perfect: it moves us to a time before

---

*Unhappy the languages that do not have the imperfect and try to render Nerval's opening. A nineteenth-century English translation (*Sylvie: A Recollection of Valois* [New York: Rout-ledge and Sons, 1887]) tried this: "I quitted a theater where I used to appear every night," while a more recent one went for: "I came out of a theater where I used to spend money every evening," and we have no idea where that mention of spending money comes from, but perhaps the translator wants us to realize that this was a habit, a vice, something that had been going on too long (Nerval, *Selected Writings*, trans. Geoffrey Wagner [New York: Grove Press, 1957]). What lengths people will go to make up for the absence of the imper-fect! The most recent translation, by Richard Sieburth (*Sylvie* [New York: Penguin, 1995]) seems to me more faithful: "I was coming out of a theater where, night after night, I would appear in one of the stage boxes. . . ." It is rather long, but it conveys the durative and itera-tive nature of the original imperfect.

the present in which we are speaking, but it does not tell us exactly when or how long it went on for. Hence its fascination. Proust said (speaking of Flaubert): "I confess that certain uses of the imperfect indicative—of this cruel tense which presents life to us as something ephemeral and at the same time passive, which at the very moment it summons up our actions stamps them with illusion, and obliterates them in the past without leaving us, like the simple past does, the consolation of activity—have remained for me an inexhaustible source of mysterious sadness."*

All the more reason why in *Sylvie* the imperfect is the tense that forces us to lose our sense of the confines of time. It is used with apparent generosity, and yet with mathematical caution, so much so that in the changes from the first to the second version of *Sylvie* Nerval adds one imperfect but eliminates another. In the first chapter, when he discovers that he is rich, Jerard writes, in 1853, "Que dirait maintenant, *pensai-je,* le jeune homme de tout à l'heure" (What would the young man of a few moments ago say now, I thought) and then "Je frémis de cette pensée" (I trembled at that thought). In 1854 he corrects this to *"pensais-je"* (I was thinking). In fact this is correct, since the imperfect appears in those lines to present us with the narrator's thoughts, a stream of thoughts that lasts in time: Jerard dreams for a certain number of seconds (or minutes) of the idea of a possible conquest of the actress, without making up his mind. Then, suddenly, and only then, with the return to the simple past (*"Je frémis"*), he definitively rejects that fantasy.

On the other hand, at the end of chapter 2, in 1853 Adrienne *"repartait"* (was leaving again), whereas in 1854 Adrienne *"repartit"* (left again). Rereading the passage one sees that up until that point everything has taken place in the imperfect, almost as if to make the whole scene more nebulous, and only at that point

---

*"Journées de lecture," in *Pastiches et mélanges* (Paris: Gallimard, 1919, ed. 1958), 239 n 1.

something definitely happens that belongs not to the dreamworld but to reality. The next day Adrienne disappears. Her departure is abrupt and definitive. In fact, aside from the ambiguous oneiric episode in chapter 7, this is the last time Jerard sees her—or at least has the good fortune to be near her.

In any case, the reader is well warned right from the first chapter, where in the space of the first five paragraphs there are no fewer than fifty-three imperfects out of a total of sixty or so verb forms. In those first five paragraphs everything that is described happened habitually, for some time, every evening. Then in the sixth paragraph someone "said" something, or, rather, someone asks Jerard "who it is" that he goes to the theater to see. And Jerard "said" her name. The nebulous temporality becomes more concrete, becomes solid at a precise moment: the story starts at that point, or, rather, that point signals $Time^1$, from which Jerard (who is recalling this in $Time^N$) makes the story of his journey start.

The extent to which the imperfect nebulizes time can be seen in the Châalis chapter. The person who intervenes twice in the present indicative (the first time to describe the abbey, the second to tell us that in summoning up those details the speaker wonders whether they are real or not) is Nerval—or Jerard in $Time^N$. Everything else is in the imperfect—except where syntax will not permit it. The analysis of the verb tenses in this chapter would require too many grammatical subtleties. But all we need to do is reread the chapter several times, listening attentively to the music of those tenses, and we realize why not only we but also Nerval himself hesitates to say whether this is a nightmare or a memory.

The use of the imperfect takes us back to the distinction between story, plot, and discourse. The choice of a verb tense takes place on the level of discourse, but the vagueness thus established at the discursive level impinges on our capacity to reconstruct the story by way of the plot. This is why critics are unable to agree on the sequence of events, at least so far as the first seven chapters are concerned. In order to extricate ourselves from the tangle of tenses, let us label as "the first dance" the one that takes place in front of the castle with Adrienne (perhaps at Orry), as "the second dance" the one at the festival with the swan (the first trip to Loisy), and as "the third dance" the one Jerard gets to just as it ends, after his journey in the carriage.

When does the episode of the night at Châalis happen? Before or after the first visit to Loisy? Again, remember that we are not dealing with a forensic problem here. It is the unconscious reply to this question that the reader is seeking, the one that plays the greatest role in creating the mist-effect.

One critic (and this shows just how powerful the mist-effect is) has even advanced the hypothesis that Châalis comes *before* the first dance on the lawn—on the grounds that in chapter 2, paragraph 5, it is said that after the dance "we would never see her again." But this cannot be before the dance, and for three reasons: first, Jerard *recognizes* Adrienne at Châalis, whereas he sees her for the first time at the dance (and this is confirmed in the third chapter); second, the young girl is already "transfigured" by her monastic vocation that night, whereas in the second chapter we were told that she would devote herself to the religious life only after the dance; and third, the scene of the first dance is described at the beginning of the fourth chapter as a childhood memory, and one cannot see how, when they were even younger, Jerard and Sylvie's brother had gone on a cart through the woods at night to watch a sacred mystery play.

In that case Châalis comes between the first and second dance. But this would presuppose that in the time between those two events Jerard had gone once more to Loisy. And in that case why is Sylvie sulky with him upon his arrival at the second dance, as though she still felt the humiliation she had suffered in Adrienne's presence? But this could be another mist-effect. The text does not in fact state that Sylvie is sulking with him because of that ancient betrayal—if anything it is Jerard who thinks this. Both she and her brother reproach him for not having been in touch "for so long." What is to say that this long time extends from the first dance? Jerard could have returned in the meantime, on any occasion, and enjoyed an evening with her brother. And yet this solution is not convincing because that evening Jerard gives the impression of seeing Sylvie for the first time since the first dance, finding her transformed and more fascinating than before.

So Jerard could have gone to Châalis after the second dance (in $Time^{-1}$). But how could that be if, according to most critics, the second dance happens three years before the evening at the theater, and once more, on arriving, Jerard is rebuked for not having been in touch for so long? Here too, perhaps we are victims of a mist-effect. The text does not in fact say that the second dance ($Time^{-1}$) happened three years before the evening at the theater. The text (chapter 3, third paragraph) says of Sylvie, "Why have I forgotten her for three years?" It says not that three years have gone by since the second dance, but (paragraph seven) that Jerard had been wasting the inheritance left him by his uncle for three years, and one can imagine that in those three years of high living he had forgotten about Sylvie. Between the second dance and the evening at the theater many more years could have passed.

But whatever hypothesis is chosen, how does one place Châalis with respect to the year of 1832, when Adrienne dies? It certainly would be touching to think that Adrienne dies (is dying, is already dead) when Jerard sees (or dreams he sees) her at Châalis.

It is such calculations, apparently so persnickety, that explain why we readers (like Proust) feel obliged constantly to turn back to earlier pages of the story to understand "where we are." Of course, in this matter too, it could be Labrunie who is confused. But if his overeager biographers were not so obsessive in providing us with the unfortunate writer's clinical charts, we would simply say, when we read the text, that we do not know where we are because Nerval did not want us to know. Nerval does the opposite of the author of a detective novel, who plants clues in the text so that when we reread it we tell ourselves that we should have guessed the truth immediately. Nerval puts us off the scent, and wants us to lose "the sequence of events."

And that is why Jerard tells us (in the first chapter) that he could not keep track of the order of events and (at the beginning of chapter 14) that he tried to pin down his own chimeras "without paying attention to their order." In the universe of *Sylvie*, where someone said that time passes in fits and starts, "the clocks do not work."

Elsewhere, taking as an example the clock described in chapter 3, I said that a "symbolic mode" is inserted into a text when there is a description of something that does not have any relevance for the purposes of the plot.* The case of the clock in the second chapter is a perfect illustration. Why stop to describe that antique when it cannot actually say what even the concierge's cuckoo clock knows? Because it is a condensed symbol of the whole story, and first of all for the Renaissance world it evokes, which is the world of the Valois, and secondly because it is there to tell us (to tell the reader more than Jerard, perhaps) that we will never recover the sequence of time. Through a symmetry that has already been mentioned, a broken clock returns in chapter 12. If it appeared only there, it would be simply an enjoyable childhood detail: but it is the return of a theme. Nerval is telling us that right from the beginning, for him, time was destined to become confused or, as Shakespeare would have said, the time is out of joint—for Jerard as much as for the reader.

---

*See my *Semiotics and the Philosophy of Language* (Bloomington: Indiana University Press, 1984).

OBJECTS OF DESIRE

Why is it that the order of events cannot be recovered? Because in the course of time Jerard shifts his desire onto three different women, though the sequence is not linear and heading in one direction, but goes in a spiral. Inside this spiral Jerard identifies, in sequence, one or other of the women as the object of his desire, but often he confuses them, and in any case, as each woman reappears in turn (rediscovered or remembered) she no longer possesses the properties she had previously.

Jerard has an object of desire, and he draws its outline for us right from the start of the tale. It is an ideal of femininity as either goddess or queen, so long as she is "inaccessible." However, in the following chapters he does still try to reach something. But as soon as his object of desire comes close to him, Jerard finds a reason for distancing himself from it. So the mist-effect concerns not just the time sequences, and space, but also desire.

In the first chapter it seems that Jerard desires dreams and finds reality repugnant, and that his ideal is incarnated by the actress:

DREAM	ACTRESS	REALITY
Uncertainty and indolence	What does it matter if it is him or someone else?	Heroic gallantry
Vague enthusiasms	She satisfied my every desire	Chasing after benefices
Religious aspirations	The divine Hours of Herculaneum	The lost hours of day
Drunk with poetry and love	She made people thrill with joy and love	Skepticism, bacchanalia
Metaphysical phantoms	Pale as the night	The real woman
Inaccessible goddess and queen	He did not care who she was	Vice

Up until this point the stage is certainly more real than the auditorium, and compared with the actress the spectators are nothing but "empty appearances." But in the second chapter Jerard seems to desire something more tangible, even if only by recalling the one moment when he came close to it. The person who has all the virtues of the actress, who had been seen all alone on the stage, is now Adrienne, glimpsed in the pale circle of the lawn by night.

AURÉLIE (chapter 1)	ADRIENNE (chapter 2)
Pale as the night	The brightness of the rising moon falls only on her
She lived only for me	I was the only boy in that dance
The warble of her voice	With a fresh, penetrating voice
Magic mirror	A will-o'-the-wisp escaping
An apparition	A phantom barely touching the green grass
Beautiful as the day	A mirage of glory and beauty
Like the Divine Hours	The blood of the Valois ran in her veins
Her smile fills him with bliss	They thought they were in paradise

This is why Jerard wonders (in the third chapter, second paragraph) whether he is not in love with a religious woman in the guise of an actress—and this question will haunt him till the end.

However, Adrienne possesses not only, let's say, ideal qualities but also physical properties, thanks to which, in the second chapter, she wins out over Sylvie, who bears the hallmarks of a rather slight rustic gracefulness. But in chapter 4, when some years later Jerard sees Sylvie again, now that she is no longer a child but a young girl in the bloom of adolescence, it is she who has acquired all the graces of Adrienne, who has now disappeared, and of Aurélie (albeit in a pale reflection of the latter), whose memory now fades.

ADRIENNE (chapter 2)	SYLVIE (chapter 2)	SYLVIE (chapter 4)
"Grande"	*"Petite fille"*	*"Ce n'était plus cette petite fille"*
Beautiful	Lively and fresh	She had become so beautiful
Blonde	Tanned complexion	White arms
Tall and slim	Still a child	Her slender figure
Descendant of the Valois	From the nearby village	Worthy of ancient art
Mirage of glory and beauty	Regular profile	Athenian features
She remained alone and triumphant	(She did not deserve the crown)	Irresistible charm
Intangible, vague love	Tender friendship	Her divine smile

Not only does Jerard entertain suspicions, fears, desires, illusions right to the end, and in the face of considerable evidence that Aurélie and Adrienne are the same person, but at times he thinks that what he desired in the first two women can be given to him by Sylvie. For reasons never stated, after the second dance, when he has even celebrated a kind of symbolic marriage with her, he leaves her. When he comes to her at the third dance, to escape the impossible fascination of Aurélie, he finds her similar to the woman he is fleeing, and understands that either Sylvie is lost for him or he is lost to her. It could be said that at each fade-out, when one female figure dissolves and becomes another, what was unreal becomes real; but precisely because it is now within reach, it changes again into something else altogether.

Jerard's secret curse is that he always has to reject what he previously desired, and precisely because it becomes just what he wanted it to become. Look how in chapter 13 Aurélie becomes exactly what he had dreamed of unconsciously: she had belonged to another, and the other man disappears overseas; actresses did not have a heart, and now she shows herself ready to love. . . . But alas, what becomes approachable can no longer be loved. Precisely because she has a heart, Aurélie will go off with the person who really does love her.*

This agonizing wishing and then unwishing is given an almost neurotic manifestation in the interior monologue in chapter 11. Stung by the ambiguous allusion to Adrienne's fate, Jerard, who up until a moment before had desired Sylvie, discovers that it would be sacrilegious for him to seduce someone he regarded as a sister. Immediately (and with irritating fickleness) his thoughts and desire turn once more to Aurélie. Yet at the beginning of the next chapter he is once more ready to throw himself at Sylvie's feet and offer her his house and his uncertain fortune. With "three women around his heart, dancing around him," as Dante might have said, Jerard loses his sense of their identity and desires and loses all three.

1832

In any case, Nerval encourages us to forget. And to help us (or lose us), he puts onstage a forgetful Sylvie, who only at the end remembers that Adrienne died in 1832.

This is the element that most upsets the critics. Why give such a crucial piece of information only at the end, whereas, as a rather naive note in the Pléiade edition remarks, we would have expected it at the beginning? Here Nerval performs one of those

---

*Mirène Ghossein, in a term paper during my course at Columbia University in 1984, observed a continual dyscrasia between what is set up as a Platonic ideal, and what is revealed as a disappointing shadow in the cave. I do not know if Nerval was thinking of Plato, but certainly the mechanism is this: as something gradually comes within reach (real in the normal sense of the term), it becomes a shadow and cannot stand comparison with, is no longer equal to, the ideal image conjured up.

"completing analepses" or "returns," as Genette calls them, where the narrator, pretending he has forgotten a detail, remembers it much later in the development of the action.* It is not the only one in the story; the other is the incidental remark about the actress's name, which appears only in chapter 11: but there seems to be more of a reason for this latter return, because it is only then that Jerard, sensing that his idyll with Sylvie is about to end, begins to think of the Actress as a Woman whom he might perhaps approach. The completing analepsis regarding the date seems to be at the very least scandalous, all the more so since it is preceded by a delaying tactic, which is difficult to justify at first sight.

In chapter 11 we find one of the most ambiguous expressions of the whole story: *"cela a mal tournée."* For whoever rereads the tale, that allusion by Sylvie in some way anticipates the final revelation, but for whoever reads it for the first time it delays it. Sylvie does not quite say that Adrienne ended up unhappily, but that her story ended unhappily. Consequently I cannot agree with those who translate it into Italian as *"le è andata male"* (she ended up unhappily), nor with the more cautious translators who say *"è andata male"* (ended up unhappily—not daring to interpret that very obvious *"cela"* leaves one with the suspicion that the subject is Adrienne). In fact, Sylvie says that "that story ended unhappily." Why do we have to respect that ambiguity (so much so that some people understand it to mean that, hearing this hint, Jerard convinces himself even more that it means Adrienne has become the actress)? Because it reinforces and justifies the delay,

---

*The "completing analepsis" is sometimes not a calculated technique but a stopgap, as in the case of many nineteenth-century writers of serial novels. By expanding to excess the dimensions of their novels in installments, they would find themselves obliged either to make amends for details they had forgotten or to justify, with a brusque retrospective explanation, events they were forced to make happen. For a discussion of this technique, see, for instance, my "Rhetoric and Ideology in Sue's *Les Mystères de Paris,*" now in *The Role of the Reader* (Bloomington: Indiana University Press).

which means that it is only in the last line of the text that Sylvie definitively destroys all of Jerard's illusions.

The fact is that Sylvie is not reticent. For whom would this information be essential? For Jerard, who on the basis of his memory of Adrienne, and of her possible identity with Aurélie, has created an obsession. But would it be essential for Sylvie, to whom Jerard has not yet revealed his own obsessions (as he will with Aurélie), except through vague allusions? For Sylvie (an earthly creature), Adrienne is even less than a phantom (she is only one of the many women who had passed that way). Sylvie does not say that Jerard has been tempted to identify the religious woman with the actress, she does not even know for certain whether this actress exists, nor who she is. She is totally outside this metamorphic world in which one image fades into another and overlays it. So it is not that she delivers the final revelation in small doses, drop by drop. Nerval does this, not Sylvie.

Sylvie speaks in a vague way not out of guile but "absent-mindedly," because she finds the affair irrelevant. She participates in the destruction of Jerard's dream precisely because she "is unaware of it." Her relationship with time is serene, made up of some nostalgia to which she is now reconciled or some tender memories, neither of which threaten her tranquil present. For this reason, of the three women, she is the one who remains the most inaccessible at the end. Jerard has even had a magic moment with Adrienne, and from what one can understand has enjoyed amorous intimacy with Aurélie, but with Sylvie nothing, except an extremely chaste kiss—and at Othys the even chaster fictional nuptials. The minute Sylvie comes fully to embody the reality principle (and pronounces the only undoubtedly true, historical statement in the whole story: a date), she is lost forever. At least as a lover: for Jerard she is by now only a sister, and, what's more, married to his (foster-)brother.

So much so that one would be tempted to say that it is precisely for this reason that the story is entitled *Sylvie* and not—like a later, flamboyant work—*Aurélie.* Sylvie represents the real time that was lost and never found—precisely because she is the only one who stays.

But this would imply a thesis, an ambitious thesis, and one that acquires all its importance precisely from the comparison between Proust and Nerval. Nerval seems to go in search of lost time but is incapable of finding it, and he celebrates only that emptiness of his own illusion. The final date pronounced by Sylvie would seem to sound therefore like a funeral bell that *closes* the story.

This would help us understand the affectionate and almost filial interest shown by Proust for this literary father, who failed in a desperate enterprise (and perhaps this is why Labrunie killed himself). Proust then sets out to avenge this paternal defeat with his own victory over Time.

But when is it that Sylvie reveals to Jerard that Adrienne had died some time previously? In *Time*[13] ("the following summer," when the theater company gives performances at Dammartin). However one works out the figures, she certainly does it long before *Time*[N], when Jerard begins his narration. Consequently, when Jerard starts to conjure up the night at the theater, only to go back to the time of the dance on the lawn, and to tell us of his trembling at the thought that Adrienne was the actress, and of the illusion of still being able to see her near the convent of Saint-S***—during this period of time (and narration), when he makes us share in his uncertainties, *he already knew* that Adrienne had definitely died in 1832.

So it is not that Jerard (or Nerval along with him) stops narrating when he realizes that everything is over: on the contrary, it is precisely when he has understood that all is over that he starts his narration (and it is a narration about a Jerard who did not know, nor could he have known, that everything was by now over).

Is the person who acts like this someone who has not succeeded in dealing with his past? Not a bit: this is someone who notices that one can start to revisit the past only when the present is by now canceled, and only memory (even though, or precisely because, it is not too ordered) can give us back something for which—if it is not worth living—it is at least worth dying.

But in that case Proust would not have seen Nerval as a weak, defenseless father, a forerunner to be rehabilitated, but, rather, as a strong, overstrong father, one to be outdone. And he would devote his life to this challenge.*

---

*There are many works that have helped me understand Nerval. I will cite only some of those from which I took various suggestions. In the special issue of *VS*, 31/32 (*Sur "Sylvie"*) (1982), see Daniele Barbieri, "Etapes de topicalisation et effets de brouillard," Beppe Cottafavi, "Micro-procès temporels dans le premier chapitre de *Sylvie*," Isabella Pezzini, "Paradoxes du désir, logique du récit" (and see also the same author's "Promenade a Ermenonville" in her *Passioni e narrazione* (Milan: Bompiani, 1996)), Maria Pia Pozzato, "Le brouillard et le reste," Patrizia Violi, "Du côté du lecteur." Among French critics I should mention Albert Béguin, *Gérard de Nerval* (Paris: Corti, 1945), Jacques Bony, *Le récit nervalien* (Paris: Corti, 1990), Frank Paul Bowman, *Gérard de Nerval. La conquête de soi par l'écriture* (Orléans: Paradigme, 1997), Pierre-Georges Castex, introduction and commentary to *Sylvie* (Paris: SEDES, 1970), Léon Cellier, *Gérard de Nerval* (Paris: Hatier, 1956), Michel Collot, *Gérard de Nerval ou la devotion à l'imaginaire* (Paris: PUF, 1992), Uri Eisenzweig, *L'espace imaginaire d'un récit: 'Sylvie' de Gérard de Nerval* (Neuchâtel: La Baconnière, 1976), Jacques Geninasca, "De la fête à l'anti-fête," and "Le plein, le vide et le tout," in *La parole littéraire* (Paris: PUF, 1997), Raymond Jean, *Nerval par lui-même* (Paris: Seuil, 1964), and his introduction and notes to *Sylvie. Aurélie* (Paris: Corti, 1964), Michel Jeanneret, *La lettre perdue. Ecriture et folie dans l'oeuvre de Gérard de Nerval* (Paris: Flammarion, 1978), Aristide Marie, *Gérard de Nerval, le poète et l'homme* (Paris: Hachette, 1914), Pierre Moreau, *Sylvie et ses soeurs nervaliennes* (Paris: SEDES, 1966), Georges Poulet, "Nerval," in *Le metamorfosi del cerchio* (Milan: Rizzoli, 1971), Dominique Tailleux, *L'éspace nervalien* (Paris: Nizet, 1975). I will mention also the introductions and notes by Henri Lemaître in the Garnier edition of the *Oeuvres,* the commentaries by Jean Guillaume and Claude Pichois, and their collaborators, in the third volume of the *Oeuvres complètes* in the Bibliothèque de la Pléiade edition, and Vincenzo Cerami, introduction to *Le figlie del fuoco* (Milan: Garzanti, 1983). I have taken many ideas from Gérard Genette, *Figure III* (Turin: Einaudi, 1976).

A reworking of part of the afterword to my Italian translation of Gérard de Nerval's *Sylvie* (Turin: Einaudi, 1999). I have already discussed, in *Six Walks in the Fictional Woods* (Cambridge, MA, and London: Harvard University Press, 1994), how I first wrote a short article on this novella ("Il tempo di *Sylvie*" (Time in *Sylvie*), *Poesia e critica*, 2 [1962]), then conducted a series of seminars on it at the University of Bologna in the 1970s (from which stemmed three graduating theses), then took it up again for a course of lectures at Columbia University in 1984, and made it the subject of the Norton Lectures at Harvard University in 1993, as well as of two other courses, at Bologna in 1995 and at the École Normale Supérieure, Paris, in 1996. The most interesting outcome of these many papers of mine was the special issue of the journal *VS*, 31/32 (1982) (*Sur "Sylvie"*).

WILDE: PARADOX AND APHORISM

There is nothing more difficult to define than an aphorism. This Greek term, originally meaning "something put aside as an offering," "an oblation," comes to mean in the course of time "a definition, saying, or concise proverbial statement." An aphorism is thus, according to the Italian Zingarelli dictionary, a "brief maxim expressing a norm of existence or a philosophical conclusion."

What distinguishes an aphorism from a maxim? Nothing, except its brevity.

It takes little to console us since it takes little to afflict us.
                              (Pascal, *Pensées*, Brunschwicg ed., 136)

If we did not have defects ourselves we would not take such delight in noting those of others.
                              (La Rochefoucauld, *Maxims*, 31)

Memory is the diary that we all carry about with us.
                              (Wilde, *The Importance of Being Earnest*)

Several thoughts that I have and that I could not sum up in words were actually derived from language.
                              (Kraus, *Half-Truths and One-and-a-Half Truths*)

These maxims are also aphorisms, while those that follow are too long to be aphorisms:

> What an advantage nobility is: already at eighteen years of age it places a man in an elevated position, and makes him known and respected, in a way that another could manage to deserve only in fifty years. This is an advantage of thirty years gained without effort.
>
> (Pascal, *Pensées,* Brunschwicg ed., 322)

> No artist has ethical sympathies. An ethical sympathy in an artist is an unpardonable mannerism of style.
>
> (Wilde, Preface to *The Picture of Dorian Gray*)

Alex Falzon, in editing Wilde's *Aphorisms* (Milan: Mondadori, 1986), defines an aphorism as a maxim where what counts is not only the brevity of its form but also the wit of its content. In doing so, he follows a widespread tendency to privilege the grace or brilliance of the aphorism over the acceptability of what is said in terms of truth. Naturally, as far as maxims and aphorisms are concerned, the concept of truth is relative to the intentions of its author: saying that an aphorism expresses a truth means saying that it is meant to express what the author intends as a truth and which he wants to convince his readers of. However, in general, maxims or aphorisms do not necessarily aim to be witty. Nor do they always mean to offend current opinion. Rather, they aim to go more profoundly into a matter on which current opinion seems superficial, and has to be corrected.

Here now is one of Chamfort's maxims: "He who is frugal is the richest of men; he who is miserly, the poorest" (*Maxims and Thoughts,* I, 145). The witticism lies in the fact that public opinion tends to consider a person frugal when he does not waste the few resources he has in order to meet his needs sparingly, while the miser is someone who amasses resources beyond his needs. The maxim would appear to go against public opinion, unless we agree that while "richest" is understood to refer to resources, "poorest" is meant to refer not just to its moral sense, but also to the satisfaction of daily needs. Once the rhetorical game has been cleared up, this maxim no longer goes against public opinion but corroborates it.

When, on the other hand, an aphorism goes violently against public opinion, so much so that at first it appears false and unacceptable, and only after a judicious deflation of its hyperbolic form seems to bring some crumb of truth, which is just barely acceptable, then we have a paradox.

Etymologically, *paradoxos* is what goes *parà ten doxan,* beyond current opinion. Thus originally the term denoted a statement that was far from everyone's beliefs, strange, bizarre, unexpected, and in this sense we find it also in Isidore of Seville. That this unexpected statement might yet be a harbinger of truth seems to me to be an idea that makes only slow progress. In Shakespeare a paradox is false at a certain point, but with the passing of time becomes true. See *Hamlet* III.1.110 ff.:

OPHELIA. What means your lordship?
HAMLET. That if you be honest and fair, your honesty should admit no discourse to your beauty.
OPHELIA. Could beauty, my lord, have better commerce than with honesty?
HAMLET. Ay, truly, for the power of beauty will sooner transform honesty from what it is to a bawd than the force of honesty can translate beauty into his likeness. This was sometime a paradox, but now the time gives it proof.

Logical paradoxes are a separate category; these are self-contradictory statements whose truth or falsehood cannot be proved—like, for instance, the paradox of the Cretan liar. But gradually the para-rhetorical sense comes in, for which I refer to the Italian Battaglia dictionary definition:

> Thesis, concept, statement, conclusion, witticism, mostly formulated during an ethical or doctrinal discourse, which contrasts with widespread or universally held opinion, with common sense and experience, with the belief system to which it refers or with principles or elements of knowledge that are taken as given (and often does not possess the power of truth, being merely reduced to a sophism, dreamed up through love of eccentricity or to display dialectical skill; but it can also contain, beneath an apparently illogical and disconcerting shape, a grain of objective validity, which will in the end establish itself in opposition to the ignorance and simplistic approach of those who uncritically follow majority beliefs).

Thus the aphorism seems to be a maxim that is meant to be recognized as true, though it deliberately appears witty, whereas the paradox presents itself as a maxim which is prima facie false but which, on mature reflection, apparently aims at expressing what the author considers to be true. Because of the gap that exists between the expectation of public opinion and the provocative form it assumes, the paradox appears witty.

The history of literature is rich in aphorisms and not quite so rich in paradoxes. The art of aphorism is easy (and proverbs are also aphorisms: you've only one mother; a dog's bark is worse than his bite), whereas the art of paradox is difficult.

Some time ago I dealt with an author who was a master of aphorisms, Pitigrilli.* Below are several of his most brilliant maxims;

---

*"Pitigrilli: l'uomo che fece arrossire la mamma," in *Il superuomo di massa* (2nd ed; Milan: Bompiani, 1978).

while some of them are undoubtedly quite witty, they aim to state a truth that does not go against commonly held opinions:

> Gourmet: a cook who has been to high school.
> Grammar: a complicated instrument that teaches you
>   languages but prevents you from ever speaking.
> Fragments: a fortunate excuse for writers who cannot put a
>   whole book together.
> Dipsomania: a scientific word that is so nice it makes you
>   want to start drinking.

Others, rather than express a presumed truth, affirm an ethical decision, a rule of action:

> I can understand kissing a leper but not shaking hands
>   with a cretin.
> Be indulgent with the person who has done you wrong,
>   because you never know what others have in store
>   for you.

However, in the very collection, entitled *Dizionario antiballistico* (Milan: Sonzogno, 1962), in which he collected his own and others' maxims, sayings, and aphorisms, Pitigrilli, who always wanted above all to be taken for a cynic, even if it meant confessing his own escapades openly, warned how insidious aphorisms can be:

> In this spirit of confidentiality, I acknowledge that I have
> abetted the reader's hooliganism. Let me explain: in the
> street, when a fight breaks out or there is a traffic accident,
> there suddenly emerges from the bowels of the earth an in-
> dividual who tries to poke one of the two disputants with
> his umbrella, usually the driver. The unknown hooligan has
> thus projected his latent anger. The same happens in books:

when the reader who has no ideas, or only ideas in an amorphous state, finds a picturesque, brilliant or explosive phrase, he falls in love with it, adopts it, comments on it with exclamations like "Excellent!," "Quite right!," as though he had always seen things that way, and as if that phrase were the quintessence of his way of thinking, of his philosophical system. He "takes a stance," as Il Duce used to say. I offer the reader a chance to take a stance without having to go deep into the jungle of various literatures.

In this sense an aphorism expresses a commonplace in a brilliant way. To call a harmonium "a piano that got fed up with life and turned to religion" merely reformulates with a powerful image what we already knew and believed, namely, that a harmonium is a church instrument. To call alcohol "a liquid that kills the living and preserves the dead" adds nothing to what we knew about the risks of intemperance or about what happens in anatomy museums.

When Pitigrilli makes his protagonist in *Esperimento di Pott* (Milan: Sonzogno, 1929) say that "intelligence in women is an anomaly one occasionally comes across, like albinos, left-handed people, hermaphrodites and those born with more than ten fingers or toes" (p. 132), he was saying exactly what the male reader (and probably also the female reader) in 1929 wanted to hear.

But in criticizing his *vis aphoristica*, Pitigrilli also tells us that many brilliant aphorisms can be reversed without losing their force. Let us look at some examples of reversal that Pitigrilli gives us in his *Dizionario* (op. cit., pp. 199 ff.):

Many despise riches but few know how to be liberal with
    them.
*Many know how to be liberal with riches, but few despise
    them.*

We make promises according to our fears and keep them
  according to our hopes.
*We make promises according to our hopes and keep them
  according to our fears.*
History is nothing but one of liberty's adventures.
Liberty is nothing but one of history's adventures.
Happiness resides in things, not in our tastes.
Happiness resides in our tastes, not in things.

In addition he drew up lists of maxims by different authors,
which certainly contradict each other, and yet seemed always to
express an established truth:

One only deceives oneself out of optimism (Hervieu).
One is more often deceived by diffidence than by confidence
  (Rivarol).
People would be happier if kings were philosophers and
  philosophers were kings (Plutarch).
*The day I want to punish a province I will have it ruled by a
  philosopher* (Frederick II).

I propose the term "transposable aphorism" for these reversible aphorisms. A transposable aphorism is a malaise of the
urge to be witty, or in other words, a maxim that is untroubled
by the fact that the opposite of what it says is equally true so long
as it appears to be funny. But the paradox is a genuine reversal of
a commonly held viewpoint, and it presents an unacceptable
world, provoking resistance and rejection. And yet if we make
the effort to understand it, it produces knowledge; in the end it
seems funny because we have to admit it is true. The transposable aphorism contains a very partial truth, and often after it has
been reversed, it reveals to us that neither of its two propositions
is true: it seemed true only because it was witty.

The paradox is not a variation of the classical *topos* of "the world upside down." The latter is mechanical, it foresees a universe where animals talk and humans make animal noises, fish fly and birds swim, monkeys celebrate mass and bishops swing through the trees. It proceeds through accumulation of *adynata* or *impossibilia* without any logic. It is a carnival game.

In order for it to become a paradox the reversal has to follow a logic and be circumscribed to a portion of the universe. A Persian arrives in Paris and describes France the way a Parisian would describe Persia. The effect is paradoxical because it forces one to see everyday things not according to established opinion.

One of the proofs for distinguishing a paradox from a transposable aphorism consists of trying to reverse the paradox. Pitigrilli quotes a definition of Zionism from Tristan Bernard, which was clearly valid before the establishment of the state of Israel: "One Jew asking another Jew for money to send a third Jew to Palestine." The fact that this paradox can't be reversed is a true sign that its original form genuinely contained a truth, or at least what Bernard wanted us to accept as truth.

Now let us consider a series of Karl Kraus's famous paradoxes.*
I will not attempt to reverse them because, if you think about them a little, it is not possible. They contain an unconventional truth that goes against the grain of common opinion. They cannot be twisted to express the opposite truth.

> The scandal starts when the police put an end to it.
> To be perfect all she needed was just one defect.
> The ideal of virginity is the ideal of those who want to
>   deflower.

---

*Karl Kraus, *Half-Truths and One-and-a-Half Truths,* ed. and trans. Harry Zohn (Manchester: Carcanet, 1986).

Sexual relations with animals are forbidden, but
  slaughtering animals is allowed. But has nobody
  reflected on the fact that that might be a sexual crime?
Punishment serves to frighten those who do not want to
  commit sins.
There is an obscure corner of the earth that sends explorers
  out into the world.
Children play at being soldiers. But why do soldiers play at
  being children?
Mad people are definitively recognized as such by
  psychiatrists because after being interned they exhibit
  agitated behavior.

Of course, Kraus too falls into the sin of transposable aphorisms. Here are some of his sayings that can be contradicted easily, and therefore reversed (the reversals are, obviously, my own):

Nothing is more unfathomable than the superficiality of a
  woman.
Nothing is more superficial than the unfathomability of a
  woman.
Easier to forgive an ugly foot than ugly socks!
Easier to forgive ugly socks than an ugly foot!
There are women who are not beautiful but have an air of
  beauty.
There are women who are beautiful but do not have an air of
  beauty.
Superman is a premature ideal that presupposes man.
Man is a premature ideal that presupposes superman.
The true woman deceives for pleasure. The others seek
  pleasure to deceive.
The true woman seeks pleasure to deceive. The others deceive
  for pleasure.

The only paradoxes that almost never seem to be transposable are those by Stanislaw J. Lec. Here is a short list from his *Mysli nieuczesane* (*Uncombed Thoughts*):

If one could only pay the death penalty by sleeping
    through it in installments!
I dreamed of reality: what a relief to wake up!
Open Sesame: I want to get out!
Who knows what Columbus might have discovered had
    America not blocked his way!
Horrible is the gag smeared with honey.
The prawn goes red after death: what exemplary
    refinement in a victim!
If you knock down monuments, spare the pedestals: they
    can always be used again.
He possessed knowledge, but was unable to make her
    pregnant.
In his modesty he considered himself an incurable
    scribbler. But he was actually just an informer.
Burning pyres don't light up the darkness.
You can die on Saint Helena without being Napoléon.
They embraced each other so tightly there was no room
    left for feelings.
He covered his head in ashes: those of his victims.
I dreamed of Freud. What does that mean?
Cavorting with dwarves ruins your backbone.
He had a clean conscience: he had never used it.
Even in his silence there were grammatical mistakes.

I admit I have a weakness for Lec, but until now I have found only one of his aphorisms to be transposable:

Reflect before thinking.
Think before reflecting.

Now we come to Oscar Wilde. When we consider the countless aphorisms scattered throughout his works, we have to admit that this is a fatuous author, a dandy who does not distinguish between aphorisms, reversible aphorisms, and paradoxes, so long as he manages to *épater le bourgeois*. What is more, he has the nerve to present as aphorisms witty statements that, aside from the wit, turn out to be wretched commonplaces—or at least commonplaces for the Victorian middle classes and aristocracy.

Nevertheless, this kind of experiment can help us see whether and to what extent an author who made provocative aphorisms the true essence of his novels, plays, and essays was a real author of penetrating paradoxes or a sophisticated collector of bons mots. My experiment is purely exploratory of course, and aims to encourage (and why not?) someone to do a thesis that will take the research to a systematic conclusion.

I will herewith provide a series of genuine paradoxes, and challenge you to try to reverse them (excluding the production of nonsense or of a maxim that is false for people with common sense):

> Life is simply a *mauvais quart d'heure* made up of exquisite moments.
> Selfishness is not living as one wishes to live; it is asking others to live as one wishes to live.
> The ugly and the stupid have the best of it in this world. They can sit at their ease and gape at the play. If they know nothing of victory, they are at least spared the knowledge of defeat.
> A sensitive person is one who, because he has corns himself, always treads on other people's toes.
> Everybody who is incapable of learning has taken up teaching.
> When people agree with me I always feel that I must be in the wrong.

A man who is much talked about is always very attractive.
   One feels there must be something to him, after all.
Every great man has his disciples, and it is always Judas
   who writes the biography.
I can resist everything except temptation.
Falsehoods [are] the truth of other people.
The only duty we owe to History is to rewrite it.
A thing is not necessarily true because a man dies for it.
Relations are simply a tedious pack of people, who haven't
   the remotest knowledge of how to live, nor the
   smallest inkling of when to die.

However, there are countless Wildean aphorisms that seem
to be easily reversible (the reversals are obviously my own):

To live is the rarest thing in the world. Most people exist,
   that is all.
*To exist is the rarest thing in the world. Most people live, that
   is all.*
Those who see any difference between soul and body have
   neither.
Those who see no difference between soul and body have neither.
Life is far too important a thing ever to talk seriously
   about it.
Life is too unimportant to joke about.
The world is divided into two classes; those who believe
   the incredible, like everyone else, and those who do the
   improbable, like me.
*The world is divided into two classes; those who believe the
   improbable, like everyone else, and those who do the
   incredible, like me.*
*The world is divided into two classes; those who do the
   improbable, like everyone else, and those who believe the
   incredible, like me.*

Moderation is a fatal thing. Nothing succeeds like excess.

Excess is a fatal thing. Nothing succeeds like moderation.

There is a fatality about good resolutions—they are always
made too late.

*There is a fatality about wicked resolutions—they are always
made at the right time.*

To be premature is to be perfect

To be premature is to be imperfect.

To be perfect is to be premature.

Ignorance is like a delicate exotic fruit; touch it and the
bloom is gone.

*Knowledge is like a delicate exotic fruit: touch it and the
bloom is gone.*

The more we study Art the less we care for Nature.

The more we study Nature the less we care for Art.

Sunsets are quite old-fashioned. They belong to the time
when Turner was the last note in art. To admire them
is a distinct sign of provincialism.

*Sunsets are back in fashion. They belong to the time when
Turner was the last note in art. To admire them is a
distinct sign of one's modernity.*

Beauty reveals everything because it expresses nothing.

Beauty reveals nothing because it expresses everything.

No married man is ever attractive, except to his wife. And
often, I'm told, not even to her.

*Every married man is attractive, except to his wife. But often,
I'm told, even to her.*

Dandyism, in its own way, is an attempt to assert the
absolute modernity of beauty.

*Dandyism, in its own way, is an attempt to assert the absolute
unmodernity of beauty.*

Conversation should touch everything but should
concentrate itself on nothing.

*Conversation should touch on nothing but should concentrate
    itself on everything.*
I love talking about nothing. It's the only thing I know
    everything about.
*I love talking about everything. It's the only thing I know
    nothing about.*
Only the great masters of style ever succeed in being obscure.
Only the great masters of style ever succeed in being clear.
Anyone can make history. Only a great man can write it.
Anyone can write history. Only a great man can make it.
The English have everything in common with America
    nowadays except, of course, language.
*The English have nothing in common with America
    nowadays except, of course, language.*
It is only the modern that ever becomes old-fashioned.
It is only the old-fashioned that ever becomes modern.

If we had to stop here our verdict on Wilde would be quite severe: the very incarnation of the dandy (though Lord Brummel
and even Wilde's own beloved Des Esseintes got there first), he
does not bother distinguishing paradoxes, those bearers of out-
rageous truths, from aphorisms, which contain acceptable truths,
or from reversible aphorisms, which are mere jeux d'esprit that
are indifferent to the truth. And in any case, Wilde's ideas on art
would appear to authorize his behavior, seeing that no aphorism
ought to aim at either utility, truth, or morality, but only beauty
and elegance of style.

However, this pursuit of aesthetic and stylistic provocation
would not be enough to absolve Wilde, since he did not manage
to distinguish between paradoxical provocation and mere fatuousness. As we know, to be true to his own principles he should
have been sent to prison not for having loved Lord Douglas but
for having sent him letters with lines like this: "It is a marvel that

those red rose-leaf lips of yours should have been made no less for music of song than for madness of kisses"—and not only for this, but also for having maintained during his trial that the letter was a stylistic exercise and a kind of sonnet in prose.

The Picture of Dorian Gray was condemned by the London judges for thoroughly stupid reasons, but from the point of view of literary originality, despite its undoubted charm, it is merely an imitation of Balzac's *Peau de chagrin* (*The Wild Ass's Skin*) and broadly copies (even though this was admitted indirectly) Huysmans' *A rebours*. Mario Praz noted that *Dorian Gray* also owes very much to Lorrain's *Monsieur de Phocas,* and even one of Wilde the aesthete's fundamental maxims ("No crime is vulgar, but all vulgarity itself is a crime") is a version of Baudelaire's "A dandy can never be a vulgar man: if he commits a crime, he would lose none of his reputation, but if this crime were caused by a trivial motive, the damage done to his honor would be irreparable."

Nevertheless, as Alex Falzon commented in the Italian edition of Wilde's aphorisms cited above, it is difficult to collect aphorisms by an author who has never written a book of aphorisms—so that what we consider aphorisms were created not to shine alone, devoid of any context, but in a narrative or theatrical work, and therefore said by someone in a particular context. For instance, can one consider an aphorism weak if the author puts it in the mouth of a ludicrous character? Is what Lady Bracknell says in *The Importance of Being Earnest* an aphorism: "To lose one parent, Mr Worthing, may be regarded as a misfortune; to lose both looks like carelessness"? Hence the legitimate suspicion that Wilde did not believe in any of the aphorisms he pronounced, nor even in the best of his paradoxes: he was only interested in putting on stage a society capable of appreciating them.

In places he actually says as much. Consider this dialogue from *The Importance of Being Earnest*:

ALGERNON: All women become like their mothers. That is
their tragedy. No man does. That's his.
JACK: Is that clever?
ALGERNON: It is perfectly phrased! And quite as true as any
observation in civilised life should be.

Thus Wilde should be seen not as an immoral creator of aphorisms but, rather, as a satirical author, a critic of society's morals.
The fact that he lived within that society's set of morals is a different matter, for that was his misfortune.

Let us reread *The Picture of Dorian Gray.* With just one or
two exceptions, the most memorable aphorisms are voiced by ludicrous characters like Lord Wotton. Wilde does not offer them
to us as aphorisms for life, which he himself could guarantee.

Lord Wotton pronounces, albeit wittily, an endless series of
commonplaces about the society of his time (and precisely for
this reason Wilde's readers enjoyed his false paradoxes): A bishop
keeps on saying at the age of eighty what he was told to say when
he was a boy of eighteen. The commonest thing is delightful if
only one hides it. The one charm of marriage is that it makes a
life of deception absolutely necessary for both parties (though
later Lord Wotton will say that the real drawback of marriage is
that it makes one unselfish). I don't suppose that ten per cent of
the proletariat live correctly. Nowadays a broken heart will run to
many editions. Young men want to be faithful, and are not; old
men want to be faithless but cannot. I don't want money: it is
only people who pay their bills who want that, and I never pay
mine. I do not desire to change anything in England, except the
weather. To get back one's youth, one has merely to repeat one's
follies. Men marry because they are tired, women because they
are curious. No woman is a genius. Women are a decorative sex.
Women are wonderfully practical, much more practical than we
are: we often forget to say anything about marriage and they always remind us. When we are happy we are always good, but

when we are good we are not always happy. The real tragedy of the poor is that they can afford nothing but self-denial (who knows if Wotton had read *The Communist Manifesto,* where he would have discovered that the poor have nothing to lose but their chains?). To adore is better than being adored: being adored is a nuisance. For every effect we produce we make an enemy, so to be popular we have to be mediocre. Anybody can be good in the country; there are no temptations there. Married life is nothing but habit. Crime is the exclusive preserve of the lower classes: crime is for them what art is for us, a way out of the ordinary sensations. Murder is always a mistake: one should never do anything that one cannot talk about after dinner. . . .

Alongside this series of banalities, which become brilliant only because he fires them out one after the other (just as in lists where the most trite words can astonish us through the incongruous relationship they set up with other equally trite words), Lord Wotton shows a particular genius for identifying commonplaces that would not be worthy even of being used in wrapping papers for chocolates, and then making them interesting by reversing them:

Being natural is simply a pose, and the most irritating pose
     I know.
The only way to get rid of a temptation is to yield to it.
I adore simple pleasures. They are the last refuge of the
     complex.
What I want is information: not useful information, of
     course, but useless information.
'I assure you there is no nonsense about the Americans.'
     'How dreadful!'
I can sympathize with everything except suffering.
Nowadays most people . . . discover when it is too late that
     the only things one never regrets are one's mistakes.
I don't think I am likely to marry. I am too much in love
     [but this is Dorian, infected by his master].

My dear boy, the people who love only once in their lives
are really the shallow people.

There is always something infinitely mean about other
people's tragedies.

Whenever a man does a thoroughly stupid thing, it is
always from the noblest of motives.*

Discord is to be forced to be in harmony with others.

A man can be happy with any woman as long as he does
not love her.

It is better to be beautiful than to be good.†

Ugliness is one of the seven deadly virtues.

The only people to whose opinions I listen now with any
respect are people much younger than myself.

Only shallow people do not judge by appearances.

It is perfectly monstrous the way people go around,
nowadays, saying things against one behind one's back
that are absolutely and entirely true.

The only difference between a caprice and a lifelong
passion is that the caprice lasts a little longer.

One cannot deny that Lord Wotton invents some effective
paradoxes however, such as:

I choose my friends for their good looks, my acquaintances
for their good characters, and my enemies for their
good intellects.

American girls are as clever at concealing their parents as
English women are at concealing their past.

---

*This reverses the commonplace whereby one does wonderful things for noble reasons, but
it too can be reversed: when a person does a particularly noble deed, it is always for the most
stupid of motives.

†This reverses a commonplace, but it continues with "But no one is readier than myself to
recognize that it is better to be good than to be ugly," and so resorts to a commonplace of
the lowest order, of the kind made popular on Italian TV screens by talk-show hosts: "It is
better to be beautiful, rich, and healthy than to be ugly, poor, and sick."

Philanthropic people lose all sense of humanity. It is their
distinguishing characteristic.

I can stand brute force, but brute reason is quite
unbearable.

I like Wagner's music better than anybody's. It is so loud
that one can talk the whole time without other people
hearing what one says.

When one is in love, one always begins by deceiving one's
self and one always ends by deceiving others.

A *grande passion* is the privilege of people who have
nothing to do.

Women inspire us with the desire to create masterpieces
and always prevent us from carrying them out.

The man who would call a spade a spade should be
compelled to use one.

But Lord Wotton's paradoxes are more commonly reversible
aphorisms (the reversals are, of course, my own):

Sin is the only real colour element left in modern life.
Virtue is the only real colour element left in modern life.
Humanity takes itself too seriously. It is the world's original
sin. If the caveman had known how to laugh, history
would have been different.
*Humanity does not take itself seriously enough. It is the
world's original sin. If the caveman had known how not
to laugh, history would have been different.*
Women represent the triumph of matter over mind, just as
men represent the triumph of mind over morals.
*Men represent the triumph of matter over mind, just as
women represent the triumph of mind over morals.*

The truth is that *Dorian Gray* portrays the inanity of Lord
Wotton, and at the same time denounces it. One character says

of him: "Don't mind him, my dear . . . He never means anything he says." The author says of him: "He played with the idea and grew wilful; tossed it into the air and transformed it; let it escape and recaptured it; made it iridescent with fancy and winged it with paradox. [. . .] He felt that the eyes of Dorian Gray were fixed on him, and the consciousness that amongst his audience there was one whose temperament he wished to fascinate seemed to give his wit keenness and to lend colour to his imagination."

Lord Wotton delights in what he thinks are paradoxes, but his acquaintances do not hold paradoxes in high esteem:

'They say that when good Americans die they go to Paris,' chuckled Sir Thomas, who had a large wardrobe of Humour's cast-off clothes. . . . 'Paradoxes are all very well in their way . . . ,' rejoined the baronet.

It is true that Lord Erskine says: "Was that a paradox? I didn't think so. Perhaps it was. Well, the way of paradoxes is the way of truth. To test reality we must see it on the tightrope. When the verities become acrobats, we can judge them." Lord Erskine was not wrong, but Lord Wotton—not having anything to believe in—was mean with paradoxes, and on his tightrope it was common sense rather than Truth that performed acrobatics. But what did matter to Lord Wotton in any case?

'And now my dear young friend, if you will allow me to call you so, may I ask if you really meant all that you said to us at lunch?'

'I quite forget what I said,' smiled Lord Henry. 'Was it all very bad?'

In *Dorian Gray* few terrible things are said, but many are done. But basically Dorian does them because his friends have ruined him with their false paradoxes. In the end this is the lesson we can take from the novel. But Wilde would even deny this lesson, because he says clearly in the preface that "No artist has ethical sympathies. An ethical sympathy in an artist is an unpardonable mannerism of style." And the style of *Dorian Gray* resides totally in the portrayal of fatuousness. Consequently, even though Wilde was himself a victim of the very cynicism that he so ostentatiously displayed, and that so delighted readers and audiences, we should not do him the injustice of quoting his aphorisms in isolation, as though they were intended or were able to teach us something.

It is true that some of the best Wildean paradoxes appear in those *Phrases and Philosophies for the Use of the Young*, which he published as maxims for life in an Oxford journal:

Wickedness is a myth invented by good people to account for the curious attractiveness of others.

Religions die when they are proved to be true. Science is the record of dead religions.

The well-bred contradict other people. The wise contradict themselves.

Ambition is the last refuge of the failure.

In examinations the foolish ask the questions that the wise cannot answer.

Only the great masters of style ever succeed in being obscure.

The first duty in life is to be as artificial as possible. What the second duty is no one has discovered.

Nothing that actually occurs is of the smallest importance.

Dullness is the coming of age of seriousness.

When one tells the truth, one is sure, sooner or later, to be found out.

Only the shallow know themselves.

The extent to which he considered these teachings to be true is evident in the replies he gave at his trial, when those sentences were objected to: "I rarely think that anything I write is true." Or: "That is a pleasing paradox, but I do not set very high store on it as an axiom." In any case, if "a truth ceases to be a truth when more than one person believes in it," to what collective consensus could a truth uttered by Wilde aspire? And since "in all unimportant matters, style, not sincerity, is the essential, and in all important matters, style, not sincerity, is the essential," it is right not to ask Wilde for a strict distinction between (true) paradoxes, (obvious) aphorisms, and (false, or devoid of any truth value) reversible aphorisms. What he exhibits is a *furor sententialis* (which is a pleasurable rhetorical incontinence), not a passion for philosophy.

Wilde would have sworn by one single aphorism, and he staked his life on it in the end: "All art is quite useless."

Paper given at a conference on Oscar Wilde held at the University of Bologna on 9 November 2000.

A PORTRAIT OF THE ARTIST
AS BACHELOR

I am probably the least suitable speaker to celebrate Joyce's bachelor of arts degree. After all, an article published in *St. Stephen's Magazine* in 1901 claimed that it was ideas from Italy that had corrupted Joyce. But I did not ask to give this commemorative address: that is the responsibility of University College. As for the title of my lecture, perhaps my intertextual wordplay is not terribly original, but then I am only "a playboy of the southern world."

I do, however, feel ill at ease with the title I have chosen: I would have liked to speak of the time when Jim, at Clongowes Wood College, announced his age by saying, "I am half past six." But let us not stray from the subject, which is, of course Joyce as *bachelor*.

All of you know probably that *bachelor* has become a magic word in many studies of contemporary semantics, ever since it was passed down from author to author as the supreme example of an ambiguous term possessing at least four different meanings. A *bachelor* is (i) an unmarried male adult; (ii) a young knight in the service of another; (iii) a person who has obtained his first degree; and (iv) a male seal who has not yet managed to mate during the mating season. Nevertheless, Roman Jakobson has pointed out that despite their semantic differences, these four homonyms have an element of incompleteness in common, or at least of something unfinished. In any context, a *bachelor* is, then, someone who has not yet reached a state of maturity. The young male is not yet a husband or mature father, the page is not yet a knight who has received investiture, the young B.A. graduate is not yet a Ph.D., and the poor male seal has not yet discovered the joys of sex.

When our Jim left University College he was still an incomplete Joyce, in that he had not yet written those works without which Joyce would have remained little more than a bigheaded novice. However, I would like to underline the fact that despite this, at the end of his studies Jim was not so incomplete as one would like to believe, and that it was precisely during those years of study that he clearly outlined, in his first attempts at writing, the directions he would later take in his maturity.

Jim began his degree in 1898, studying English under the supervision of Father O'Neill, a pathetic enthusiast of the Bacon-Shakespeare controversy, Italian with Father Ghezzi, and French with Edouard Cadic. This was the period of neo-Thomist studies, which often provide the quickest route to misunderstanding Aquinas, but while he was at the College, and before the *Pola Notebook* and *Paris Notebook,* Jim had certainly understood something about Aquinas. He once said to Stanislaus that Thomas Aquinas is a very complex thinker because what he says resembles exactly what ordinary people say, or what they would like to say—and for me this means that he had understood an awful lot, if not everything, of the philosophy of Saint Thomas.

In "Drama and Life," a lecture read on 20 January 1900 to the University College Literary and Historical Society, Joyce announced in advance the poetics of *Dubliners*: "Still I think out of the dreary sameness of existence, a measure of dramatic life may be drawn. Even the most commonplace, the deadest among the living, may play a part in a great drama."

In "Ibsen's New Drama," published 1 April 1900 in the *Fortnightly Review,* we can identify that fundamental idea of artistic impersonality, which we find later in the *Portrait.* Referring to a work of drama, he writes: "Ibsen [. . .] sees it steadily and whole, as from a great height, with perfect vision and an angelic dispassionateness, with the sight of one who may look on the sun with open eyes," and the God of the *Portrait* will be "within or behind or beyond or above his handiwork, invisible, refined out of existence, indifferent, paring his fingernails."

In "James Clarence Mangan," a lecture also given to the to the Literary and Historical Society on 15 February 1902 and published the following May in *St Stephen's Magazine,* we find that "Beauty, the splendour of truth, is a gracious presence when the imagination contemplates intensely the truth of its own being, or the visible world, and the spirit which proceeds out of truth and beauty is the holy spirit of joy. These are realities and these alone give and sustain life." This is without doubt the first adumbration of the notion of epiphany as it would be developed in his subsequent works.

In "The Study of Language," an essay written during his first year at university (1898–99), we find an astonishing statement that lies at the root of the structure of *Ulysses:* the young author speaks of an artistic language that escapes from "the hardness which is sufficient for flat, plain statements, by an overadded influence of what is beautiful in pathetic phrases, swelling of words, or torrents of invective, in tropes and varieties of figures, yet preserving even in moments of the greatest emotion, an innate symmetry."

In this same text we can also identify a distant foretaste of *Finnegans Wake* and of his future reading of Vico, when Joyce writes that "in the history of words there is much that indicates the history of men, and in comparing the speech of today with that of years ago, we have a useful illustration of the extent of external influences on the very words of a race."

Moreover, Joyce's fundamental obsession, his search for artistic truth through the manipulation of all the languages of the world, is revealed in another passage of this early essay when Jim, still in his first year, writes that "the higher grades of language, style, syntax, poetry, oratory, rhetoric, are again the champions and exponents, in what way soever, of truth."

If it is true that every author develops a single seminal idea in the course of his whole life, this seems particularly clear in the case of Joyce: while not yet a *bachelor,* he knew exactly what he had to do—and he said so, albeit in an unformed and rather naive way, within these four walls. Or, if you prefer, he decided to make his maturity fulfill what he had managed to foresee while studying in these lecture rooms.

In the first year of his degree Jim meditated on the representation of the Sciences in Santa Maria Novella, and concluded that Grammar had to be "the primary science." He thus dedicated most of his life to the invention of a new grammar, and the search for truth became for him the search for a perfect language.

In the year when Dublin is being celebrated as the European cultural capital, it is appropriate to reflect on the fact that the search for a perfect language was and continues to be a typically European phenomenon. Europe was born from a single nucleus of languages and cultures (the Greco-Roman world) and later had to face its fragmentation into different nations with different languages. The ancient world was bothered neither by the problem of a perfect language nor by that of the multiplicity of languages. The Hellenistic *koiné* first, and later the Latin of the Roman Empire, guaranteed a satisfactory system of universal communication from the Mediterranean basin to the British Isles. The two peoples that had invented the language of philosophy and the language of law identified the structure of their languages with the structures of human reason. Greeks spoke *the language.* All the others were barbarians, which etymologically means "those who stammer."

The fall of the Roman Empire marked the beginning of a period of linguistic and political division. Latin became corrupt. The barbarians invaded, with their own languages and customs. Half of the Roman lands went to the Greeks of the Eastern Empire. Part of Europe and the whole Mediterranean basin began to speak Arabic. The dawn of the new millennium saw the birth of the national vernaculars that we still speak today on this continent.

It was precisely at this historical moment that Christian culture began to reread the Bible passage on the *confusio linguarum* that had taken place during the building of the Tower of Babel. It was only in these centuries that men began to dream of the possibility of rediscovering or reinventing a pre-Babelic language, a language common to all humanity, capable of expressing the nature of things through a kind of innate homology between things and words. This search for a universal system of communication has taken on different forms from then to the present day: there have been those who have tried to go back in time in an effort to rediscover the language that Adam originally spoke with God; others moved forward, trying to build a language of reason endowed with the lost perfection that initially belonged to Adam's language. Some tried to pursue Vico's ideal of finding a language of the mind common to all peoples. International languages like Esperanto were invented, and people are still working to outline a "language of the mind" common to men and computers . . .

However, in the course of these researches, there were cases when someone claimed that the only perfect language was that spoken by his own compatriots. In the seventeenth century George Philipp Harsdörfer claimed that Adam could not have spoken anything but German, since only in German do word stems offer a perfect reflection of the nature of things (later, Heidegger would say that one could philosophize only in German and, in a generous concession, Greek). For Antoine de Rivarol

(*Discours sur l'universalité de la langue française*, 1784), French was the only language in which the syntactic structure of sentences reflected the real structure of human reason, and therefore it was the only logical language in the world (German sounded too guttural, Italian too sweet, Spanish too redundant, English too obscure).

It is well known that Joyce became an enthusiast of Dante Alighieri in this College, and that he remained an enthusiast for the rest of his life. All his Dante references are to *The Divine Comedy*, but there are valid reasons for believing that he also had a certain familiarity with the Italian poet's ideas on the origins of language, and with his plan for creating a perfect, new poetic language, as Dante himself expressed it in his *De Vulgari Eloquentia* (*On Vernacular Eloquence*). In any case Joyce must have found clear references to this subject in *The Divine Comedy*, and in *Paradiso* 26 a new version of the old question about Adam's language.

De Vulgari Eloquentia was written between 1303 and 1305, before *The Divine Comedy*. Although it looks like a doctrinal dissertation, the work is in fact a self-commentary, in which the author tends to analyze his own methods of artistic production, implicitly identifying them with the model of all poetic discourse.

According to Dante the plurality of vernacular languages had been preceded, before the sin of Babel, by a perfect language that Adam used to speak with God, and his descendants used to speak with each other. After the confusion caused by Babel, languages multiplied, first in the various geographical areas of the world and then inside what we call today the romance area, where the languages of *sí, d'oc,* and *d'oïl* became differentiated. The language of *sí,* or Italian, divided into a multiplicity of dialects, which at times differed even from one area of a city to another. This differentiation was caused by the unstable and inconstant nature of man, his customs and his verbal habits, in both time and space. It was precisely to make up for these slow, inexorable changes in natural language that the inventors of grammar tried to create a kind of unchangeable language that would stay the same in time and space, and this language was the Latin spoken in medieval universities. But Dante was searching for a vernacular Italian language, and thanks to his poetic culture and the contacts he made as an itinerant exile, he experienced both the variety of Italian dialects and the variety of European languages. The aim of *De Vulgari Eloquentia* was to find a more dignified and noble language, and for that reason Dante proceeded by way of a rigorous critical analysis of dialectal Italian. Since the best poets had, each in his own way, departed from their regional dialect, this suggested the possibility of finding a "noble dialect," a "*vulgare illustre*" ("an illustrious vernacular," i.e. one that "diffused light") worthy of taking its place in the royal palace of a national kingdom, were the Italians ever to have one. This would be a dialect common to all Italian cities but to none in particular, a kind of ideal model which the poets came close to and against which all existing dialects would have to be judged.

Consequently, to combat the confusion of different languages, Dante seemed to be proposing a poetic idiom that had affinities with Adam's language and that was the same as the poetic language of which he proudly considered himself the founder. This perfect language, which Dante hunts down as though it were a "scented panther," appears from time to time in the works of those poets that Dante considers great, albeit in a rather unformed way, not clearly codified, and with grammatical principles that are not quite explicit.

It was in this context—faced with the existence of dialects, natural but not universal languages, and of Latin, universal but artificial—that Dante pursued his dream of restoring an Edenic language that was at the same time both natural and universal. But unlike those who would later seek to rediscover the original Hebraic language, Dante intended to re-create the Edenic condition with a stroke of modern invention. The illustrious vernacular, for which his own poetic language was to be a model, would help the "modern" poet heal the post-Babel wound.

This audacious conception of his own role as restorer of a perfect language explains why, instead of condemning the multiplicity of languages, Dante brings out their biological strength in *De Vulgari Eloquentia,* their capacity for renewal *in the course of time.* It is precisely on the basis of this creativity of language that he believes himself capable of inventing and launching a perfect, modern, and natural language, without going back to lost models. If Dante had believed that the primordial language was to be identified with Hebrew he would have immediately decided to learn it and write in the language of the Bible. But Dante never thought about that possibility, because he was certain he could still find, through a perfecting of the various Italian dialects, that universal language of which Hebrew had simply been the most venerable incarnation.

Many of the arrogant statements of the young Joyce seem to allude to the same task of restoring the conditions of a perfect language through his own personal literary invention, with the aim of forging "the uncreated conscience" of his race, a language that would be not arbitrary like ordinary language but necessary and existing for a reason. In this way the young *bachelor* understood Dante's idea perfectly, and also mysteriously, and he would pursue it throughout his life.

However, Dante's project, like every other blueprint for a perfect language, involved finding a language that would allow humanity to escape the post-Babelic labyrinth. One can, as Dante did, accept the positive plurality of languages, but a perfect language ought to be clear and lucid, not labyrinthine. Joyce's project, on the other hand, as it moved progressively away from his first Thomist aesthetic toward the vision of the world expressed in *Finnegans Wake,* seems to be that of overcoming the post-Babelic chaos not by rejecting it but by accepting it as the only possibility. Joyce never tried to place himself on this side or the far side of the Tower, he wanted to live inside it—and you will allow me to speculate whether by chance his decision to start *Ulysses* from the top of a tower is not an unconscious prefiguration of his final objective, namely, that of forging a "polyguttural" and "multilingual" crucible that would represent not the end but the triumph of the *confusio linguarum*.

What can the ultimate origin of such a decision have been?

Around the first half of the seventh century A.D. there appeared in Ireland a grammatical treatise entitled *Auraicept na n-Éces* (*The Precepts of the Poets*). The basic idea of this treatise is that in order to adapt the Latin grammatical model to Irish grammar one must imitate the structures of the Tower of Babel: there are eight or nine (depending on the various versions of the text) parts of speech, namely, nouns, verbs, adverbs, and so on, and the number of basic elements used to build the Tower of Babel was eight or nine (water, blood, clay, wood, and so on). Why this parallel? Because the seventy-two doctors of the school of Fenius Farsaidh, who had planned the first language to emerge after the chaos of Babel (and it goes without saying that this language was Gaelic), had tried to build an idiom that, like the original, was not only homologous with the nature of things but also able to take into account the nature of all the other languages born after Babel. Their plan was inspired by Isaiah 66.18: "I shall come, that I will gather all nations and tongues." The method they had used consisted in selecting the best from every language, fragmenting, so to speak, the other languages, and recombining the fragments into a new and perfect structure. One is tempted to say that, by doing this, they were really genuine artists, since, as Joyce says, "the artist who could disentangle the subtle soul of the image from its mesh of defining circumstances most exactly and 're-embody' it in artistic circumstances chosen as the most exact for it in its new office, he was the supreme artist" (*Stephen Hero*, page 78).

Cutting into segments—which is the basic concept in the analysis of linguistic systems—was so important for these seventy-two learned men that (as my source suggests)* the word *teipe,* which was used for "to segment" and therefore to select, to model, indicated automatically the Irish language as a *berla teipide.* Consequently, the *Auraicept,* as a text that defined this event, was considered to be an allegory of the world.

It is interesting to note that a somewhat similar theory had been expressed by a contemporary of Dante, the great twelfth-century Cabalist Abraham Abulafia, according to whom God had given Adam not a specific language but a kind of method, a universal grammar, which, although it was lost after the sin of Babel, had survived among the Jewish people, who had been so skillful in using this method that they had created the Hebrew language, the most perfect of the seven post-Babelic languages. The Hebrew that Abulafia talks about was not a collage of other languages, however, but rather a totally new corpus produced by combining the twenty-two original letters (the elementary segments) of the divine alphabet.

By contrast, the Irish grammarians had decided not to go back and look for the Adamic language, but had preferred to build a new, perfect language, their own Gaelic.

Did Joyce know of these early medieval grammarians? I have not found any reference to the *Auraicept* in his work, but I was intrigued by the fact, quoted by Ellmann, that on 11 October 1901 young Jim went to John F. Taylor's lecture to the Law Students' Debating Society. This lecture not only celebrated the beauty and perfection of Irish but also formulated a parallel between the right the Irish people had to use its own language and the right Moses and the Jews had to use Hebrew as the language

---

*See Diego Poli, "La metafora di Babele e le *partitiones* nella teoria grammaticale irlandese dell'*Auraicept na n-Éces,*" in *Episteme. Quaderni Linguistici e Filologici,* 4 (1986–89), ed. Diego Poli (Macerata: Istituto di Glottologia e Linguistica Generale), 179–98.

of revelation, rejecting the Egyptian language that had been imposed on them. As we know, Taylor's idea was amply exploited in the "Aeolus" chapter of *Ulysses,* which is dominated by the parallel between Hebrew and Irish, a comparison that represents a kind of linguistic counterpart to the parallel between Bloom and Stephen.

Allow me then to raise a doubt. In *Finnegans Wake* (p. 356) there is the word "taylorised," which Atherton interprets as a reference to the Neoplatonist Thomas Taylor.* I, on the other hand, would like to interpret this as a reference to John F. Taylor. I have no proof of it, but I find it interesting that this quotation comes in a context (*Finnegans Wake,* p. 353 ff.) where Joyce begins speaking of the "abnihilisation of the etym," and uses expressions like "vociferagitant, viceversounding," and "alldconfusalem," and ends with "how comes every a body in our taylorised world to selve out thisthis," with a reference to the "primeum nobilees" and to the word "notomise." It seems probable that the idea of inventing languages by dissecting and cutting up the roots of words was inspired by that early lecture by Taylor, accompanied by some indirect knowledge of the *Auraicept.* But since there is no textual proof of all this, I cannot present my suggestion as anything other than an attractive hypothesis, or simply a personal fancy.

There is no evidence of Joyce's familiarity with medieval Irish traditions. In the lecture "Ireland, Island of Saints and Sages," given in Trieste in 1907, Joyce insisted on the antiquity of the Irish language, identifying it with Phoenician. Joyce was not an accurate historian, and during the lecture he confused Duns Scotus Eriugena (who was definitely a ninth-century Irish writer) with John Duns Scotus (born in Edinburgh in the thirteenth century, though in Joyce's time many were convinced he was Irish) and treated them as the same person; he also believed that

---

* *The Books at the Wake* (London: Faber, 1959).

the author of the *Corpus Dionysianum,* whom he called Dionysius the Pseudo-Areopagite, was Saint Denys, patron saint of France—and, since this attribution was also false and one does not know whether Dionysius really was some Dionysius or other, the real author of the *Corpus* was in any case a Pseudo-Dionysius the Areopagite and not Dionysius the Pseudo-Areopagite. But at University College Joyce had studied only Latin, French, English, mathematics, natural philosophy, and logic—not medieval philosophy. Whatever the case, the analogies between the claims of the Irish grammarians and the search by Joyce for a perfect poetic language are so surprising that I will try to find other links.

Although Joyce's ideas about the ancient Irish traditions were imprecise, for the purpose of inventing his own poetic language he came to know rather well one text he mentioned explicitly, for the first time, in his Trieste lecture on Ireland: *The Book of Kells.*

As a young man Joyce had certainly seen *The Book of Kells* at Trinity College, and later he mentioned a reproduction of it: *The Book of Kells, described by Sir Edward Sullivan and illustrated with 24 plates in colour* (2nd ed., London–Paris–New York, 1920). Joyce had given a copy of it to Miss Weaver at Christmas 1922.

Recently, when writing the introduction to the marvelous facsimile edition of the manuscript,* I pointed out that this masterpiece of Irish art had been preceded by a "murmur," and I am certain that Joyce was influenced by that murmur, even if in an indirect way. Two days ago I spent an afternoon in the most magical place in Ireland (for the second time in my life), the Seven Churches of Clonmacnoise, and once more I understood that nobody, even someone who has never heard of the Irish grammarians or works such as *The Book of Kells, The Book of Durrow,*

---

* *The Book of Kells (Ms 58, Trinity College Library Dublin),* commentary and ed. by Peter Fox. Fine Art Facsimile Publishers of Switzerland (Lucerne: Faksimile Verlag, 1990).

The Lindisfarne Gospels, and *The Book of the Dun Cow,* can look at that landscape and those ancient stones and not hear the murmur that accompanied the birth and the thousand-year life of *The Book of Kells.*

The history of Latin culture before the year 1000, particularly between the seventh and tenth centuries, charts the development of what has been called "Hisperic aesthetics," a style that emerged and developed from Spain to the British Isles, and even parts of Gaul.* The classical Latin tradition had previously described (and condemned) this style as "Asianic" and later "African," as opposed to the balance of the "Attic" style. In his *Institutio Oratoria* (XII.79), Quintilian had already emphasized that the best style must display "magna, non nimia, sublimia non abrupta, fortia non temeraria, severa non tristia, gravia non tarda, laeta non luxuriosa, iucunda non dissoluta, grandia non tumida" (grandeur, not excess, sublimity not harshness, strength not rashness, severity not grimness, gravity not dullness, joy not abandon, pleasantness not decadence, greatness not pomposity). Not just Roman orators but also ancient Christian rhetoric denounced the *kakozelón,* or damaging affectation, of the Asianic style. For an example of how profoundly scandalized the fathers of the church were when faced with examples of this "mala affectatio," see the invective by Saint Jerome (in *Adversus Iovinianum,* I): "Such is the barbarism displayed by these writers, and so confused does their discourse become thanks to these stylistic vices, that we have reached the point where we do not understand who is talking and what is being discussed. Everything (in these works) is expanded only to then burst like a weak serpent which splits in two as it tries to contort itself. . . . Everything is caught up in such inextricable verbal knots that one could quote Plautus here:

---

*See *The Hisperica Famina. I: The A-Text,* ed. Michael Herren (Toronto: Pontifical Institute of Medieval Studies, 1974), and *The Hisperica Famina. II: Related Poems,* ed. Michael Herren (Toronto: Pontifical Institute of Medieval Studies, 1987).

'Here nobody except the Sibyl could understand anything.' What are these verbal monstrosities?"

This broadside sounds like the spiteful description a traditionalist might make about a page from *The Book of Kells* or *Finnegans Wake*. But in the meantime something was to change: those qualities that, according to classical tradition, had been classified as vices would become virtues in the poetics of Hisperic writers. A page of Hisperic writing no longer obeyed the laws of traditional syntax and rhetoric, the models of rhythm and meter were overthrown in order to produce expressions that had a baroque flavor. Sequences of alliteration that the classical world would have considered cacophonous began to produce a new music, and Aldhelm of Malmesbury (*Epistula ad Eahfridum, PL,* 89, 91) had fun composing sentences where each word began with the same letter: "Primitus pantorum procerum praetorumque pio potissimum paternoque praesertim privilegio panegyricum poemataque passim prosatori sub polo promulgantes. . . ." The Hisperic style's lexis became enriched with incredible hybrid words, borrowing Hebrew and Hellenistic terms, and the text was studded with cryptograms and enigmas that defied any attempt at translation. If the ideal of classical aesthetics was clarity, the Hisperic ideal would be obscurity. If classical aesthetics exalted proportion, Hisperic aesthetics would prefer complexity, the abundance of epithets and paraphrases, the gigantic, the monstrous, the unrestrained, the immeasurable, the prodigious. The very search for nonstandard etymologies would lead to the breaking down of the word into atomic elements, which would then acquire enigmatic meanings.

The Hisperic aesthetic would epitomize the style of Europe in those dark ages when the old continent was undergoing demographic decline and the destruction of the most important cities, roads, and Roman aqueducts. In a territory covered in forests not only monks but also poets and miniaturists would look out on the world as a dark, menacing wood, teeming with monsters and crisscrossed with labyrinthine paths. In these difficult and chaotic centuries, Ireland would bring Latin culture back to the continent. But those Irish monks who wrote down and preserved for us that small amount of the classical tradition they had managed to salvage would take the initiative in the world of language and visual imagination, groping for the right path in the dense forest, like Saint Brendan's comrades, who sailed the seas with him, encountering monsters and lost islands, meeting a giant fish on which they disembarked when they mistook it for an island, an island inhabited by white birds (the souls who fell with Lucifer), miraculous fountains, Paradise trees, a crystal column in the middle of the sea, and Judas on a rock, beaten and tormented by the incessant pounding of the waves.

Between the seventh and ninth centuries, it was perhaps on Irish soil (but certainly in the British Isles) that there appeared that *Liber Monstrorum de Diversis Generibus*,* which seems to describe many of the images that we find in *The Book of Kells*. The author admits in the opening pages that although many authoritative books had already recounted similar lies, he would never have thought of presenting them again if "the impetuous wind of your requests had not unexpectedly arrived to throw me—a terrified sailor—headlong into a sea of monsters. [. . .] And without doubt it is impossible to count the number of kinds of monstrous marine animals which with enormous bodies the size of high mountains whip up the most gigantic waves and shift huge expanses of water with their torsos, almost seeming to uproot the water from the depths only to then heave themselves toward the quiet estuaries of rivers: and as they swim along, they raise spume and spray with a thunderous noise. In huge ranks, that monstrous, enormous army crosses the swollen plains of blue water, and sweeps the air with lashes of the whitest spray, white as marble.

Liber Monstrorum de Diversis Generibus, ed. Corrado Bologna (Milan: Bompiani, 1977).

And then churning up the waters with a tremendous backwash, waters already in a ferment because of the huge mass of their bodies, they head for land, offering to those standing on the shore watching them not so much a spectacle as a scene of horror."

However fearful the author may have been about telling lies, he cannot resist the colossal beauty of this fascinating falsehood because it allows him to weave a tale as infinite and varied as a labyrinth. He tells his story with the same pleasure as the *Vita S. Columbani* describes the sea around the island of Hibernia, or as in the *Hisperica Famina* (a work with which the author of the *Liber Monstrorum* must have had a certain familiarity), where adjectives like "astriferus" or "glaucicomus" are used to describe the breakers (and Hisperic aesthetics would privilege neologisms such as "pectoreus," "placoreus," "sonoreus," "alboreus," "propriferus," "flammiger," and "gaudifluus").

These are the same lexical inventions praised by Virgil the Grammarian in his *Epitomae* and *Epistulae*.* Many scholars now maintain that this mad grammarian from Bigorre, near Toulouse, was in fact an Irishman, and everything—from his Latin style to his vision of the world—would seem to confirm this. This Virgil lived in the seventh century and therefore, presumably, one hundred years before the production of *The Book of Kells*. He would cite passages from Cicero and Virgil (the famous one) that these authors could never have written, but then we discover, or presume, that he belonged to a circle of rhetoricians, each of whom had taken the name of a classical author. Perhaps, as has been surmised, he wrote to mock other orators. Influenced by Celtic, Visigoth, Irish, and Hebrew culture, he described a linguistic universe that seems to spring from the imagination of a modern surrealist poet.

He maintains that there exist twelve varieties of Latin and that in each of them the word for "fire" can be different: "ignis,"

---

*Virgilio Grammatico Marone, *Epitomi ed Epistole,* ed. G. Polara (Naples: Liguori, 1979).

"quoquihabin," "ardon," "calax," "spiridon," "rusin," "fragon," "fumaton," "ustrax," "vitius," "siluleus," "aenon" (*Epitomae,* IV.10). A battle is called "praelium" because it takes place at sea ("praelum"), because its importance brings about the supremacy ("praelatum") of the marvelous (*Epitomae,* IV.10). Geometry is an art that explains all the experiments with herbs and plants, and that is why doctors are called geometers (*Epitomae,* IV.11). The rhetorician Aemilius made this elegant proclamation: "SSSSSSSSSSS. PP. NNNNNNNN. GGGG.R.MM.TTT.D. CC. AAAAAAA. IIIIVVVVVVVV. O. AE. EEEEEE." This is supposed to mean "the wise man sucks the blood of wisdom and must be rightly called leech of the veins" (*Epitomae,* X.1). Galbungus and Terrentius clashed in a debate that lasted fourteen days and fourteen nights, discussing the vocative of "ego," and the matter was of supreme vastness because it was a question of determining how one should address oneself with emphasis: "Oh, I, have I acted correctly?" *(O egone, recte feci?).* This and much more is told us by Virgil, making us think of the young Joyce wondering whether baptism with mineral water was valid.

Each one of the texts I have mentioned could be used to describe a page of *The Book of Kells* or, for that matter, a page of *Finnegans Wake,* because in each of these texts language does what the images do in *The Book of Kells.* Using words to describe *The Book of Kells* is tantamount to reinventing a page of Hisperic literature. *The Book of Kells* is a flowery network of intertwined and stylized animal forms, of tiny monkeylike figures amid a labyrinth of foliage covering page after page, as if it were always repeating the same visual motifs in a tapestry where—in reality— each line, each corymb, represents a different invention. It has a complexity of spiral forms that wander deliberately unaware of any rule of disciplined symmetry, a symphony of delicate colors from pink to orangey yellow, from lemon yellow to purplish red. We see quadrupeds, birds, greyhounds playing with a swan's beak, unimaginable humanoid figures twisted around like an athlete on horseback who contorts himself with his head between his knees until he forms an initial letter, figures as malleable and flexible as rubber bands inserted amid a tangle of interlacing lines, pushing their heads through abstract decorations, coiling around initial letters and insinuating themselves between the lines. As we look, the page never sits still, but seems to create its own life: there are no reference points, everything is mixed up with everything else. *The Book of Kells* is Proteus's realm. It is the product of a sober hallucination that has no need of mescaline or LSD to create its abysses, not least because it represents not the delirium of a single mind but, rather, the delirium of an entire culture engaged in a dialogue with itself, quoting other Gospels, other illuminated letters, other tales.

It is the lucid vertigo of a language that is trying to redefine the world while it redefines itself in the full knowledge that, in an age that is still uncertain, the key to the revelation of the world can be found not in the straight line but only in the labyrinth.

It is not, therefore, by accident that all this inspired *Finnegans Wake* at the point when Joyce tried to create a book that would represent both an image of the universe and a work written for an "ideal reader affected by an ideal insomnia."

Also with regard to *Ulysses*, Joyce had already declared that many of the initials in *The Book of Kells* possessed the character of an entire chapter in his book, and he had explicitly asked that his work be compared to those miniatures.

The chapter in *Finnegans Wake* that clearly refers to *The Book of Kells* is the one conventionally called "The Manifesto of Alp." This chapter tells the story of a letter found on a pile of dung, and the letter has been seen as a symbol of all attempts at communication, of all the literature in the world, and of *Finnegans Wake* itself. The page in *The Book of Kells* that most inspired Joyce is the "tenebrous Tunc page" (folio 124r). If we allow our gaze to wander over this *Tunc* page, simultaneously reading, however haphazardly, some lines of Joyce, we have the impression that this is a multimedia experience, where the language reflects the illuminated images and the illuminated images stimulate linguistic analogies.

Joyce speaks of a page where "every person, place and thing in the chaosmos of Alle anyway connected with the gobbly-dumped turkey was moving and changing every part of the time." He talks of a "steady monologue of interiors," where "a word as cunningly hidden in its maze of confused drapery as a fieldmouse in a nest of coloured ribbons" becomes an "Ostrogothic kakography affected for certain phrases of Etruscan stabletalk," made of "utterly unexpected sinistrogyric return to one peculiar sore point in the past . . . indicating that the words which follow may be taken in any order desidered."

What, then, does *The Book of Kells* represent? The ancient manuscript speaks to us of a world made up of paths that fork in opposite directions, of adventures of the mind and imagination that cannot be described. It is a structure in which every point can be connected to any other point, where there are no points or positions but only connecting lines, each of which can be interrupted at any moment because it will instantly resume and follow the same direction. This structure has no center nor periphery. *The Book of Kells* is a labyrinth. This is the reason it succeeded in becoming in Joyce's excited mind the model of that infinite book that was still to be written, to be read only by an ideal reader affected by an ideal insomnia.

At the same time *The Book of Kells* (along with its descendant, *Finnegans Wake*) represents the model of human language and, perhaps, the model of the world in which we live. Perhaps we are living inside a *Book of Kells*, whereas we think we are living inside Diderot's *Encyclopédie*. Both *The Book of Kells* and *Finnegans Wake* are the best image of the universe as contemporary science presents it to us. They are the model of a universe in expansion, perhaps finite and yet unlimited, the starting point for infinite questions. They are books that allow us to feel like men and women of our time, even though we are sailing in the same perilous sea that led Saint Brendan to seek out that Lost Island that every page of *The Book of Kells* speaks of, as it invites and inspires us to continue our search to finally express perfectly the imperfect world we live in.

Jim the *bachelor* was not in fact incomplete, because he had seen, albeit as if through a haze, what his duty was and what we had to understand—namely, that the ambiguity of our languages, the natural imperfection of our idioms, represents not the post-Babelic disease from which humanity must recover but, rather, the only opportunity God gave to Adam, the talking animal. Understanding human languages that are imperfect but at the same time able to carry out that supreme form of imperfection we call poetry represents the only conclusion to every search for perfection. Babel was not an accident, we have been living in the Tower from the beginning. The first dialogue between God and Adam may well have taken place in *finneganian,* and it is only by going back to Babel and taking up the one opportunity we have that we can find our peace and face the destiny of the human race.

This whole story began in Dublin, when a boy began to be obsessed by the images in *The Book of Kells,* and perhaps by those in *The Book of Durrow,* of *Lindisfarne* and *The Dun Cow* . . .

"Once upon a time there was a Dun Cow coming down along the maze and this Dun Cow that was down along the maze met a nicens little boy named baby Jim the bachelor . . ."

This is translated from a revised Italian version of a lecture given on 31 October 1991 at University College Dublin to commemorate the anniversary of the conferral of the degree of Bachelor of Arts on James Joyce. The original English version is now in Umberto Eco and Liberato Santoro Brienza, *Talking of Joyce* (Dublin: University College Dublin Press, 1998).

BETWEEN LA MANCHA AND BABEL

In thanking this university (Castilla–La Mancha) for the honorary degree bestowed on me, I am pleased to see that this ritual is taking place in La Mancha, and at the very time we are celebrating Jorge Luis Borges.* For there once was, and perhaps there still is, a library in a village in this region, whose name people have never wanted to mention. This library, filled entirely with adventurous romances, was a library *with a way out.* Indeed, the wonderful story of Don Quixote begins at precisely the moment when our hero decides to leave the site of his bookish fantasies to venture out into life. He does so essentially because he is convinced that he has found truth in those books, so that all he needs to do is to imitate them, and reproduce their feats.

Three hundred fifty years later, Borges would tell us the story of a library *with no way out,* where the search for the true word is endless and utterly hopeless.

There is a profound analogy between these two libraries: Don Quixote tried to find in the world the facts, adventures, and

---

*For this, see the following essay on Borges and the anxiety of influence.

damsels his library had promised him: and consequently he wanted to believe and did believe that the universe was like his library. Borges, less of an idealist, decided that his library was like the universe—and one understands then why he never felt the need to leave it. Just as one cannot say, "Stop the world, I want to get off," likewise one cannot escape from the Library.

There are many stories of libraries: there are the lost libraries, like that of Alexandria, and there are the libraries we enter and leave immediately, because we realize that they contain only absurd stories and ideas. The Library of Saint-Victor was like that, the one Pantagruel entered several decades before Quixote was born, where he was delighted by those hundreds of volumes that promised the wisdom of ages, but as far as we know he left it almost instantly to do something else. He has left us only the curiosity and the desire to know what those volumes were about, and the pleasure of repeating their names like a litany: *Bragheta Juris, De Babuinis et Scimiis cum Commento Dorbellis, Ars Honeste Petandi in Societate, Formicarium Artium, De Modo Cacandi, De Differentiis Zupparum, De Optimitate Tripparum, Quaestio Subtilissima utrum Chimera Bombinans in Vacuo Possit Comedere Secundas Intentiones, De Baloccamentis Principum, Baloccatorium Sorboniformium, Campi Clysteriorum, Antidotarium Animae, De Patria Diabolorum . . .*

We can cite titles from the libraries of both Rabelais and Cervantes, since they were finite libraries, limited by the universes their books spoke about: the former talked of the Sorbonne, the latter of Roncesvalles. We cannot cite titles from Borges's library since the number of books in it is limitless, and because it is the shape of the library more than the subjects of its books that interests us.

Libraries of Babel were dreamed of even before Borges. One of the properties of Borges's library is that it not only contains countless volumes in endless, repeated rooms but can display volumes containing all the possible combinations of twenty-five letters of the alphabet, so that one cannot imagine any combination of characters that the library has not foreseen.

This was the ancient dream of the Cabalists, because only by combining endlessly a finite series of letters could one hope to formulate one day the secret name of God. And if I do not quote, as all of you might have expected, Raymond Lull's wheels, that is because even though he wanted to produce an astronomical number of propositions, he intended only to conserve those that were true, and reject all the rest. However, by putting together both Lull's wheels and the combinatory utopia of the Cabalists, people in the seventeenth century hoped to be able to name every single individual in the world, and thus to escape the curse of language, which forces us to designate individuals with general terms, *haeccitates* with *quidditates,* leaving us always—as happened in the Middle Ages—with a bitter taste in the mouth as a result of the *penuria nominum.*

It was for this reason that Harsdörfer (in his *Matematische und philosophische Erquickstunden,* 1651) planned to display on five wheels 264 elements (prefixes, suffixes, letters, and syllables), generating through their various combinations 97,209,600 German words, including nonexistent ones. Clavius (*In Spheram Ioannis de Sacro Bosco,* 1607) calculated how many terms could be produced with the twenty-three letters of the alphabet, combining them in twos, then threes and so on, right down to considering words with twenty-three letters. Pierre Guldin (*Problema Arithmeticum de Rerum Combinationibus,* 1622), by calculating all the terms of variable length that an alphabet could generate, from two to twenty-three letters, reached the figure of seventy thousand billion billion words—to record these on registers of a thousand pages, with one hundred lines per page and sixty characters per line, would have required 8,052,122,350 libraries, each one measuring 432 feet per side. Mersenne (*Harmonie universelle,* 1636), taking into account not only words but also "chants" (that is to say, musical sequences), noted that the chants that can be generated by twenty-two notes number around twelve billion billion (so that if one wanted to write down all of them, at a thousand a day it would take almost twenty-three million years).

It is to mock these very combinatorial dreams that Swift put forward his antilibrary, or, rather, a perfect, scientific, universal language in which there would no longer be any need for books, words, or alphabetical symbols:

> We next went to the School of Languages, where three Professors sat in Consultation upon improving that of their own country.
>
> The first project was to shorten Discourse by cutting Polysyllables into one, and leaving out Verbs and Participles; because in Reality all things imaginable are but Nouns.
>
> The other, was a Scheme for entirely abolishing all Words whatsoever: And this was urged as a great Advantage in Point of Health as well as Brevity. For, it is plain, that every word we speak is in some Degree a Diminution of our Lungs by Corrosion; and consequently contributes to the shortning of our Lives. An Expedient was therefore offered, that since Words are only Names for *Things,* it would be more convenient for all Men to carry about them, such *Things* as were necessary to express the particular Business they are to discourse on. And this Invention would certainly have taken place, to the great Ease as well as Health of the Subject, if the Women in Conjunction with the Vulgar and Illiterate had not threatened to raise a Rebellion, unless they might be allowed the Liberty to speak with their Tongues, after the Manner of their Forefathers: Such constant irreconcilable Enemies to Science are the common People. However, many of the most Learned and Wise adhere to the new Scheme of expressing themselves by *Things*; which hath only this Inconvenience attending it; that if a Man's Business be very great, and of various Kinds, he must be obliged

in Proportion to carry a greater Bundle of *Things* upon his Back, unless he can afford one or two strong Servants to attend him. I have often beheld two of these Sages almost sinking under the weight of their Packs, like Pedlars among us, who when they met in the Streets, would lay down their Loads, open their Sacks, and hold Conversation for an Hour together; then put up their Implements, help each other to resume their Burthens, and take their Leave. (*Gulliver's Travels*, III.5)

Notice, however, how even Swift could not avoid producing something very close to the Library of Babel. For in order to name everything in the universe men would need a dictionary made up entirely of things, and the size of this dictionary would match the extent of the entire cosmos. Once more there would be no difference between Library and universe. In Swift's project we would be *in* the library, or rather, part of the library itself, and we would not be able to come out of it, nor could we even speak of it since, just as in the Library of Babel one can only be in one hexagon at a time, in the world we live in we could speak only of what is around us depending on the place we are in, pointing with our finger at what surrounds us.

But let us imagine for the sake of argument that Swift's vision had triumphed and men did not speak anymore. Even in this case, as Borges warned us, the library would contain the autobiographies of angels and a detailed history of the future. And it was this particular Borgesian allusion that inspired Thomas Pavel, in his book *Fictional Worlds*,* to invite us to take part in a fascinating mental experiment. Let us imagine that an omniscient being is capable of writing or reading a Magnum Opus containing all the true statements regarding both the real world and all possible

---

*Thomas Pavel, *Fictional Worlds* (Cambridge, MA: Harvard University Press, 1986).

worlds. Naturally, since one can speak of the universe in different languages, and each language defines it in a different way, there must exist a set of all Magna Opera. Now let us suppose that God entrusts some angels to write Daily Books for each man, where they record all the statements (regarding the possible worlds of his desires and hopes and the real world of his actions) that correspond to a true statement in one of the books that make up the set of all Magna Opera. The Daily Book of each individual must be displayed on the Day of Judgment, along with the collection of those Books that evaluate the lives of families, tribes, and nations.

But the angel writing a Daily Book not only writes down true statements: he links them together, evaluates them, constructs them into a system. And since individuals and groups alike will have defending angels on the Day of Judgment, these defenders will rewrite for each of them another, endless series of Daily Books, where the same statements will be connected in a different way, and compared differently with the statements in one of the Magna Opera.

Since infinite alternative worlds are part of every one of the infinite Magna Opera, the angels will write countless Daily Books, in which there will be a jumble of statements that are true in one world but false in another. If we then imagine that some angels are not very skillful, and they mix up statements that a single Magnum Opus records as mutually contradictory, we will end up with a series of Compendia, Miscellanies, and compendia of fragments of miscellanies, which will amalgamate different layers of books of different origin, and at that point it will be very difficult to say which books are true and which are fictitious, and in relation to which original book. We will have an astronomical infinity of books, each of which hovers between different worlds, and the result will be that we regard as fictitious stories that others have considered true.

Pavel writes these things to make us understand that we are already living in such a universe, except that instead of being written by archangels, these books are written by us, from Homer to Borges; and he implies that the bastard ontology of fiction is not an exception compared with the "pure" ontology of those books that speak about the real world. He suggests that the legend he retells depicts quite well our situation as regards the universe of statements we regularly regard as "true." The result is that the vertigo we feel when we notice the ambiguous borders between fiction and reality is not only the same as that which seizes us when faced with the books written by angels but also the same as that which ought to seize us when faced with the series of books that, with authority, represent the real world.

The idea of the Library of Babel has now linked up with the equally vertiginous idea of the plurality of Possible Worlds, and Borges's imagination has inspired in particular the formal calculus of modal logicians. Not only that, but the Library described by Pavel, which naturally is also made up of works by Borges, including his story about the Library, seems curiously to resemble Don Quixote's library, which was a library of impossible stories that took place in possible worlds, where the reader lost his sense of the borders between fiction and reality.

There is another story invented by an artist that has also influenced the imagination of scientists—maybe not logicians, but certainly physicists and cosmologists—and that is *Finnegans Wake* by Joyce. Joyce did not dream up a possible library: he simply put into practice what Borges would later suggest. He used the twenty-six alphabetical symbols of English to produce a forest of nonexistent words with multiple meanings, he certainly put forward his book as a model of the universe, and he definitely intended that the reading of it should be endless and recurrent, so much so that he wished for "an ideal reader affected by an ideal insomnia."

Why do I mention Joyce? Perhaps and above all because, along with Borges, he is one of the two contemporary writers I have most loved and who have most influenced me. But also because we have now come to the point where we should ask ourselves about the parallels and differences between these two authors who have both turned universal language and culture into their playing field.

I would like to place Borges in the context of contemporary experimentalism, which, according to many people, is defined as a literature that interrogates itself about its own language, or about the language we use, and puts it on trial by deconstructing it down to its original roots. That is why when we think about experimentalism we think about Joyce, and the Joyce of *Finnegans Wake,* where not only English but the languages of all peoples, ground down to a vortex of free-floating fragments, are put together again and then deconstructed once more in a whirlwind of new lexical monstrosities, which coagulate for a second only to dissolve once more, as in a cosmic dance of atoms, in which writing is shattered down to its etyms—and it is no accident that it was the phonic analogy between etym and atom that induced Joyce to speak of his work as "the abnihilation of the ethym."

Obviously, Borges did not put language into crisis. You just have to read the smooth prose of his essays, the traditional grammatical structure of his stories, the plain, conversational comprehensibility of his poems. In this respect Borges is as far as it is possible to be from Joyce.

Of course, like every good writer, Borges reinvigorates the language he writes in, but he does not make a display of the way he tears it apart. If Joyce's linguistic experimentalism is to be considered revolutionary, Borges must be regarded as a conservative, the delirious archivist of a culture whose respectful custodian he claims to be. Delirious, I say, but also a conservative archivist. And yet it is this very oxymoron ("delirious archivist") which gives us the key to discussing Borges's experimentalism.

Joyce's project was to make universal culture his field of play. Well, this was also Borges's project. If in 1925 Borges exhibited some difficulty in reading *Ulysses* (see *Inquisiciones*) and in 1939 (in the November issue of *Sur*) looked with cautious curiosity at Joyce's calembours—though according to Emir Rodríguez Monegal, Borges himself invented an exquisitely Joycean pun word "whateverano" (meaning "what a summer" and "whatever is summer")—in at least two later poems (in the collection *Elogio de la sombra*) he declares his admiration for Joyce and his debt to him:

> *Que importa mi perdida generación,*
> *Ese vago espejo,*
> *Si tus libros la justifican.*
> *Yo soy los otros. Yo soy de todos aquellos*
> *Que ha rescatado tu obstinado rigor.*
> *Soy los que no conoces y los que salvas.*

> What does my lost generation matter,
> That lovely mirror,
> If it was justified by your books.
> I am the others. I am all those
> That your obstinate rigor rescues.
> I am those you do not know and those you save.

What, then, links these two authors who both chose universal culture as their playing field, for their salvation or damnation?

I believe that literary experimentalism works on a space we might call the world of languages. But a language, as linguists know, has two sides. On one side the signifier, on the other the signified. The signifier organizes sounds, while the signified arranges ideas. And it is not that this organization of ideas, which constitutes the form of a particular culture, is independent from language, because we know a culture only through the way in which language has organized the still-unformed data about our contact with the continuum of the world. Without language there would be no ideas, but a mere stream of experience that has not been processed or thought about.

Working experimentally on language and the culture it conveys means therefore working on two fronts: on the signifier front, playing with words (and through the destruction and reorganization of words ideas are reorganized); and playing with ideas, and therefore pushing words to touch on new and undreamed-of horizons.

Joyce played with words, Borges with ideas. And at this point we discern the different ideas the two writers held about what they played with and its infinite capacity for being segmented.

The atomic particles of words are their stems, syllables, and phonemes. One can, at the extreme limit, recombine sounds and produce a neologism or pun, or recombine letters and produce an anagram, a kabbalistic procedure whose magic Borges knew well.

The atomic element of ideas, or signifieds, is instead always an idea or another signified. One can break down the word "man" into "male human animal" and "rose" into "flower with fleshy petals," one can yoke together ideas to interpret other ideas, but one cannot *go beneath that.*

We could say that working on the signifier acts at a subatomic level, whereas working on the signifieds acts on atoms, which cannot be broken down further, in order to reorganize them later into new molecules.

Borges took this second option, which was not the route Joyce took but is just as rigorous and absolute and leads toward the limits of what is possible and thinkable. Borges had models for doing this, of course, whom he openly cites (and so you see that the apparently rather irrelevant quotations I produced a moment ago were not unjustified). One of these was Raymond Lull with his *Ars Magna,* in whom Borges rightly foresaw the forerunner of modern computer science. The other, less well known, is John Wilkins, who (in his *Essay Towards a Real Character,* 1688) tried to achieve that perfect language sought after by Mersenne, Guldin, and the other authors of his century—except that Wilkins did not wish to combine letters devoid of sense to assign a name to every single person or thing, but wanted to combine what he and others called "real characters," which were inspired by Chinese ideograms, in which an idea corresponds to every basic sign, so that by combining these signs in order to name things, the nature of the thing itself was to be made manifest through its name.

His project could not succeed, and I have tried to explain this in my book *The Search for a Perfect Language.** But the extraordinary fact is that Borges had not read Wilkins: he had merely secondhand information from the *Encyclopaedia Britannica* and a few other books, as he confesses in his essay "The analytical language of John Wilkins" (*Otras inquisiciones*). And yet Borges was able to condense the essence of his thought and to identify the weaknesses of his project better than many other scholars who have spent their lives reading the enormous folio volume of 1688. Not only this, but in discussing his ideas he noticed that Wilkins's discourse had something in common with other seventeenth-century figures who had wrestled with the problem of alphabetic combinations.

Borges, who delighted in other universal and secret languages, knew well that Wilkins's project was impossible, because it presupposed taking into account all the objects in the world, the ideas to which they referred, and a unitary criterion for ordering our atomized ideas. And it is this hurdle that defeats all utopians who aspire to a universal language. But let us examine the conclusion Borges drew from this consideration.

Once he had understood and declared that one cannot arrive at a unitary classification of the universe, Borges became fasci-

---

* *The Search for the Perfect Language*, trans. James Fentress (London: Fontana, 1997).

nated by the opposite project: that of overthrowing and multi-plying all classifications. It is in this very essay on Wilkins that we find the mention of that improbable Chinese encyclopedia (*The Celestial Emporium of Benevolent Knowledge*), where we find in turn the most amazing model of uncategorized and incongru-ous classification (which would later inspire Michel Foucault in the opening passage of *The Order of Things.*)

The conclusion Borges draws from the failure of classifica-tions is that we cannot know what the universe is. Furthermore, he says that "one can entertain the idea that there is no universe in the organic, unifying sense that this ambitious word possesses." But immediately afterward he points out that "the impossibility of penetrating the divine design of the universe cannot, however, dissuade us from trying to trace human designs." Borges knew that some patterns, like that of Wilkins and many in science, try to reach a provisional and partial order. But he chose the oppo-site path: if the atoms of knowledge are many, the poet's game consists in making them rotate and recombine ad infinitum, in the endless combinations not only of linguistic etyms but also of ideas themselves. In fact, the Library of Babel is made up of mil-lions of new Chinese encyclopedias of Benevolent Knowledge whose totality is never achieved. Borges found this library to be a storehouse of the culture of several millennia and of diaries of each archangel, but he did more than just explore it: he played at putting different hexagons in contact with one another, at insert-ing pages from one book into those of another (or at least at dis-covering the possible books in which this disorder had already taken place).

When it comes to the latest form of contemporary experi-mentalism, postmodernism, there is much talk of playing with intertextuality. But Borges had gone beyond intertextuality to anticipate the age of hypertextuality, in which one book not only talks of another, but one can penetrate one book from within another. In not only designing the form of his library but also prescribing in every page how one should peruse it, Borges had designed the World Wide Web ahead of its time.

Borges had to choose between dedicating his life to the search for God's secret idiom (a search he tells us about) or celebrating the millennial universe of knowledge as a dance of atoms, an interweaving of quotations, a welding together of ideas to produce not only everything that is and has been but also that which will be or could be, as is the duty or the potential of the librarians of Babel.

Only in the light of this Borgesian experimentalism (playing with ideas, not words) can one understand the poetics of *The Aleph,* that magic object in which one can see at a glance the countless and separate objects that make up whatever populates the universe. One has to be able to see everything at once, and change the criterion of what links things together, and be able to see something else, changing at every vision of the "Celestial Emporium."

At this point the question of whether the Library is infinite or of indefinite size, or whether the number of books inside it is finite or unlimited and recurring, becomes a secondary question. The true hero of the Library of Babel is not the library itself but its Reader, a new Don Quixote, on the move, adventurous, restlessly inventive, alchemically combinatory, capable of overcoming the windmills he makes rotate ad infinitum.

For this Reader, Borges has suggested a prayer and an act of faith, and it comes in the other poem dedicated to Joyce:

> *Entre el alba y la noche está la historia*
> *Universal. Desde la noche veo*
> *A mis pies los caminos del hebreo,*
> *Cartago aniquilada, Infierno y Gloria.*
> *Dame, Señor, coraje y alegría*
> *Para escalar la cumbre de este día.*

Between dawn and night lies universal
History. From the depths of night I see
At my feet the wandering of the Jew,
Carthage annihilated, Hell, and the Glory of Heaven.
Grant me, Lord, the happiness and courage
To touch the summit of my day.

This is a revised version of a lecture given on 22 May 1997 at the University of Castilla–La Mancha on the occasion of being awarded an honorary degree.

BORGES AND MY ANXIETY OF INFLUENCE

I have always maintained that one should never invite heart patients to a cardiologists' conference. However, now that I am here, my duty should be, apart from thanking you for the many kind things you have said about me in the last few days, to stay silent and be consistent with my idea that a written text is a manuscript in a bottle. This does not mean that a manuscript can be read any way we like, but it should be read when the old man's gone, to use another popular expression. That is why, as I listened to each paper over the past few days, I have been jotting down questions to answer and points to elaborate, but in the end I have decided not to discuss the papers individually.

I prefer to take advantage of the suggestions received from all of you to discuss the concept of influence. It is a crucial concept for criticism, for literary history, for narratology; but it is also dangerous. Over the last few days I have noticed this danger repeatedly, and for that reason I wish to pursue these reflections.

When we speak of a relationship of influence between two authors, A and B, we are in one of two situations:

(1) A and B were contemporaries. We could, for instance, discuss whether there was any influence between Proust and Joyce. There was not; they met just once, and each of them said more or less of the other: "I don't like him, and I have read little or nothing of anything he's written."

(2) A came before B, as was the case with the two writers discussed in the last few days, so the debate is concerned only with the influence of A on B.

Nevertheless, one cannot speak of influence in literature, in philosophy, or even in scientific research, if one does not place an X at the top of the triangle. Shall we call this X culture, the chain of previous influences? To be consistent with our exchanges over the last few days, let's call it the universe of the encyclopedia. One has to take this X into account, and above all in the case of Borges, since, like Joyce, although in a different way, he used universal culture as an instrument of play.

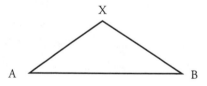

The relationship between A and B can take place in different ways: (1) B finds something in the work of A and does not realize that behind it lies X; (2) B finds something in the work of A and through it goes back to X; (3) B refers to X and only later discovers that X was already in the work of A.

I do not intend to construct a typology of my relationship with Borges. Instead I will quote some examples in an almost haphazard order, and leave to someone else the question as to how these examples correspond to different positions in this triangle. Moreover, it is often the case that these moments are confused because any consideration of influence must take account of the temporality of memory: an author can easily recall something he read in another author in—let's say—1958, forget that thing in 1980 while writing something of his own, and rediscover it (or be induced to remember it) in 1990. One could carry out a psychoanalysis of influences. For instance, in the course of my fictional work critics have found influences of which I was totally conscious, others that could not possibly have been influences because I had never known the source, and still others that astonished me but that I then found convincing—as when Giorgio Celli, discussing *The Name of the Rose,* spotted the influence of the historical novels of Dmitri Merezkovskij, and I had to admit that I had read them when I was twelve, even though I never thought of them while I was writing the novel.

In any case, the diagram is not quite so simple, because in addition to A, B, and the sometimes millennial chain of culture represented by X, there is also the Zeitgeist. The Zeitgeist must not be considered a metaphysical or metahistorical concept; I believe it can be broken down into a chain of reciprocal influences, but what is extraordinary about it is that it can work even in the mind of a child. Some time ago I found in an old drawer something I had written at the age of ten, the diary of a magician who claimed he was the discoverer, colonizer, and reformer of an island in the Glacial Arctic Ocean called Acorn. Looking back on it now, this seems a very Borgesian story, but obviously I could not have read Borges at the age of ten (and in a foreign language). Nor had I read the utopian works of the sixteenth, seventeenth, or eighteenth centuries, with their tales of ideal communities. However, I had read many adventure stories, fairy tales of course, and even an abbreviated version of *Gargantua and Pantagruel,* and who knows what chemical reactions had taken place in my imagination.

The Zeitgeist can even make us think of reversals of time's arrow. I remember writing some stories about planets at the age of sixteen (so around 1948): the plots had as protagonists the Earth, the Moon, Venus falling in love with the Sun, etc. They were in their own way *Cosmicomic* stories. I sometimes amuse myself wondering how Calvino managed to burgle my house years later and find these youthful writings, which existed only in a single copy. I'm joking, of course, but the point is that sometimes one must believe in the Zeitgeist. In any case, I know you will not believe me, but Calvino's cosmic stories are better than mine.

Lastly, there are themes common to many authors because they come, as it were, directly from reality. For example, I remember how after *The Name of the Rose* was published a number of people pointed to other books in which an abbey was burned, many of which I had not read at all. And nobody bothered to mention the fact that in the Middle Ages it was quite common for abbeys, as it was for cathedrals, to burn.

Now, without sticking rigorously to my diagram, I would like to introduce into my triad—*intentio auctoris, intentio operis, intentio lectoris*—the *intentio intertextualitatis,* which must play a role in this discussion. Allow me to reflect, once more in no particular order, on three types of relationship with Borges: 1) the cases where I was fully conscious of Borgesian influence; 2) the cases where I was not aware of it, but subsequently readers (among whom I would also count you over the past few days) forced me to recognize that Borges had influenced me unconsciously; 3) the cases where, without adopting a triangle based on preceding sources and the universe of intertextuality, we are led to consider as straight two-way influence cases of three-way influence—namely, the debts Borges owed to the universe of culture, so that we cannot attribute to Borges what he always proudly declared he took from culture. It was no accident that yesterday I called him a "delirious archivist": Borges's delirium could not exist without the archive on which he was working.

I believe that if someone had gone to him and said: "You invented this," he would have replied: "No, no, it was already there, it already existed." And he would have proudly taken as his own model that phrase of Pascal's that I placed as an epigraph to my book *A Theory of Semiotics*: "And don't let anyone tell me that I have not said anything new: *la disposition des matières est nouvelle.*"

I say this not to deny my debts to him, which are many, but to lead you back, and to lead myself back, to a principle that I think is fundamental for all those who have taken part in this conference, certainly for me, and certainly for Borges: this most important point is that books talk to each other.

In 1955 Borges's *Ficciones* came out in Italy, with the title *La biblioteca di Babele* in Einaudi's Gettoni series. It had been recommended to Einaudi by Sergio Solmi, a great poet whom I really loved, particularly for an essay of his on science fiction as a version of the fantastic, which he had written some years before. You see the role the Zeitgeist plays: Solmi discovers Borges while he is reading American writers of science fiction, who write (perhaps consciously) in the tradition of the utopian tale that begins in the seventeenth to eighteenth centuries. Let us not forget that Wilkins also wrote a book on the inhabitants of the moon, and therefore he too, like Godwin and others, was already traveling to other worlds. I think it was one evening in 1956 or '57 that Solmi told me as we strolled together in the Piazza del Duomo in Milan: "I advised Einaudi to publish this book; we have not managed to sell even five hundred copies, but you should read it because it is very good." That was how I first fell in love with Borges, and I remember going to friends' houses and reading them excerpts from *Pierre Menard*.

At that time I was beginning to write those parodies and pastiches that later would become *Diario minimo* (*Misreadings*). Influenced by what? Perhaps the strongest influence there was Proust's *Pastiches et mélanges,* so much so that when *Diario min-*

imo came out in French I chose the title *Pastiches et postiches.* But I recall that when I later published *Diario minimo,* in 1963, I thought of giving it a title that alluded to a title of Vittorini's, *Piccola borghesia,* except that I would have liked to change the title to *Piccola Borges-ia.* The point of this, then, is to explain how a network of influences and echoes began to come into play.

However, I could not have allowed myself a reference to Borges at that time, because in Italy he was still known to very few people. It was only in the following decade that the publication of all his other works established Borges definitively in Italy, principally thanks to Domenico Porzio, a very dear friend of mine and a man of great intellectual openness and wide reading, though a traditionalist critic. While polemics about the neo-avanguardia raged in Italy, Borges was not considered an avant-garde writer. This was the time when the poetry anthology *I novissimi* appeared and then the Gruppo 63, and their models were Joyce and Gadda. The neo-avant-garde was interested in an experimentalism that worked on the signifier (their model was that of the illegible book); Borges, on the other hand, who wrote in a classical style, worked on the signifieds, and therefore as far as we were concerned at the time he was beyond the pale, a disturbing presence, one not easily categorized. In crude terms, while Joyce or Robbe-Grillet was on the left, Borges was on the right. And since I would not want this distinction to be understood in political terms, we could also say the opposite, and their opposition would stay the same.

In any case, for some of us Borges was a "secret love." He was reclaimed only later by the neo-avant-garde, after a lengthy and circuitous process.

In the early 1960s fantasy was either traditional fiction or science fiction, so it was possible to write an essay on science fiction and the fantastic without addressing the theory of literature. I believe that interest in Borges began midway through the sixties, with what was called the structuralist and semiological movement.

Here I must correct another error that is continually made, even in what claim to be scholarly works: today it is said that the Italian neo-avant-garde (Gruppo 63) was structuralist. In truth, nobody in that group was interested in structuralist linguistics except myself, but in my case it was a private hobby that began in university circles, between Pavia (Segre, Corti, Avalle) and Paris (my own and others' encounters with Barthes).

Why do I say that the interest in Borges began with structuralism? Because Borges carried out his experimental work not on words but on conceptual structures, and it was only with a structuralist methodology that one could begin to analyze and understand his work.

When I later wrote *The Name of the Rose* it was more than obvious that in constructing the library I was thinking of Borges. If you go and read my entry "Codice" (Codex) in the Einaudi Encyclopaedia, you will see that in one of its sections I carry out an experiment on the Library of Babel. That entry was written in 1976, two years before I began *The Name of the Rose,* which indicates that I had been obsessed by Borges's library for some time. When I began the novel later, the idea of the library came naturally to me and with it the idea of a blind librarian, whom I decided to call Jorge da Burgos. I really do not remember whether it was because I had decided to give him that name that I went to see what was happening at Burgos, or whether I called him that because I already knew that in that period *pergamino de paño,* that is to say, paper instead of parchment, had been produced at Burgos. Sometimes things happen very quickly, as one reads here and there, and one cannot remember what came first.

After that everyone asked me why Jorge becomes the "bad guy" in my story, and I could only reply that when I gave my character this name I did not know what he would do later (and that is what happened in my other novels as well, so that the game of finding precise allusions to this or that, which many people play, is generally a waste of time). Nevertheless, I cannot rule out the possibility that at the point when this ghost of Borges appeared I was influenced by the plot of his "Death and the Compass," which certainly had made an enormous impression on me.

But you see how strange the game of influences is: if someone had asked me about influences at the time when I was depicting the mutual seduction between Jorge and William, I would have said that I was thinking of Proust, of that scene where Charlus tries to seduce Jupien, which is described with a metaphor of the bee buzzing around the flower.

I also had other models. For instance, the model of Mann's *Doctor Faustus* was fundamental, because the way Adso relives his own story as an old man, telling us how he saw it as a young man, was in some sense the way old Serenus Zeitblom looked at the story of Adrian Leverkühn. Here is another good example of unknown influences, because few critics have spotted the *Doctor Faustus* model, whereas many have seen instead an allusion to the dialogues between Naphta and Settembrini in *The Magic Mountain.*

To turn to other examples, I was grateful to the speaker who underlined the possible influence of *Bouvard et Pécuchet* on *Foucault's Pendulum.* For the fact is that while writing that novel, I thought a lot about Flaubert's book. I even promised to go and reread it, but then in the end I decided not to, because in some sense I wanted to be its Pierre Menard.

An opposite case is provided by my encounter with the Rosicrucians, which determined the structure of *Foucault's Pendulum.* Right from my youth I had devoted a shelf of my library to occult sciences; then one day I came across a totally stupid book on the Rosicrucians, and that was where I got the idea of doing a Bouvard and Pécuchet for occult idiocy. After that I collected texts by second-rate occultists on one hand, and on the other historically reliable literature on the Rosicrucians. Only when my novel was far advanced did I reread "Tlön," where Borges talks of the Rosicrucians—as he often did, taking information at second hand (from De Quincey) and yet understanding everything about it better than scholars who have dedicated their whole lives to the subject.

In the course of this research I found a photocopy of an out-of-print book, Arnold's monograph. When the *Pendulum* eventually came out, I said that Arnold's old work should be translated into Italian; immediately afterward a French publisher decided to reprint the book and asked me to write a preface for it, and only in that preface do I refer, this time consciously, to Borges, beginning precisely with "Tlön, Uqbar, Orbis Tertius."

But who can deny that from the time I read "Tlön" so many years previously, the word "Rosicrucian" might have lodged in some remote corner of my brain, so that decades later (when I read the book by the idiotic Rosicrucian) it reappeared thanks also to a Borgesian memory?

These past few days I have been led to reflect instead on how much I have been influenced by the "Pierre Menard model." This is a story that I have never tired of quoting since I first read it. In what sense has it determined the way I write? Well, I would say that the real Borgesian influence on *The Name of the Rose* does not lie in having imagined a labyrinthine library; after all, the universe is full of labyrinths from the time of Cnossos onward, and theorists of postmodernism regard the labyrinth as a recurring image in almost all contemporary literature. It lies rather in the fact that I knew I was rewriting a medieval story, and that this rewriting of mine, however faithful to the original, would have a different meaning for contemporary readers. I knew that if I rewrote what had really happened in the fourteenth century, with the Fraticelli movement and Fra Dolcino, the reader (even if I did not want him to) would see almost literal references to the Red Brigades—and I was really delighted to discover that Fra Dolcino's wife was called Margherita like the wife of Renato Curcio. The Menard model worked, and consciously so, since I knew that I was writing the name of the wife of Dolcino, and that the reader would think that I was thinking of Curcio's wife.

After the "Menard model" I would like to discuss the "Averroes model." The story of Averroes and the theater is another of Borges's tales that have come to fascinate me more and more. In fact, the only essay I have ever written on the semiotics of the theater begins with the story of Averroes.* What is so extraordinary about that story? It is that Borges's Averroes is stupid not in personal terms but culturally, because he has reality before his eyes (the children playing) and yet he cannot make that relate to what the book is describing to him. Incidentally, I have been thinking in the past few days that, taken to its extreme, Averroes's situation is that of the poetics of "defamiliarization," which the Russian formalists describe as representing something in such a way that one feels as if one were seeing it for the first time, thus making the perception of the object difficult for the reader. I would say that in my novels I reverse the "Averroes model": the (culturally ignorant) character often describes with astonishment something he sees and about which he does not understand very much, whereby the reader is led to understand it. That is to say, I work to produce an intelligent Averroes.

As someone said, it may be that this is one of the reasons for the popularity of my fiction: mine is the opposite of the "defamiliarization" technique; I make the reader familiar with something he did not know until then. I take a reader from Texas, who has never seen Europe, into a medieval abbey (or into a Templar commandery, or a museum full of complicated objects, or into a baroque room) and make him feel at ease. I show him a medieval character who takes out a pair of glasses as if it were completely natural, and I depict his contemporaries, who are astonished at

---

*See "Interpreting drama," *The Drama Review*, 21.1 (March 1977), now in *The Limits of Interpretation* (Bloomington: Indiana University Press).

this sight; at first the reader does not understand why they are amazed, but in the end he realizes that spectacles were invented in the Middle Ages. This is not a Borgesian technique; mine is an "anti-Averroes model," but without Borges's model before me I would never have been able to conceive of it.

These are the real influences, much more so than others, which are only apparent. Let us go back to the labyrinthine disorder of the world, which seems to be directly Borgesian. But in this instance I had found it in Joyce, as well as in some medieval sources. *The Labyrinth of the World* was written by Comenius in 1623, and the concept of the labyrinth was part of the ideology of mannerism and the baroque. It is no accident that a fine book on mannerism, Hocke's *Die Welt als Labyrinth,* was written in our own time, starting from Comenius's idea. But that is not all. That every classification of the universe leads to the construction of a labyrinth or of a garden of forking paths was an idea that was present both in Leibniz and—in a very clear and explicit way— in the introduction to Diderot and D'Alembert's *Encyclopédie.* These are probably also Borges's sources. Here then is a case where it is not clear, not even to me, whether I (B) found X by going through writer A, or whether I (B) first discovered some aspects of X and then noticed how X had also influenced A.

And yet the Borgesian labyrinths probably made the many references to the labyrinth that I had found elsewhere coalesce in me, so much so that I have wondered whether I could have written *The Name of the Rose* without Borges. This is a counterfactual hypothesis of the kind: "If Napoléon had been a Somalian woman, would he have won at Waterloo?" In theory, taking Father Emanuele's machine (seeing that someone here quoted the Jesuit from my book *The Island of the Day Before*) and making it rotate at maximum speed, the libraries already existed, the arguments over laughter did take place in the medieval world, the collapse of order was a story that began, if you like, from

Occam onward, mirrors were already celebrated in the *Roman de la rose* and had been researched by the Arabs, and then when I was very young I had been fascinated by a Rilke poem on mirrors. Would I have been able to catalyze all these elements without Borges? Probably not. But would Borges have written what he wrote if the texts I have mentioned had not been behind him? How is it that he catalyzed the idea of the labyrinth and the idea of the mystery of mirrors? Borges's work also consisted in taking from the immense territory of intertextuality a series of themes that were already whirling around there, and turning them into an exemplary pattern.

Now I would like to highlight all those cases where the search for two-way influence is dangerous, since one loses sight of the networks of intertextuality. Borges is a writer who has mentioned everything. One cannot identify in the history of culture a single theme he has not touched on, even if only fleetingly. Just yesterday I listened to a speaker who suggested that Borges could have influenced Plato when he was writing the *Parmenides* since he, Borges, had portrayed the same characters as Plato. I do not remember who evoked the Bacon-Shakespeare controversy yesterday: certainly Borges talks of it, but on this subject there is an endless bibliography, which begins in the seventeenth century, continues with monumental (and crazy) works in the nineteenth century, and extends to this day with pseudosecret societies that continue to look for the traces of Francis Bacon in Shakespeare's works. Obviously an idea like this (that the work of the great bard was written by someone else, who has left constant clues in the text if you read between the lines) could not but fascinate Borges. But that certainly does not mean that an author who cites the Shakespeare controversy today is quoting Borges.

Let us consider the problem of the rose. As I have said on several occasions, the title *The Name of the Rose* was chosen by some friends who looked at the list of ten titles I had scribbled down at the last minute. In fact the first title was *Delitti all' abbazia* (Murders at the Abbey) (a clear quotation of *Murder at the Vicarage,* which is a recurrent theme in English crime novels), and the subtitle was *Storia italiana del XIV secolo* (An Italian Tale from the Fourteenth Century) (a quotation from Manzoni's subtitle to *The Betrothed*). Subsequently this title seemed a bit heavy to me. I made a list of titles, among which I liked best *Blitiri* ("blitiri," like "babazuf," is a term used by the late Scholastics to indicate a word devoid of meaning), and then, seeing that the last line of the novel quoted a verse by Bernard of Morlaix that I had chosen for its allusion to Nominalism ("Stat rosa pristina nomine, etc."), I also put down *The Name of the Rose.* As I have said elsewhere, it seemed a good title to me because it was generic, and because in the course of the history of mysticism and literature the rose had taken on so many different meanings, often contradictory ones, that I hoped it would not lend itself to one-sided interpretations.

But it was pointless: everyone tried to find a precise meaning and many saw in it a reference to Shakespeare's "A rose by any other name," which means exactly the opposite of what my source intended. At any rate, I can swear that I never gave a thought to the appearances of the rose in Borges. Nevertheless, I find it wonderful that Maria Kodama made an allusion to Angelus Silesius the other day, probably unaware of the fact that some years ago Carlo Ossola wrote a very learned article on the links between my title and Silesius.* Ossola noticed that in the closing pages of my novel there is a collage of mystic texts from the period when the aged Adso is writing, but that I also inserted, in a wicked anachronism, a quotation from Angelus Silesius, which I had

---

*Carlo Ossola, "La rosa profunda. Metamorfosi e variazioni sul *Nome della rosa,*" *Lettere italiane* 36.4 (1984), subsequently in "Purpur Wort," in his *Figurato e rimosso. Icone di interni del testo* (Bologna: Il Mulino, 1988).

found somewhere or other, without knowing (at the time) that Silesius had also dealt with the rose. Here is a fine example of how the triangle of influences becomes more complex, but there was no straight two-way influence.

Another Borgesian theme that has been mentioned is the Golem. I inserted this theme into the *Pendulum* because it is part of the bric-a-brac that makes up occult lore, but my most direct source was obviously Meyrink, not to mention the famous film, closely followed by the kabbalistic texts I had studied through Scholem.

It has been pointed out in these last few days that many ideas that Borges later worked on had been expounded by Peirce and Royce. I believe that if you scour the index of names for all of Borges's works you will find neither Peirce nor Royce. And yet it is highly possible that Borges was influenced by them via other writers. I have many experiences that are, I think, common to all who possess very many books (I now have around forty thousand volumes, between Milan and my other houses) and to all who consider a library not just a place to keep books one has already read but primarily a deposit for books to be read at some future date, when one feels the need to read them. It often happens that our eye falls on some book we have not yet read, and we are filled with remorse.

But then the day eventually comes when, in order to learn something about a certain topic, you decide finally to open one of the many unread books, only to realize that you already know it. What has happened? There is the mystical-biological explanation, whereby with the passing of time, and by dint of moving books, dusting them, then putting them back, by contact with our fingertips the essence of the book has gradually penetrated our mind. There is also the casual but continual scanning explanation: as time goes by, and you take up and then reorder various volumes, it is not the case that that book has never been glanced at; even by merely moving it you looked at a few pages, one today, another the next month, and so on until you end up by reading most of it, if not in the usual linear way. But the true explanation is that between the moment when the book first came to us and the moment when we opened it, we have read other books in which there was something that was said by that first book, and so, at the end of this long intertextual journey, you realize that even that book you had not read was still part of your mental heritage and perhaps had influenced you profoundly. I think one can say this of Borges and his relation to Royce or Peirce. If this is influence, it is not two-way influence.

The theme of the double: Why did I put a double in *The Island of the Day Before*? Because Tesauro (in the chapter on novels in his *Cannocchiale aristotelico*) says that you have to do so if you want to write a novel in the baroque manner. Following Tesauro's rules, I put the twin brother in the opening chapter of my novel, but then I did not know what to do with him. At a certain point I found a way of using him, however. Would I have put him in if (leaving aside Tesauro's suggestion) I had not been influenced also by the theme of the double in Borges? And what if I had had in mind instead the theme of the double in Dostoyevsky? And what if Borges had been influenced by Tesauro, whom he perhaps absorbed indirectly through other baroque authors?

In these games of intertextuality and influences one must always be careful not to go for the most naive solution. Some of you at this conference recalled how Borges refers to a monkey hitting the keys of a typewriter at random and in the end writing *The Divine Comedy*. But be careful, for the argument that, if one denies the existence of God, then one must admit that the creation of the world happened rather as in the case of the famous monkey, was used countless times by fundamentalist believers in the nineteenth century (and also later) against the theory of evolution, as well as against the theory of the random formation of the cosmos. In fact, this theme is more ancient even than that;

we could trace it back to Democritus's and Epicurus's discussions of the clinamen . . .

This morning someone mentioned, referring to Fritz Mauthner, the question of whether real characters are like the characters of an ancient Chinese language (which then leads to Borges's idea of the Celestial Emporium). But it was Francis Bacon who first said that real characters had to be the same as Chinese ideograms, and that was what started the whole search for the perfect language in the seventeenth century. It was against this idea that Descartes launched his attack. Borges certainly knew this, either through Mauthner or directly from Descartes' famous letter to Father Mersenne, but did he also know Francis Bacon's discussion on real characters and Chinese ideograms? Or did he rediscover the topic through his reading of Athanasius Kircher? Or reading some other author? I believe it is fruitful to let the wheels of intertextuality rotate fully in order to see how the interplay of influence works in unexpected ways. Sometimes the most profound influence is the one you discover afterward, not the one you find immediately.

Now I would like to underline some aspects of my work that can *not* be called Borgesian, but as we are coming toward the end, I will mention only two.

First and foremost is the matter of quantity. Naturally one can write Leopardi's "L'infinito," which is a very short work, and one can write Cantù's *Margherita Pusterla,* which is a long and unbearable book; but on the other hand *The Divine Comedy* is long and sublime, while a brief sonnet by Burchiello is simply entertaining. The opposition between minimalism and maximalism is not one that entails value. It is an opposition of genre or procedure. In this sense Borges certainly is a minimalist, while I am a maximalist. Borges writes under the sign of rapidity, moves quickly to the conclusion of his story, and in this sense it is hardly surprising that Calvino admired him. I, on the other hand, am a writer who delays (as I wrote in my *Six Walks in the Fictional Woods*).

Perhaps also for quantitative reasons, I think one could define my writing as neo-baroque. Borges is fascinated intellectually by the baroque and the way the baroque maneuvers concepts, but his writing is not baroque. His style is limpidly classical.

But I prefer to pick out some strong Borgesian ideas, which cannot be reduced to a single quotation, and which probably constitute his most profound legacy, and therefore represent the way he influenced not just me but many others.

Someone mentioned narrative as a model of knowledge. Certainly Borges's fabulist narratives have influenced us in showing how one can make philosophical, metaphysical statements while telling a parable. Here too, of course, we have a topic that begins with Plato, or even with Jesus—if I may say so—and finishes with Lotman (with a textual modality as opposed to a grammatical modality), with Jerome Bruner's psychology (narrative models actually aid perception itself), and with the frames of artificial intelligence. But it seems certain to me that Borges's power of influence has been fundamental in this sense.

Now I would like to consider the call (and that is why I spoke of Borges as a delirious archivist) to reread the whole encyclopedia in the light of suspicion, and in a counterfactual way to seek the revelatory word in the margins, to reverse the situation, to make the encyclopedia play against itself.

It is very difficult to escape the anxiety of influence, just as it was very difficult for Borges to be a precursor of Kafka. Saying that there is no idea in Borges that did not exist before is like saying there is not a single note in Beethoven that had not already been produced before. What remains fundamental in Borges is his ability to use the most varied debris of the encyclopedia to make the music of ideas. I certainly tried to imitate this example (even though the idea of a music of ideas came to me from Joyce). What can I say? Compared with Borges's divine melodies, so instantly singable (even when they are atonal), memorable, and exemplary, I feel as if I blow into an ocarina.

But I hope that still someone will be found after my death who is even less skillful than me, someone for whom I will be recognized as the precursor.

An abbreviated version of a paper given at the conference on "Relaciones literarias entre Jorge Luis Borges y Umberto Eco," held at the University of Castilla–La Mancha (with the assistance of the Department of Italian Studies and the Emilio Goggio Chair of the University of Toronto).

ON CAMPORESI: BLOOD, BODY, LIFE

It is difficult to say who Piero Camporesi is. Over the course of fifteen books he has studied the various aspects of what is called "the material life"—our customs, behaviors, and in particular the "lower" functions, those connected with the body, food, blood, feces, sex—and thus he is certainly a cultural anthropologist. And yet one expects a cultural anthropologist to carry out "fieldwork," exploring the customs and myths of some civilization that still exists.

Camporesi, on the other hand, reads texts. He reads *literary* texts, or, rather, texts that belong to the history of literature. In fact, if you go and check what his academic field is you will see that he is a historian of literature (Italian literature, as is indicated in the list of faculty at Bologna University, but Camporesi makes frequent incursions into other literatures).

However, Camporesi reads and discovers texts that histories of literature have ignored, because they deal with everyday questions, moral or physical problems. Some official histories of literature have taken these texts into consideration, but from the point of view of their style, not of their content. Camporesi, on the other hand, has spent his life rediscovering and rereading them as witnesses to a way of life. Camporesi is therefore a cultural anthropologist who, in order to find material, does not go and study the men of today, whether "savage" or "primitive," but rather the (very civilized) men of the past.

I would like to explain myself better: Camporesi is the kind of man who goes into a room where there is a carpet with beautiful patterns and colors, which everyone has always looked at as a work of art; he takes it by the edge, turns it over, and shows us that the underside of that carpet was teeming with worms, cockroaches, grubs, a whole unknown and *underground* life. A life that nobody had ever discovered. And yet it was on the underside of the carpet all the time.

Camporesi has spent his life reading and rereading these forgotten texts, these texts that were staring everyone in the face but which no one had yet read in that way, to tell us how in past centuries the world was inhabited by vagabonds, charlatans, healers, thieves, murderers, madmen inspired by God, fake and genuine lepers. He has rediscovered the millennial dreams of a land of Cockaigne, the dreams of peoples who were oppressed by famine: he has rediscovered the rituals of Carnival, of witches' Sabbaths, of diabolical hallucinations.

He has brought to light texts that help us understand how in the past people had different ideas of their own bodies, and of food (Camporesi is a gourmet, and he understands what the smell of cheese or the taste of milk meant in those times). He has reread passages by religious preachers about the Inferno and its torments (which meant rediscovering a vision of the body as a site and occasion of pain, punishment, and endless suffering), he has looked at the way men ate, cooked, how they clicked their tongue when swallowing, how they heightened their sexual appetite through unguents and elixirs, how in the eighteenth century they welcomed those exotic and (at that time) marvelous beverages such as coffee and chocolate, how miners, weavers, barbers, surgeons, doctors, and healers worked, what image was held of the poor, the disinherited, the scoundrel, the thief, the murderer, and the desperado.

All the things Camporesi discovers were already there, as clear as day, in books that had piled up over the course of centuries. Camporesi simply knows how to *reread* these books.

He is, then, a historian of literature, who invites us to rediscover the least celebrated literary texts. He is a cultural anthropologist, but one who rediscovers the customs of ancient civilizations through the traces they have left in various texts.

It is difficult to say who Camporesi is. I confess that if I had to reread at a single sitting all the books he has written, I would be seized with nausea: they amount to a sequence of insights on the way bodies were loved, dismembered, fed, anatomized, devoured, rejected, humiliated. . . . Camporesi's cultural anthropology is shocking, ruthless, richly documented, and true. If someone decided to read all of Camporesi's books one by one, the reader would feel horror, satiety, and a desire to escape from this orgy of fibers, intestines, mouths, buboes, vomit, and greed. Camporesi's books must be sipped slowly, bit by bit, to escape the obsession with the body triumphant, with all its miseries and glories. Reading them all at once would be like eating nothing but cream cakes for an entire week, or swimming for a week in one's own excrement (which amounts to much the same).

The reader of this book will find just one aspect of this unbearable representation of the human body throughout the centuries: blood, its rites, myths, and reality. As we read this book we are seized by a slight (or not so slight) anxiety. We are made of bones, flesh, and blood. Blood is important. But nowadays it is analyzed only in laboratories, and we do not have a direct relationship with our blood. If we cut ourselves with a knife, we stop the bleeding with a bandage or with a styptic pencil. When a surgeon operates on us, and the blood flows, we are asleep. If there is an accident on the highway, we call the police and the ambulance, but we try not to see the blood. And yet, as Camporesi shows us, in past centuries blood was a daily reality, people knew its smell and its stickiness.

Are we really strangers to blood? Are we really that far from those centuries Camporesi tells us about? And if so why are there still so many Satanic sects, so many blood cults? One can even find them advertised on the Internet.

Have we solved the problem of our relationship with blood? True, we no longer have public ceremonies of dismemberment, where blood flowed in rivers. But as I write, the Italian newspapers feature accounts of a Madonna who weeps blood. A superstition, of course, but is there not also an element of superstition in those charismatic sects who order their faithful to carry out a bloodbath? What is the relationship between the Madonnas who weep blood and the taste for blood that hung over the slaughter of Sharon Tate?

That brings me to what I want to say: Camporesi reconstructs customs, feelings, fears, and desires that seemed ancient to us, and invites us to *look inside ourselves,* to understand the obscure relationship between rites and myths of the past and our own urges today, and to discover the ancient man inside us, we who use the Internet and think that blood only concerns surgeons and those who study new epidemics on our planet.

Perhaps Camporesi must be read in small doses, because if we read all his books, we would invariably ask ourselves: "Who are we, we civilized men?"

This is a short book. Let us read Camporesi in a homeopathic dose. That is enough for the moment. Later perhaps you will want to read his other books.

Written as a preface to Piero Camporesi, *The Juice of Life* (New York: Continuum, 1995).

ON SYMBOLISM

I know already that whatever I say about the topic of symbolism will be refuted in an erudite essay by my friend Sandro Briosi. Moreover, I have already devoted a number of articles to this subject, in particular the entry on "Symbolism" in the *Enciclopedia Einaudi,* which later became a chapter in my *Semiotics and the Philosophy of Language* (Bloomington: Indiana University Press, 1984). Whether it is because of the aging process or the persistence of adolescent hubris, I do not believe I have changed my thinking on this question. To emend one's thinking constantly is a desirable practice, and one I often engage in—sometimes to the point of being almost schizophrenic. But there are cases where one should not parade changes just to prove one is up to date. In the field of ideas, as much as in other fields, monogamy is not necessarily a sign of absence of libido.

In order not to repeat what I have already said on symbols, I would like to deal with a particularly topical aspect of this vexed question, namely, the phenomenon of symbolic paranoia. But in order to get to that point I will have to reiterate in part what I have already said on the subject, since omitting it would in the end create an excessive gap.

"Symbol" is a word I advise my students to use very sparingly and to note the contexts in which they find it, in order to decide the meaning it has there and not elsewhere. In fact, I no longer know what a symbol is. I have tried to define the symbolic mode as a particular textual strategy. But leaving aside this textual strategy—which I will return to later—a symbol can be either something very clear (an unambiguous expression with a definable content) or something very obscure (a polyvalent expression, which summons up a whole nebula of content).

The ambiguity of symbols comes from distant roots and is justified not only by the etymology of "*symballein*" but by the very practice its etymology denotes. For one could say of those two matching pieces of token that they will be seamlessly put together again the day someone places them in the presence of each other and makes them fit together, removing them from the free flow of semiosis and turning each of them once more into a thing in the world of things; and yet what is so fascinating about each of the two separated elements is the very absence of the other, for it is only on absence and in absence that the most overpowering passions thrive.

But let us leave aside etymology. The first quandary facing us is that in certain contexts, mostly scholarly ones, we use the expression "symbol" to indicate semiotic processes that are extremely clear and incontrovertible, objects that are not ambiguous but, rather, aim at being read in the most univocal way possible. The proof of this is the chemical symbol, or certain definitions of symbol that indicate, as opposed to the fluctuating openness of the icon, the conventionality of the linguistic or grammatical sign.

Of course, even symbols in logic have something of the openness of what, from Romanticism onward, we consider to be symbolic in the obscure and polyvalent sense of the term. For they represent variables, and as such they can be linked to highly unpredictable contents. Think, for instance, of an expression of symbolic logic such as "If p, then q." We have the impression that "p" and "q" can stand for anything we like, but that is not the case. Let us imagine that instead of "p" we put the entire *Divine Comedy* and in place of "q" the assertion that "six times six equals thirty-six." This proposition would appear to be true because of the laws of material implication. However, it is impossible to invert the order of the equation. If, for example, I placed the *Divine Comedy* in the position of "q," because the totality of assertions constituted by Dante's text is false from the point of view of truth-function (it is not true that a Florentine ascended to Paradise while still alive, or that Charon exists), then by the same laws of material implication the inference would be false, despite having a true premise. Whereas everything would work if in place of "six times six makes thirty-six" we assigned to "p" the entire text of *Mein Kampf,* in that, according to the famous paradox of material implication, false plus false makes true. Semiotic balancing acts aimed at finding a relationship between symbolic logic and the obscure symbols of Romantic poetics are therefore pointless. They each have different ways of functioning, different syntax, and different natures with regard to truth.

Similarly, the use Cassirer makes of the term in his theory of symbolic forms has nothing to do with the sense that we attribute to it: instead, his is a culturological version of Kantian transcendentalism, and even Euclidean geometry is a symbolic form, where we breathe the sense of the infinite and the undecideable only in the continuation of the parallel lines that his fifth postulate promises us in a way that is itself undecideable in terms of the truth of the statement.

We could stick to a sensible definition, which also applies to a whole series of daily experiences: the symbolic is identified by the existence, in every language, of levels of secondary meaning. This is the route taken by Todorov in his book on symbols. But to identify the symbolic with every instance of secondary meaning would lead us to confuse phenomena that are very different from each other.

There are two levels of meaning in any discourse that has two senses: the classic riddle is an example. But the two levels are structured, often on the basis of treacherous homonyms, according to two isotopies that can be traced without difficulty. Just like a message in code, the double sense needs to be deciphered, and once it has been decoded we have two senses that are indisputable, without any room for demurral.

Metaphor does not belong to the order of the symbolic. It can be open to multiple interpretations and can, as it were, be continued along the line of the second or third isotopy that it generates. But there are rules governing interpretation: that our planet is, as Dante says, "the threshing floor that makes us all so fierce" (*Par.* 22.151) might suggest thousands of poetic inferences, but it will not convince anyone, so long as there are cultural conventions we all agree on, that it is a place where peace and benevolence flourish. Moreover, I remain one of those who believe that the first signal of metaphorical usage consists in the fact that, taken literally, a metaphorical expression would appear false or weird, or nonsensical (the earth is not a threshing floor). This is not the case in the symbolic mode, which, as we shall see, conceals its own potential for meaning behind the deceptive appearance of something inexplicably obvious.

All the more reason, then, that allegory does not belong to the order of the symbolic either, since it is a continuous double sense based not on homonyms but on an almost heraldic codification of certain images.

The modern Western tradition is by now used to distinguishing allegory from symbolism, but the distinction is a rather late one: its articulation begins in Romanticism, and is particularly striking in Goethe's famous aphorisms (*Maximen und Reflexionen*):

> Allegory transforms the phenomenon into a concept and
> the concept into an image, but in such a way that
> the concept in the image is always to be considered

circumscribed and complete in the image, and has to
be given and to express itself through it (1.112).

Symbolism transforms the phenomenon into an idea and
the idea into an image, in such a way that the idea
in the image remains always infinitely effective and
inaccessible and, even if articulated in every language,
remains nevertheless inexpressible (1.113).

It makes a considerable difference whether the poet seeks
the particular as a function of the universal or whether
he sees the universal in the particular. In the first case
we have allegory, where the particular is valid only as
an example, as an emblem of the universal, whereas
in the second case the true nature of poetry is revealed: the particular case is expressed without thinking about the universal or alluding to it. Now whoever
catches this living particular seizes at the same time
the universal without realizing it, or only realizing it
later on (279).

True symbolism is that in which the particular element
represents the more general, not as a dream or a
shadow but as a living, instantaneous revelation of
the inscrutable (314).

The classical and medieval world, on the other hand, understood "symbol" and "allegory" to be synonyms. Examples of this
abound, from Philo to grammarians such as Demetrius, from
Clement of Alexandria to Hippolytus of Rome, from Porphyry
to Pseudo-Dionysius the Areopagite, and from Plotinus to Iamblichus, where the term "symbol" is also used for those didactic
and conceptualizing representations that elsewhere would be
called allegories.

It is true that scholars have described the world of the High
Middle Ages as the "symbolic universe," a universe where, ac-

cording to the words of Duns Scotus Eriugena (*De Divisione Naturae*, V.3), "*nihil enim visibilium rerum corporaliumque est, ut arbitror, quod non incorporale quid et intelligibile significet*" (there is, I believe, no visible or corporeal thing that does not signify something non-corporeal and intelligible). The world, then, is apparently, as Hugh of St. Victor would say later, "*quasi quidam liber scriptus digito Dei*" (like some book written by the finger of God). So must it not have been the case that that world where "*nostrum statum pingit rosa*" (a rose depicts our condition) (Pseudo-Alain of Lille, *Rhythmus Alter*) was a world populated by symbols?

According to Huizinga (chapter 15 of his *Waning of the Middle Ages*), the medieval symbolic universe was very close to the universe of Baudelaire's *Corréspondences*:

> The medieval spirit was never so convinced of any great truth as it was of the words of St. Paul: "*Videmus nunc per speculum in aenigmate, tunc autem facie ad faciem* (now we see through a glass darkly, then we will see face to face)." The Middle Ages never forgot that any object would be absurd if its meaning were limited to its immediate function and its place in the world of phenomena, and that all things extend far into the world beyond. This idea is familiar also to us, as an unformulated sensation, when for instance the noise of the rain on the leaves in the trees or the light of the lamp on the table, in a moment of tranquillity, gives us a more profound perception than daily observation, which merely serves practical activity. It can sometimes appear in the form of a morbid oppression, which makes us see things already laden with personal menace or with a mystery that one ought to recognize but cannot. More often, however, it will fill us with the tranquil and reassuring certainty that our existence too participates in that secret sense of the world.

But this is the interpretation of someone who has already seen Verlaine and Rimbaud wandering, on the borders of his own country, as exiles searching for the absolute, listening to the sound of the same rain on the leaves and letting their hearts fill with languor, or hallucinating about the chromaticism of vowels. Was this really the symbolism of the High Middle Ages, not to mention the late medieval period?

In order to accept the Neoplatonic inheritance it was essential to conceive, as Dionysius the Areopagite does, an idea of the One as unfathomable and contradictory, where the divinity is called the "most luminous obscurity of the silence which arcanely teaches . . . the most luminous darkness" (*Theologia mystica,* passim). It is true that for Dionysius the concepts of the One, the Good, and the Beautiful are applied to God, as though they were on a par with Light, Lightning, and Jealousy; but these concepts will be used to describe him solely in a "hypersubstantial" way: he may be these things, but in a way that is commensurately but also incomprehensibly more intense. What is more, Dionysius reminds us (and this is emphasized by his commentators), precisely in order to make clear that the names we attribute to God are inadequate, that it is important for them to be, as far as possible, different, incredibly unsuitable, almost provocatively offensive, extraordinarily enigmatic, as though the common quality that we are searching for between the symbolizing element and what is symbolized were indeed recognizable but only at the cost of inferential gymnastics and disproportionate proportions: and in order that the faithful, when naming God as Light, should not get the wrong idea that there exist celestial substances that are luminous and surrounded by haloes, it will be much better to name God using the names of monstrous beings, such as the bear or the panther, or through obscure dissimilarities (*De Coelesti Hierarchia,* 2).

Now this way of speaking, which Dionysius himself calls "symbolic" (e.g., *De Coelesti Hierarchia,* 2 and 15), has nothing to do with that illumination, that ecstasy, that rapid, lightning vision that all modern theories of symbolism see as peculiar to a symbol. The medieval symbol is a way of approaching the divine, but it is not the epiphany of something numinous, nor does it reveal to us a truth that can be articulated solely in terms of myth and not in terms of rational discourse. Rather, it is the preamble to a rational discourse, and its duty is to make clear, at the point when it seems didactically useful and appropriate to its role as preamble, its own inadequacy, its own (almost Hegelian) destiny to become real by a subsequent rational discourse. In other words, the medieval world was anxious about symbols, medieval man felt dismay, fear, and reverence before the bear and the panther, before the rose and the oak, but these were pagan remnants. Not only theology but medieval bestiaries themselves are firmly intent on deciphering these symbols, on turning them into metaphors or allegories, to stop their fluctuation.

In any case, the same thing happens with what Jung calls archetypes, which I would put under the broader category of what I term, using a metaphor, "totemic objects," which are imperious and stimulating in their very enigmatic nature. Jung was the first to explain how as soon as these archetypal images fascinate the mind of the mystic, dragging him toward an infinite drift of sense, some religious authority immediately intervenes to gloss them, subject them to a code, make them become a parable. And at that point the totemic object becomes a symbol in the more banal sense of the term, the one that makes us call the badges of political parties symbols, on which we mark our (often automatic) X of agreement. Endowed with connotative appeals at various levels (in the sense that one can become attached to or die for a flag, a cross, a crescent moon or a hammer and sickle), they are there to tell us what we have to believe in and what we have to reject. The Sacred Heart of the Vendée was no longer the same Sacred Heart that had dazzled Saint Margaret Mary Alacoque. It had changed from being the experience of something numinous to a political flag.

This idea of the symbol as an apparition that refers to a reality that cannot be expressed in words, a reality that is contradictory and ungraspable, becomes established in the West only with the spread of hermetic writings, and requires a very "strong" Neoplatonism. But as soon as the excitement caused by the flashes of the divine in Hermes Trismegistus's obscure discourse becomes a fashion, a style, a "koine," here too there suddenly emerges the desire, previously medieval, now Hermetic, to capture the symbol and give it a socializable sense.

It is curious how the baroque age was the most fertile in the production or, rather, invention of totemic objects, namely, its blazons, devices, and emblems; and it is curious how the baroque world spoke of them as symbols every time it could. *Syntagma de Symbolis* would be the title of one of the most famous commentaries on Alciati, Bocchi would write of *Symbolicarum Quaestionum,* Picinelli of *Mundus Symbolicus,* and Scarlatino of *Homo Figuratus et Symbolicus.* Emanuele Tesauro explains what these symbols are in his *Cannocchiale aristotelico:* "A symbol is a metaphor signifying a concept through some Figure which is visible."

In this celebration of symbols there always clearly emerges a dogmatic desire to write commentaries, in other words, to decipher. Venerable volumes astonish us with their iconological baggage made up of apparently oneiric images: these are real illustrious corpses of icons, a paradise for a psychoanalyst who does not want to read the gigantic accompanying commentary. But if we do turn to the commentary, it leads us step by step, and with considerable redundance, toward the most exact (though also the most clever) deciphering of every figure, in order to draw out a single moral lesson.

In this context the enterprise of Athanasius Kircher is quite ridiculous, aiming as it does to rediscover the mysteries of ancient Egyptian writing. It has a privileged position, since it sits opposite something that resembles a device or emblem, but one

for which no Alciati, Valeriano, or Ferro has supplied the interpretation. These are old and well-known images, and once they
are handed down no longer by a Christian (or pagan) tradition
but by Egypt's own divinities, they acquire a sense that is different from the one they had in moralizing bestiaries. References to
scripture, now absent, are replaced by allusions to a vaguer reli-
giosity, one dense with mysterious promises. The hieroglyphics
are seen as initiatic symbols.

These are for Kircher "symbols," and therefore expressions of
a hidden, unknown content, one that has many meanings and is
rich in mystery. Unlike a conjecture, which allows us to move from
a visible symptom to some definite cause, "a symbol is a mark signifying some more arcane mystery, which is to say that the nature
of a symbol is to lead us mentally, through some similarity, to the
understanding of something very different from things that are offered to our external senses; something whose nature is to be concealed or hidden beneath the veil of an obscure expression [. . .]. It
is not formed by words, but is expressed only through marks, characters, figures" (*Obeliscus Pamphilius*, II, 5, pp. 114–20).

These are "initiatic" symbols because the fascination of
Egyptian culture is based on the fact that the knowledge it promises is enclosed within the unfathomable and indecipherable circle
of an enigma in order to remove it from the profane curiosity of
the vulgar crowd. Furthermore, Kircher reminds us that a hiero-
glyph is a symbol of something sacred (and in that sense all
hieroglyphs are symbols, but not vice versa), and its power is due
to the fact it is not accessible to the uninitiated.

If it were accessible, the baroque age would have had to invent its own writing of the unfathomable. That is what Kircher
wants, and he delights in this with delirious enthusiasm in the
letter to the emperor that opens his *Oedipus Aegyptiacus*:

I parade before your eyes, most sacred Caesar, the polymor-
phous reign of Hieroglyphic Morpheus: by this I mean a

theater decked out with an immense variety of monsters, and these not naked monsters of nature, but so adorned with enigmatic Chimeras of a most ancient knowledge that here I am confident that sagacious minds can trace the boundless treasures of science, which is not without benefit for literature. Here the Dog of Bubastis, the Saitic Lion, the Mendesian Goat, the terrifying Crocodile with the horrendous opening of its jaws, all reveal the occult meanings of the divinity, of nature, of the spirit of Ancient Wisdom, beneath the shadowy play of images. Here the thirsty Dipsodes, the poisonous Asps, the wily Ichneumons, the cruel Hippopotami, the monstrous Dragons, the swollen-bellied toad, the snail with its spiral shell, the hairy caterpillar, and countless specters parade the miraculous, ordered chain that is revealed in the tabernacles of nature. Here are presented a thousand exotic species of things transformed into one image and then another by metamorphosis, turned into human figures and then restored again to their former shape in a mutual intertwining, the feral with the human, the human with the craft of the divine; and finally the divinity who, as Porphyry says, flows throughout the universe, and engineers a monstrous marriage with all beings; where now, sublime in their variety of faces, raising their canine necks, are displayed the Cynocephalus, and the foul Ibis, and the Sparrowhawk covered with its beaked mask [. . .] and where also, luring us with its virginal looks, under the covering of the Scarab, the sting of the Scorpion is concealed [. . . all this and more in a list that goes on for four pages] we can meditate in this all-changing theater of Nature, spread out as it is before our gaze, under the allegorical veil of an occult meaning.

It is precisely because of the fascination of the secret meanings in the ancient Egyptian language that Kircher celebrates it as opposed to the bland and highly codified iconic language of the Chinese, where every ideogram corresponds to a precise idea; something that might have fascinated Bacon but not him. Egyptian symbols "*integros conceptos ideales involvebant*" (enclosed complete ideal concepts), and by "involvebant" Kircher did not mean "collected," or "offered," but "concealed," "enclosed". . . . Egyptian icons had to be like flirtatious women, constantly luring their admirers into the vortex of an unsatisfied cognitive passion but never yielding themselves up to them.

But what does Kircher do after this preamble, for thousands of pages and throughout at least three entire works? He tries to decipher it all, makes his victory as an Egyptologist consist in revealing to us the secret meaning of these signs; he translates them, convinced that he is translating them in the only correct way possible. He makes an enormous mistake, we know, but what we object to now are not his results but his intentions. Champollion would carry out the same operation as Kircher in a more secular spirit, and without making a mistake; he would tell us that those were conventional signs, endowed with phonetic values, and would try to rid every symbol of any ambiguity. Yet Kircher had already begun the process. Those who, in a less Catholic and theological spirit than Kircher, try to preserve a charge of unresolved mystery in these hieroglyphics would turn them into party badges for down-market occultism, and in fact would be fascinated not by their unfathomable qualities but by the sense of confidence they give, these rigid emblems that they have now become. But somewhere a mystery exists, a mystery that will never be revealed, not because it is unfathomable, but because those who administer it will have decided not to fathom it so as to be able to sell it as a kind of trademark, or promise of an elixir, to collectors of the absolute or those who frequent Masonry's Grand Guignol.

Our notion of the symbolic is rooted in a universe that is by now secular, where a symbol no longer has to reveal or hide the absolutes of religion, but the absolute of poetry. Our approach to symbols is profoundly affected by French symbolism, for which Baudelaire's *Les Corréspondences* serves nicely as a manifesto: the living columns of nature allow only confused words to emerge, "*comme de longs échos qui de loin se confondent / dans une ténébreuse et profonde unité / vaste comme la nuit et comme la clarté*" (like distant echoes that dwindle in the distance / in a deep, dark unity, / vast as the night and brightness).

Only then can one say with Mallarmé "une fleur" and not decide on what the word should summon up for us, because that will be only the very absence, a pregnant absence, of all "flowerness," and therefore everything and nothing, and we will sit in a daze asking ourselves endlessly what is meant by *"le vierge, le vivace et le bel aujourd'hui."*

But at this point objects no longer exist, whether they are emblems, mysterious figures, or isolated words that have symbolic value in themselves. Not even Mallarmé's flower would be that were it not inserted into his strategy of the blank page. The symbolic becomes an effect of meaning produced by the text, and as such any image, word, or object can assume the status of a symbol.

What semiotic key can be offered, not for interpreting, but for identifying the textual strategy that I have decided to call the symbolic mode?

One suggestion was given to us some time ago, by a passionate and necessarily determined seeker after second meanings: Saint Augustine. When something in scripture appears semantically understandable but seems to us out of place, excessive, inexplicably emphatic, that is where we have to seek a hidden second meaning. Sensitivity to the symbolic mode stems from having noticed that there is something in the text that has meaning and yet could easily not have been there, and one wonders why it is there. This something is not a metaphor, because otherwise it would have gone against common sense, it would have polluted the stark purity of the degree zero of writing. It is not allegory, because it does not refer to any heraldic code. It exists, it is there, it does not disturb us that it is there, at most it might slow down our reading, but it is the surplus that it represents, its blameless incongruity, its presence looming so large in the economy of the text, that makes us suppose that its placement means it may be saying something else as well.

It is this figure's superfluity, its gratuity, that makes it totemic. It is the question it inspires in us ("Why are you here, and at this particular point?") that forces us to this interrogation that will elicit no answer. This is one of the rare cases when it is not our deconstructive hubris but the very will of the text that invites us to drift this way.

Why does Montale have to spend a good sixty "Old Lines" to tell us in the poem of that name how a horrible moth with its sharp beak ate through the thin fibers of a lampshade, insanely fluttering its wings over the papers on the table? It is the very irrelevance of the experience that makes it totemic, "*e fu per sempre / con le cose che chiudono in un giro / sicuro come il giorno, e la memoria / in sé le cresce*" (and it was forever / one with those things that close in a circle / as certain as the day, and are enhanced by memory).

Why, after warning us that he intends to show us something different from our shadow at morning striding behind us, or our shadow at evening rising to meet us, does Eliot tell us in *The Waste Land* (and it is up to us to determine whether the sense of these lines is literal or metaphorical): "I will show you fear in a handful of dust"? In this example the symbol exceeds the very powers of the metaphor. This handful of dust could certainly be a metaphor for many things, but traditionally, through association, it is for failure. How many times in our life have we ended up with nothing but a handful of dust, and we have said so using this very idiom? But is it the fear announced and produced by this that Eliot wants to evoke? Failure disappoints, hurts, and diminishes us, but it does not frighten us, since it no longer contains anything unexpected. That handful of dust stands for something else there; perhaps it has been there since the big bang, and if it is someone's failure it is that of the Demiurge. Or perhaps not; perhaps it is the epiphany of a universe without a big bang and without a Demiurge, the proof of our living-for-death (but then *The Waste Land* was written five years before Heidegger's *Being and Time*).

Epiphany: there, I've said it. Basically the Joycean concept of epiphany is the most secular, or most religious (when with Barilli it becomes "materialistic ecstasy"), version of the symbolic mode. Something appears, and we know that it is an apparition, otherwise it would not be so out of place, and yet we do not know what it is revealing to us. A symbol is an epiphany with Magi whose origins and destination we do not know, nor whom they have come to adore. The stable at Bethlehem is empty, or occupied by, let's say, an enigmatic object, a dagger, a black box, a glass ball with snow falling inside on the Madonna of Oropa, or a fragment of a railway timetable. And yet it flashes, at least for those of us who accept its invitation to the superfluous.

Returning to *The Waste Land*: Why does it say at a certain point, "There I saw one I knew, and stopped him, crying 'Stetson!'"? Because Eliot and Stetson had been together at Mylae? Because last year Stetson planted a corpse in his garden, and now it has started to sprout? Why does he have to keep the dog "far hence"?

Roberto Cotroneo, in his book *Se una mattina d'estate un bambino* (Milan: Frassinelli, 1994), attempts an explanation: of course, who else wore a Stetson but Pound? Why not Mylae when, after this first defense of the West, in order to exorcize Carthaginian power Rome introduced the cult of the Phrygian goddess, which was followed by the coming together of the two worlds, and fertility rites? Certainly, this reading is legitimate, and authorized by Eliot himself, since he begins his notes with a reference to Miss Weston. But is that the end of the story? Certainly not. The unwanted appearance of Stetson continues to disturb us, and in any case a few lines before this Eliot gives us the sign that he is fully entering the symbolic mode. He has just mentioned the fact that Saint Mary Woolnoth kept the hours "with a dead sound on the final stroke of nine," and at this point he inserts one of the few hermetic notes to his poem. Commenting on this line 68, he says: "A phenomenon which I have often noticed."

A sublime and totally superfluous observation. Why of all the events of that particular London, of that unreal city where a crowd flowed, so many that he did not think death had undone so many, where each man fixed his eyes before his feet, does Eliot have to tell us that he frequently observed that particular phenomenon, as though it were a Kantian noumenon?

And we readers, what are we meant to do? Eliot tells us immediately, borrowing an insult that lies at the origin of symbolism's poetics: "You! hypocrite lecteur!—mon semblable,—mon frère!" By translating the vocative from French to English, he has decontextualized the address. Now it means something else. We have to ask why Stetson has appeared so suddenly, whether he is just a hat, and why we are hypocritically guilty of his arrival.

Note that once more the name Stetson is not a symbol in and of itself. It becomes one because of the context. There is an unjustified focus on it.

Nor must we think that incongruity equals lack of internal logic, or that gratuitousness means frivolity. Sometimes the symbolic mode exhibits its own rigid, though perhaps paranoid, logic, and the symbol is solid, geometric, and heavy, like the galactic obelisk that appears at the beginning of *2001: A Space Odyssey.*

Nor must we think that a symbol has to be something fleeting, an image barely alluded to, appearing in the text like a brief glimpse. If for Mallarmé naming an object meant suppressing three-quarters of its poetic pleasure (which consists in the joy of guessing bit by bit— *"le suggérer, voilà le rêve!"*), nothing is merely suggested in Kafka's "In the Penal Colony"; on the contrary, everything is described in extraordinary detail. Almost like an engineering treatise, or a legal exchange with a Talmudic flavor, the story constructs its "celibate machine," and it is the entire description taken as a whole, extending page after page, that drives us to ask the reason for that presence. Not why it is there—for it is there, and that is enough—but rather what is the overall sense of this theater of cruelty. And we will continue to ask ourselves until the end of our lives, because any allegorization of the symbol would only lead us to an obvious truth, would only tell us what we already wanted to know.

And now I come to the second part of my paper. This may seem contrary to our most cherished ideas, but all the centuries that have spoken to us about symbols knew little of the symbolic mode. Perhaps that was what the pilgrims at the temple of the god at Delphi were seeking, where the oracle neither says nor hides things but only vaguely alludes. But after that point, in order to find a notion of symbol like the one we have been outlining over the millennia, to find the symbolic mode asserting itself as a conscious strategy, we have to come to the period between the nineteenth and twentieth centuries. Perhaps it was modernity that invented the notion of poetry, seeing that those who read Homer at the time or shortly afterward saw him as an encyclopedia of universal knowledge, and medieval readers used Virgil the way Nostradamus would be used later. Today it is we who demand that poetry, and often fiction, supply us not just with the expression of emotions, or an account of actions, or morality, but also with symbolic flashes, pale ersatz elements of a truth we no longer seek in religion.

Can this be enough? It will satisfy only those who have a cold awareness of the insignificance of the universe, a fervent will for redemption through the question, not through the supine acceptance of the answer.

Is this the attitude that distinguishes our times? No, and please allow me this moralistic conclusion. As soon as our age discovered the symbolic mode, it accepted only two refinements of its legacy.

The first, a learned and refined version, is that there is a deep sense concealed everywhere, that every discourse uses the symbolic mode, that every utterance is constructed along the isotopy of the *unsaid,* even when it is as simple as, "It's raining today." This is today's deconstructionist heresy, which seems to assume that a divinity or malign subconscious made us talk always and only with a second meaning, and that everything we say is inessential because the essence of our discourse lies elsewhere, in a symbolic realm we are often unaware of. Thus the symbolic diamond, which was meant to flash in the dark and dazzle us at sudden but ideally very rare moments, has become a neon strip that pervades the texture of every discourse. This is too much of a good thing.

It is not a bad interpretative strategy if interpreting means accumulating qualifications for university positions. But if everyone always says what he did not mean to say, we are all always saying the same thing. The symbolic mode no longer exists as a supreme linguistic strategy; we all speak indirectly, imprecisely, constantly using symbols because we are sick with language. Where there is no recognizable rule there cannot even be deviation from the norm. We all speak in poetry, we all reveal something, even when we are just saying that we will pay the insurance bill on Tuesday. What a curse, living in a world so damnably orphic, where there is no room for the language of the man in the street. In a world where the man in the street cannot speak, even the poet has to remain silent.

The second heresy is to be found in the information world, which, accustomed as it is now to conspiracies, coded phrases, half-spoken words, alliances promised then canceled, and whispers of divorce that are immediately denied, seeks a secret meaning in every event and in every expression. This is the curse of the contemporary writer, something I don't want to speak about since I do not want to talk about my own personal experiences; but I will construct a model of him based on the experience of a writer from the past who I imagine facing today's critics or journalists.

Let us say this writer is Leopardi, and let us invent his *Dialogo tra il Poeta e un Facitore di Rotocalchi* (Dialogue between the Poet and a Magazine Editor)...

"Signor Leopardi, the fact that you very briefly (for about fifteen lines) conducted a certain discourse on a hill where you reflected on the infinite is very stimulating and intriguing. Why did you call the hill *'ermo'* (deserted)? Allow me to say that you were obviously alluding to the mutilation of the Herms, the incident which placed Alcibiades in conflict with the Athenian government, as though you were clearly, or at least up to a point, talking about the conflict which has seen left-wing politicians lining up against Forza Italia..."

"Not at all, I called the hill *'ermo'* because I indulged in the taste for archaism, and I admit that this is the worst line of that idyll; but the hill was certainly dear to me, because I was born near there."

"And why do you imagine 'the most profound rest'? Do not try to tell me that this is not a clear and explicit allusion to the current political situation, the anxiety of the markets, and the uncertain fate of the budget bill."

"Look, I wrote 'L'infinito' between the spring and autumn of 1819, so I could not have alluded to your political situation. Allow a poet to dream, on top of a hill, deserted almost by accident, but in a totally literal way: there is no allegory, and just four rather modest metaphors: the profound rest (but even your own Lakoff would say that spatialization is an everyday way of making metaphors), the dead seasons (which is almost a mixed metaphor), the drowning of my thoughts, and the shipwreck in a sea that is not a sea . . . But as for the rest of it, there is no symbol and no allegory. Poetry does not fade into rhetoric, nor rhetoric into a legal speech . . . I was there that day, and I suddenly said to myself: 'Mamma mia, the infinite . . .' Perhaps the only symbolic element lies in the very fact that I did this even though there was no need to. But do not try to decode this. Let my moment of weakness be, just as it is, read the poem again, and then follow any line you like in your reply."

"Oh come on, my little Count, you can't pull the wool over our eyes. Three years, just three years after the Congress of Vienna, you are going on about timeless abandons, while Europe is in the process of becoming what it is . . . Will you at least allow us to read your text for what it really says?"

That is the end of my little game. Incapable as we are of finding or identifying a symbol where it actually exists, infected by the culture of suspicion and conspiracy, we look for it even where it does not exist as a textual mode. Or where, at best, not every single feature but rather the text taken as a whole, its unavoidable and open unintentionality, which makes it appear when nobody would have expected it, becomes a symbol, if you like, of the human condition.

In actual fact the world of the mass media does not go looking for symbols, because it has lost the capacity and talent for doing so. Deprived of a God to allude to, we seek allegories everywhere, mysterious connections between the stabbing of two girls (when statistics tell us that to find two murders with similarities in the space of ten years is absolutely normal), short circuits flashing in the dull texture of everyday life. And as a result we are losing the gift for identifying the symbolic mode where it does lurk.

Where everything has a second sense, everything is irredeemably flat and dull. The lust for a second sense ruins our ability to see second or even one thousand senses where they actually exist, or have been placed.

We no longer even know how to enjoy the revelation of the literal, the sense of amazement at that which is, when the maximum of polyvalence coincides with the minimum of tautology: "a rose is a rose is a rose."

The symbolic mode exists at that point where we finally will have lost the desire to decode at any cost.

Revised version of a paper given at a conference on Symbolism, held in Siena in 1994 (published in Sandro Briosi, ed., "Symbolism," special issue of *L'immagine riflessa*, n.s. IV, 1, pp. 35–53). This revised version is dedicated to Sandro Briosi, who was still with us at the time.

ON STYLE

From the way it first appeared at the beginning of the Latin world right down to contemporary stylistics and aesthetics, the term "style" exhibits a history that is anything but uniform. Even though there is an original nucleus that can be identified, which means that from the word "stilus"—the instrument from which it derives by metonymy—style becomes synonymous with "writing" and therefore with the way one expresses oneself in literary terms, it is nevertheless true that this way of writing is understood in different ways and with different intensities over the course of the centuries.

For instance, already in the early years of its usage, the term indicates literary genres that are highly codified (the sublime, middle, low style; the Attic, Asian, or Rhodian style; the tragic, elegiac, or comic style). In this, as in so many other cases, style is a way of writing dictated by rules, usually very prescriptive rules; and it was accompanied by the idea of precepts, imitation, and close adherence to models. Usually we think that it is only with mannerism and the baroque that the idea of originality and genius becomes associated with the notion of style—and not only in the arts, but also in life, since with the Renaissance idea of "*sprezzata disinvoltura*" (effortless nonchalance) the man of style will be he who has the wit, courage (and social standing) to behave in violation of the rules—or to show that he has the privilege to break them.

Nevertheless, even Buffon's famous saying, "*Le style est l'homme même*," must be understood not in an individualistic sense at this stage but rather in the sense that style is human virtue.

The idea of a style that goes against the rules appears rather with Cesare Beccaria's *Ricerca intorno alla natura dello stile* (*Inquiry into the Nature of Style*), and reappears later in organicist theories of art, so that with Goethe style will emerge when the work acquires an original, complete, inimitable harmony of its own. Finally we arrive at the Romantic notion of genius (Leopardi himself will say that style is the particular manner or facility that is called originality). So much so that by the end of the nineteenth century, with the advent of the dandy and Decadence, the concept has turned 360 degrees, to the point where style is identical with bizarre originality, the contempt for all models; and it is from this source that the aesthetics of the historical avant-garde movements will emerge.

I would single out two authors for whom style is a distinctly semiotic concept, namely, Flaubert and Proust. For Flaubert style is a way of fashioning one's work, and certainly it is inimitable, but through it a way of thinking of and seeing the world is revealed. For Proust style becomes a sort of intelligence that is transformed or incorporated into the subject matter, so much so that, for Proust, Flaubert's innovative use of the past definite, the perfect, the present participle, and the imperfect renews our vision of things almost as much as Kant.

From these sources derives the idea of style as a "way of giving form," which lies at the heart of Luigi Pareyson's aesthetics. And it is clear that at this stage, if the work of art is form, the way of giving form involves more than just lexis or syntax (as can happen in what is called stylistics), and includes every semiotic strategy deployed both on the surface and in the depths of a text's nervous system. To the realm of style (as a way of giving form) belongs not only the use of language (or of colors, or of sounds, according to the semiotic systems or universes used) but also the way of deploying narrative structures, portraying characters, and articulating points of view.

Let us take a passage from Proust's "Observations on Style," where he claims that Stendhal was less careful about style than Baudelaire. Proust suggests that Stendhal "wrote badly," and this is an obvious point, if by style we mean lexis and syntax:

> When he describes a landscape as "those enchanted places," "those delightful spaces," or one of his heroines as "that adorable woman," "that fascinating woman," he did not want to be any more precise. He was even so devoid of precision as to write: "She wrote him an endless letter." However, if one considers the huge, unconscious framework that is covered by the conscious ensemble of ideas to be an integral part of style, there is undoubtedly precision in Stendhal. I would take great pleasure in showing you that every time Julien Sorel and Fabrizio del Dongo forget their vain cares in order to live a life that is disinterested and voluptuous, they are always in some elevated place (whether it be Julien's or Fabrizio's prison or the Abbé Blanès's observatory).*

By this time speaking of style means discussing how the work of art is made, showing how it gradually emerged (even though sometimes this is only through the purely theoretical progression of a generative process), explaining why it offers itself to a certain type of reception, and how and why it arouses this reception. And, for those who are still interested in pronouncing judgments

---

*Paul Morand, *Tendres Stocks,* preface by Marcel Proust (Paris: Gallimard, 1921).

as to aesthetic value, it is only by identifying, tracking down, and laying bare the supreme workings of style that we are able to say why a given work is beautiful, why it has enjoyed different kinds of reception in the course of time, and why, although it follows models and sometimes even precepts that are scattered far and wide in the sea of intertextuality, it has been able to gather those legacies and make them blossom in such a way as to give life to something original. Only then will we be able to say why, although each of the different works by one artist aspires to an inimitable originality, it is possible to detect the personal style of that artist in each of these works.

If this is the case, I believe two points must be made here: one, that a semiotics of the arts is nothing other than searching for and laying bare the workings of style; and two, that semiotics represents the most advanced form of stylistics, and the model for all criticism.

Having said this, I do not really need to add anything further. Everyone remembers how much light has been shed on texts (already loved by all, though in an obscure way) by certain pronouncements by the Russian formalists, by Jakobson, by narratologists and analysts of poetic discourse. But we really are living in obscure times, at least in Italy, where one hears with increasing frequency polemical voices accusing semiotic studies (which they sometimes also call, with pejorative connotation, formalist or structuralist studies) of being guilty of a decline in criticism, of being pseudomathematical discourses, full of illegible diagrams, in whose mush the flavor of literature evaporates, and where the ecstasy to which the reader succumbs is plotted out as in double-entry bookkeeping—where the *je ne sais quoi* and the sublime, which were supposed to be the supreme effects of art, evaporate in an orgy of theories that crudely abuse, insult, humiliate, and crush the text, removing its freshness, magic, and capacity for ecstasy.

We must therefore ask ourselves what is meant by criticism (of art or literature), and for the sake of convenience I will restrict myself to dealing with literary criticism.

I think that first and foremost we must distinguish between discussing literary works and literary criticism. One can have the most varied discussions of literary works, and a work can be taken as a field of sociological inquiry, a document in the history of ideas, a psychological or psychiatric report, or as a pretext for a series of moral considerations. There are cultures, above all the Anglo-Saxon world, where—at least until the advent of the New Criticism—the discussion of literary works was conducted above all in moral terms. Now all these approaches are legitimate in and of themselves, except that as soon as they come into play, they presume, imply, suggest, or refer to a critical or aesthetic judgment that someone else, or perhaps even the author himself in another work, already pronounced.

This kind of discussion is the discourse of criticism in its proper sense, and it can be articulated in three ways—although we must be clear about the fact that these three ways are "critical genres," ideal types of criticism, and it is often the case that, under the aegis of one genre or mode, someone provides illustrious examples of another genre, or mixes, to good or bad effect, the three types together.

Let us call the first type the "review," where one tells readers about a book they have not yet read. A good review can also turn to more complex modes, such as the other two types, which I shall discuss later, but it is inevitably linked to immediacy, to the brief space that intervenes between a work appearing, then being read and subjected to a written verdict. In the best cases, a review can restrict itself to giving its readers a summary idea of a work that they have not yet read, and then imposing on them the critic's judgment (of taste). Its function is clearly to inform (it says that a work has been published that is roughly as described) and to offer a reliable diagnosis; the reader believes the reviewer just as he trusts the doctor who makes him say "Ah," and then immediately identifies the beginnings of bronchitis and prescribes a cough mixture. Such a diagnostic review has nothing to do with the chemical analyses or exploratory probes that nowadays the patient himself can follow on a television screen, and during which he can see and understand what the problem is, and why his body is reacting in that manner. In a review (as in the doctor's home visit) the reader does not see the work, he only hears it spoken of by a third party.

The second critical mode (the history of literature) discusses texts that the reader does know or at least ought to know, since he has previously heard people talk about them. These texts are often only mentioned, or sometimes summarized, maybe with the help of some typical quotation, and are then grouped together, assigned to various schools, and organized in chronological sequence. A history of literature can be just a dreary manual, but occasionally it becomes at the same time a survey of the works and a history of ideas, as in De Sanctis's *History of Italian Literature*. In the best cases, historical criticism pushes the reader toward a final and comprehensive understanding of the work, establishes the reader's horizon of expectations and his tastes, and opens up infinite panoramas.

Both these modes can be practiced in two different ways, which, according to Croce, can be defined as the "*artifex additus artifici*" (an artist writing about an artist) approach, or the "*philosophus additus artifici*" (a philosopher writing about an artist) approach. In the first case, rather than explaining the work to us, the critic provides us with a diary of his emotions in reading it, and unconsciously seeks to outdo in virtuosity the object of his humble devotion. Sometimes he succeeds—we know very well passages on literature that are finer, in a literary sense, than the literature they discuss, just as Proust's pages on bad music are of the highest musicality.

In the second approach the critic tries to show us, in the light of certain critical categories and criteria, why the work is beautiful. But in the case of a review he does not have sufficient space to tell us in depth how the work is made (and therefore to reveal to us the machinations of its style), while a history of literature has to maintain its analysis on a level of enforced generality. Unfortunately, it takes a hundred pages to lay bare the style of one page, and in a history of literature the proportions are inevitably the inverse.

Let us now come to the third mode, textual criticism. In it the critic has to assume that the reader knows nothing about the work, even if it is as well known as *The Divine Comedy.* He has to make the reader discover it for the first time. If the text is not brief enough to be quoted in its entirety, and subdivided into sections of prose or verse, he has to presume that the reader has access to it in some other way, since the goal of this discourse is to lead him, step by step, in the discovery of how the text has been put together and why it functions as it does. This discourse can be put forward as a confirmation ("now I will show you why everyone considers this to be a brilliant text"), as a revaluation, or as the destruction of a myth. The ways in which one can show how a text is put together (and why it is right that it is put together in this way, and how it could not be composed in any other way, and why it has to be considered as sublime precisely because it is composed in this way) can be countless. No matter how these discourses are articulated, such criticism cannot be anything other than a semiotic analysis of the text.

Consequently, if proper criticism is understanding and making others understand how a text is made, and if the review and the history of literature are unable to do this adequately, the only true form of criticism is a semiotic reading of the text.

Like proper criticism (which must lead to an understanding of the text in all its aspects and potential) the semiotic reading of a text possesses a quality that is usually and indeed inevitably missing in a critical review or history of literature: it does not *prescribe* the various ways in which the text can be pleasurable, but, rather, it shows us why the text can produce pleasure.

Because it has to make recommendations, a critical review cannot be exempt, except in cases of exceptional cowardice, from pronouncing a verdict on what the text says; historical criticism shows us at most that a work has enjoyed a varied and fluctuating critical fortune, and has aroused different responses. Textual criticism, by contrast, which is always semiotic even when it does not know it is, or even when it denies it is, fulfills that function which was admirably described by Hume in "Of the Standard of Taste," which cites a passage from *Don Quixote*:

> Two of my kinsmen were once called to give their opinion of a hogshead, which was supposed to be excellent, being old and of a good vintage. One of them tastes it; considers it, and after mature reflection pronounces the wine to be good, were it not for a final taste of leather, which he perceived in it. The other after using the same precautions, gives also his verdict in favor of the wine; but with the reserve of a taste of iron. You cannot imagine how much they were both ridiculed for their judgment. But who laughed in the end? On emptying the hogshead, there was found at the bottom, an old key with a leathern thong tied to it.*

My point is that proper criticism always has the last laugh, because it allows everyone to have his own pleasure, but it also shows the reason for that pleasure.

---

*David Hume, "Of the Standard of Taste," in *Four Dissertations and Essays on Suicide and the Immortality of the Soul,* ed. John Immerwahr, John Valdimir Price, and James Fieser (South Bend, Indiana: St. Augustine's Press, 1995), 216–17.

Of course, even textual criticism, carried out by a "*philosophus additus artifici,*" can be aware of its own excesses, which thwart its very function. It will be useful to consider some errors of textual semiotics, which have occasionally caused the rejection syndromes I spoke of just now.

There is often confusion between "the semiotic theory of literature" and "criticism that is semiotically oriented." I refer you to an old debate from the 1960s, which began with the famous catalogue issued by the publisher Il Saggiatore dedicated to "Structuralism and Criticism," a debate in which there were roughly two speaking positions, one represented by Segre, the other by Rosiello. To put it briefly, for the first option, linguistic theory was to be used to shed light on the individual work; for the second, the analysis of the individual work was to be used to shed light on the nature of language. Therefore, when the first option was at work, a group of theoretical assumptions would be used to shed light on an author's personal style, whereas in the case of the second option, the personal style was felt to be a deviation from the linguistic norm, which reinforced knowledge of the norm as such.

Now these two positions were and are equally legitimate. One can construct a theory of literature, and use individual works as documents, and one can read individual works in the light of a theory of literature, or, rather, in an attempt to make the very principles of a theory of literature emerge from the examination of individual works.

Let us take the example of one area of literary theory such as narratology, which treats texts as examples and not as objects of analysis. If the role of criticism of a narrative text is to understand that text better, what role does narratology have? First and foremost, its role is to create narratology, just as philosophy essentially is used to philosophize. It helps to understand how narrative texts function, whether they are good or bad. Secondly, it is useful to many disciplines (such as artificial intelligence, semantics, and psychology) in helping us understand how the totality of our experience is structured (maybe) always and in every case in the shape of "narrations": a narratological theory that was useful in understanding only how stories are told would not amount to very much, but if instead it teaches us how we organize our approach to the world in narrative sequences, then it is something more. Finally, it also teaches us to read better, and even (take the case of Calvino) to invent new forms of writing. So long as we know how to make it interact with a "natural" way of reading, that is to say with a critical reading that is not set in stone at the outset by certain narratological prejudices.

Now there are two ambiguities here, one of production and one of reception. The first is when the semiotician is not clear, or does not make clear, whether he is using the text to enrich his theory of narrative, or whether he is working with certain narratological categories in order to understand the particular text better. The second is when the reader (often prejudiced) takes as an exercise in criticism a discourse that was aimed instead at deriving general principles of narrativity from one or more individual texts. This would be like a psychologist who is interested in the motives that make someone kill reading a statistical essay on crime in the last twenty years and complaining that statistics have not provided an explanation of individual motivation.

We could restrict ourselves to saying to these prejudiced readers that narratological theories are of no use either to the reading or to the criticism of a text. We could say that they are simply protocols of multiple readings, and that they serve the same purpose as the theory of physics, which explains how bodies fall according to one single law without telling us whether this is good or bad, nor what the difference is between a stone falling from the Leaning Tower of Pisa and an unhappy lover plummeting from a wuthering height. We could say that their purpose is to understand not texts but the function of storytelling in its totality, and that they therefore seem more like a chapter in psychology or cultural anthropology than like a chapter in literary criticism.

And yet we would have to explain also that they have, in addition, and if nothing else, a pedagogical value. They are an instrument used by those who are teaching others to read, in order to instantly identify the crucial points to which the pupil's attention has to be drawn. And so, if nothing else, they would be useful for teaching people how to read. But since one has to teach the skill of reading even to those who are no longer illiterate, they are of use also to the mature reader, the critic, and even the writer, in order to generate reliable observation.

In short, we really need to make people understand that although a dictionary is not enough to make a good writer, nevertheless good writers often consult dictionaries. Without claiming thereby that the Zingarelli dictionary and Leopardi's *Canti* belong to the same kind of discourse.

And yet, perhaps also through the semioticians' own fault, the enemies of textual semiotics cannot distinguish between the two genres of discourse (of textual semiotics and a textual criticism that is semiotically oriented). And in confusing them they lose the sense of the third type of discourse I spoke about, the only one that can help us understand the way a text reveals how it has been given form.

When preconstituted theory precedes the reading of a text, we often mean to lay bare the tools of inquiry, which are already known, in order to show that we are familiar with them, and that we have been ingenious in constructing them, instead of possessing the artistry to conceal the art, and to make what the text finally reveals to us come directly out of the text and not out of the pyrotechnics of theoretical metalanguage. It is obvious that this method of proceeding scares the reader who wants to know something about the text, and not about the metalanguage that establishes codes of reading.

Since a textual theory sketches out the constants, while textual criticism should highlight the variables, it often happens that, having realized that the world of intertextuality is made up of constants and variables of invention, and that a work of literature is a miracle of invention that keeps at bay and conceals the variables on which it nevertheless plays, semiotic inquiry is reduced to the discovery of the same constants in every text, and thus loses sight of the inventions.

As a result of this we find people researching the structure of the Tarot cards in Calvino (as though the author had not already revealed everything on this subject to us), or formulaic exercises on life and death, identified in every text, which as a result reduces *Hamlet* to "to be / not to be," "not wanting to be / wanting not to be." In these cases, we should note, the procedure may be excellent in didactic terms, and may even succeed in showing how, whereas all of us struggle each day between wanting to be and wanting not to be, Shakespeare presents an eternal dilemma in a new way. But it is precisely from this "novelty" that our discourse should start, and narratological leveling is only a preamble to discovering the "peaks" of art.

If literary theory exists to uncover the constants in different texts, when the critic applies the theory he should not limit himself to finding the same invariables in every text (for doing so goes no further than the work of the theorist), but if anything he should start from the awareness of the constants to see how the text calls them into question, makes them interact, and covers this skeleton with different skin and muscles in each different case. The drama of Oedipus's not wanting to know in Sophocles' play is given not by this modal structure (which can be found even in the most banal scenes where the wife who has been betrayed says to her gossipy female friend: "Please, I don't want to know") but by the strategy through which the revelation is delayed, by what is at stake (parricide and incest, as opposed to a banal example of conjugal betrayal), and by the surface of the discourse.

Finally, semiotic discourse often fails to distinguish between "manner" and "style," which Hegel identifies in the first case as a repetitive obsession in the author who always continually writes the same way, and in the second case as the capacity constantly to outdo himself. And yet it is textual semiotics that is the only critique capable of bringing out such differences.

If numerous different excesses can be imputed to textual semiotics, what should we say about the defects of those who oppose it? It is certainly not our job to complain about the orgasms we are made to witness by the "*artifices additi artifici,*" who invariably provide us with a diary of their moments of languor as readers, so much so that one of their passages dedicated to author A and republished by mistake in a book dedicated to author B would go unnoticed by both editor and reviewer.

In fact, we could leave these orgasmic critics to their own delights, which do not harm anyone, and after a while show how those who are so orgasmic in words are in fact very unlibertine in reality, and abhor alterity, since in every one of their critical embraces they are simply making love to themselves. And we could also leave to their own devices those who want to write social criticism, or the history of literary institutions, or criticism of good and bad behavior, all of which are often useful and praiseworthy.

Except that in Italy, in the last ten years, there has been a kind of competition to see who can cast the fiercest anathemas against what they call "formalist-structural-semiotic" readings, as if the latter—and some people have even claimed this—were responsible for Tangentopolis, the Mafia, the collapse of the whining Left, and the rise of the triumphant Right.

This could become an embarrassing incident, in the sense that these complaints could lead the young, including young teachers, astray, diverting them from a number of directions people had taken in the last twenty years, and to good effect.

If you go into the ground floor of the Presses Universitaires bookstore in Paris and go to the second table on the right, you will find scores of manuals for all kinds of schools and at all levels on how to write an "*analyse de texte.*" Even the very pioneers of structuralism in the 1960s have been forced to rediscover not the Russian formalists or the Prague school but the legions of good old Anglo-Saxon empiricist critics and theorists, who for decades had analyzed in depth the strategies of point of view, of narrative montage, of actants and subjects in action (as in Kenneth Burke).

My generation, which was the first post-Croce generation, delighted in the revelations of Wellek and Warren, in the readings of Dámaso Alonso and Spitzer. We began to understand that reading was not just a picnic where one gathered here and there, almost by chance, the hawthorns and buttercups of "poesia," which were hidden amid the manure of structural fillers. Rather, one looked at the text as a whole, as something animated with life at every level. It seemed that even our culture had learned this.

Why is it now forgetting all this? Why are young people now being taught that to discuss a text they do not need a strong theoretical repertoire, and a capacity to examine all levels? Why are they being taught that the long and lasting labors of a critic like Contini were damaging (just because—and this is true—he overrated Pizzuto), whereas the only ideal critic (now famous again!) is one with a free mind that reacts freely to the occasional solicitations provided by the text?

Personally, I see in this tendency a reflection of other sectors of communication: criticism is being leveled down to the rhythms and rate of investment of other activities that have been proved to guarantee a profit. Why bother with reviewing, which forces one to read the book, if it sells more copies of a paper to have the literary section comment on the interview given by an author to a rival paper? Why put *Hamlet* on television, as the much-criticized TV of the 1960s used to do, when you can obtain higher ratings by putting on the same talk show, and treating the village idiot and the academic idiot on the same level? And why on earth read a text year after year if you can achieve the ecstasy of the sublime by chewing a few leaves, without wasting your nights and days discovering the sublimity of leaves in the sublime workings of chlorophyll in photosynthesis?

For this is the message that is propagated daily by the high priests of the New Post-Antique Criticism: they repeatedly tell us that whoever knows about chlorophyll and photosynthesis will for the rest of his life be insensitive to the beauty of a leaf, that whoever knows anything about the circulation of the blood will never be able to make his heart palpitate with love. And this is totally wrong, and we must say it and repeat it from the rooftops.

This is a life-or-death battle between those who love texts and those who are simply in a hurry.

But I shall allow an unimpeachable authority on the matter to speak, one so wise and reliable that we do not even know his real name, which should win over to his side the supporters, who are now everywhere, of wisdom that is traditional, unknown, and occult, or those sophisticated publishers who only publish one-book authors or authors who have not even managed that. We know this authority as Pseudo-Longinus, of the first century A.D., and we are inclined to attribute to him the invention of a concept that has always been the standard for those who proclaim that art cannot be discussed because it arouses ineffable emotions; we can record the ecstasy it produces, and at best we can retell the experience in other words, but it cannot be explained.

The concept is that of the Sublime, which in certain epochs of the history of criticism and aesthetics has been identified with the specific effect of art. And indeed, Longinus (or whoever he was) states immediately that "the Sublime does not lead its listeners to persuasion, but drives them to ecstasy." When the Sublime emerges from the act of reading (or listening) "in some sense it scatters everything, like a bolt of lightning."

The only thing is that at this point (the only point that has become famous throughout the centuries, and we are only at the end of the first section) Longinus wonders whether the Sublime can be thought about, and notes immediately that many people in his unfortunate times believe that it is an innate skill, a natural talent. But Longinus believes that natural talent can be preserved and made to bear fruit only by method, in other words by artistry, and thus he proceeds with his enterprise, which, as many people have forgotten or never known, is to define semiotic strategies that produce in the reader or listener the effect of Sublimity.

And there is no Russian formalist, no Prague-school or French structuralist, no Belgian rhetorician or German "*Stilkritiker*" who has spent as much energy as Longinus (even though only over a dozen pages or so) in exploring the strategies of the Sublime, and showing how they work. I mean showing how they work as they come into being and are then arranged on the linear surface of the text, reflecting the deepest workings of style back toward the reader's eyes.

And in fact Longinus, Pseudo or not, lists the five sources of the sublime: the capacity "to conceive noble thoughts," the ability "to display and arouse noble passions," the way "to create appropriate rhetorical figures," ingenuity in nobility of expression through "the choice of lexis and the accurate use of figures," and lastly the "general overall arrangement of the text." These are the sources of a dignified and elevated style. Because above anything else Longinus knew, against those who in his time identified the semiotic passion of the Sublime with the physical experience of excitement, that "there are some passions which are very far from the Sublime, and rather squalid, such as lamentation, dejection and fear, and at the other extreme many examples of a Sublime devoid of emotion."

And we can see Longinus embark on his search for the sublime photosynthesis that produces the feeling of Sublimity: he shows how in order to produce an effect of grandeur in describing the Divine, Homer gives us the sense of a cosmic distance by way of a brilliant hypotyposis, and conveys the sense of this cosmic expanse through a prolonged description of physical distances; elsewhere he sees how Sappho conveys interior pathos just by bringing to the foreground a battle that involves the eyes, tongue, skin, and ears; or he contrasts a shipwreck in Homer with one by Aratus of Soloi, where the latter in a sense anesthetizes the imminence of death with a simple choice of metaphor ("Only a thin bark keeps Hades at bay"), whereas in Homer Hades is not mentioned, and for that very reason looms even larger. We see him studying strategies for amplification and hypotyposis, exploring the whole panoply of figures, asyndeta, sorites, and hyperbata, and noting how conjunctions weaken the discourse, polyptoton reinvigorates it, and shifting tenses dramatize it.

But one should not think of this as nothing more than a series of stylistic analyses. Longinus deals with the opposition and interchange of characters, the shift from one verbal tense to another, the way the author addresses the reader, or identifies himself with the character, and examines the grammar of these narrative manipulations. He does not ignore periphrases and circumlocutions, idiomatic phrases, metaphors, similes, and hyperboles. It is all one huge stylistic-rhetorical machine—of narrative structures, of voices, looks, and tenses—which is seen at work, analyzing texts and comparing them, in order to reveal and make us admire the strategy of the Sublime.

It seems that only the simple-minded fall into excitement, while Longinus knows the chemistry of their passions, and for that reason enjoys even greater pleasure.

In section 39 Pseudo-Longinus sets out to deal with "the compositional harmony in the arrangement of words," a harmony that is not only a natural positioning aimed at producing persuasion and pleasure but also an astonishing tool for achieving sublimity and pathos. Longinus knows (because of the ancient Pythagorean tradition) that the flute generates passions in listeners, reducing them to a state of frenzy like so many Corybants, even though they are not musical experts; he knows that the sounds of the lyre, which on their own are devoid of sense, produce an effect of enchantment. But he knows that the flute obtains its effects "by giving a certain movement to the rhythm," and the lyre acts on the soul because of its "varying modulations" and the blending of its harmonies. What he wants to explain is not the effect, which is obvious to everyone, but the grammar of its production.

It is in this context that, when he moves on to verbal harmony, "which captures the soul along with the ear," he finds himself analyzing a phrase of Demosthenes that seems to him not just miraculous but sublime: "This decree made the danger looming over the city move on, like a cloud." And he adds:

> Here the concept is as noble as the rhythm. The entire sentence is expressed in dactylic rhythm, the most noble rhythm and the one most suitable for producing grandeur, and it is for this reason that it is typical of the heroic meter, the finest we know. Try to move the words from their present position to anywhere you like: "This decree made, like a cloud, the danger looming over the city move on," or try to get rid of just one syllable, saying "moved it on, like a cloud," and you will understand how much the harmony is consonant with its sublimity. In fact the expression "like a cloud" (*hosper nephos*) has a long first foot, with four beats; but if you eliminate one syllable and have "like cloud" (*hos nephos*), you instantly mutilate its grandeur by this reduction. On the other hand, if you add a syllable, saying "made the danger move on, as though it were (*hosperei*) a cloud," you are saying the same thing but you do not have the same rhythmic cadence, because by lengthening the final syllables the spark of the sublime is weakened and diluted.

Even without checking this against the original Greek, the spirit of this analysis is clear. Pseudo-Longinus is performing textual semiotics. And he is performing an act of criticism—at least according to the canons of his time—and explaining to us why we find something sublime, and what would need to be changed in the body of the text to lose that effect. And so, right from the most distant origins (for if we go back even further, to Aristotle's *Poetics,* we find the same thing), people knew how to read a text, and how one must not be afraid of close reading, nor of a meta-language that sometimes seems terroristic (for Longinus's time his was no less terroristic than the metalanguage that terrorizes many people today).

Consequently, we have to remain faithful to our origins, as regards both the concept of style and that of true criticism, as well as the concept of analyses of textual strategies. What the best semiotics of style has achieved and continues to achieve is the same as what our predecessors accomplished. Our only commitment is, by serious and continued work, without giving in to any blackmail, to humiliate those who are our inferiors.

Final address at the Convegno dell'Associazione Italian di Studi Semiotici on Lo stile—Gli stili, held in Feltre, in September 1995.

LES SEMAPHORES SOUS LA PLUIE

How is space represented in words? This problem has a history of its own, and the rhetorical tradition classifies the techniques of verbal representation of space (as of every other visual experience) under the heading of hypotyposis, or "evidentia," which is sometimes considered the same as, and sometimes judged to have affinities with, "illustratio," "demonstratio," "ekphrasis" or "descriptio," "enargeia," etcetera.

Unfortunately, all definitions of hypotyposis are circular, which is to say that they define as hypotyposis that figure through which visual experiences are represented or evoked through verbal procedures. Look at the definitions that come from the major exponents of classical rhetoric, from Hermogenes to Longinus, from Cicero to Quintilian, which I quote from Lausberg without specifying who said what, since one seems to borrow from the other: (i) *"credibilis rerum imago quae velut in rem praesentem perducere audientes videtur"* (a believable image of something that seems to lead the public into its very presence); (ii) *"proposita forma rerum ita expressa verbis ut cerni potius videatur quam audiri"* (a form of things proposed by the speaker in words in such a way that they seem to be visible rather than audible); (iii) *"quae tam dicere videtur quam ostendere, praesentans oculis quod demon-strat"* (things that the speaker seems to display as much as to say, presenting before our eyes what he is trying to show); (iv) *"quasi gestarum sub oculis inductio"* (a kind of parading before the eyes of things that have been done), and so on.

I have before my eyes (but this time in the literal sense of the expression) the paper on hypotyposis given by Hermann Parret at the Décade de Cerisy, which took place in July 1996, and here too this expedition into the forest of the most modern theoreticians does not seem to yield appreciable results.* Dumarsais reminds us that hypotyposis means image, or painting, and that it comes about "when, in descriptions, one depicts facts that are spoken about as though what is described were genuinely before our eyes; the speaker displays, as it were, what he recounts . . ." (*Des Tropes*), and that for others this figure of speech "allows us to touch reality with our fingers"—a fine metaphor, to be sure, but using one figure of speech to define another is not very helpful. All the more so since, as Aristotle observes, a figure that almost places things before our eyes is a metaphor—and no one will claim that a metaphor is the same thing as hypotyposis. The truth is that if by definition rhetorical figures endow a discourse with brilliance, vivacity, and persuasiveness, and if, according to Horace, one has to admit that poetry is to a certain extent *"ut pictura"* (like painting), then all such figures surprise the reader or listener and place something before their eyes in one way or another. But if that were the case, and if this metaphor were too generic, where would hypotyposis end up?

Luckily, at those very points where theoreticians are incapable of telling us what hypotyposis is, they are nearly always able to provide us with magnificent examples of it. The first three come from Quintilian (*Institutio Oratoria,* 8.3.63–69). His first one

---

*Now in Hermann Parret, "Nel nome dell'ipotiposi," in J. Petitot and P. Fabbri, eds., *Nel nome del senso* (Milan: Sansoni, 2001).

quotes a line from the *Aeneid* (5.426) where two boxers "stood up instantly erect on the tips of their toes." The second quotes Cicero's *Verrine Orations* (5.33.86): "He stood on the shore, wearing sandals, with a red pallium and a long tunic down to his feet, leaning on a vulgar little woman, he, the praetor of the Roman people," and Quintilian wonders if there is anyone so devoid of imagination as not to be able to visualize this scene and its protagonists, and even more than is said, to see their faces and eyes and their obscene caresses, and the uneasiness of the onlookers. The third example, also from Cicero, is a fragment of his speech for Q. Gallius, and refers to a dissolute symposium: "I seemed to see people going in and coming out, some staggering in drunkenness, others yawning from the drunken excess of the day before. The floor was filthy, spattered with wine, and covered with garlands of faded flowers and fish bones."

His fourth example goes like this: "Undoubtedly, in fact, whoever says 'a city has been captured,' associates with that phrase the idea of all the horrors that such a calamity usually entails, but this kind of concise statement does not arouse profound emotion. If instead the concepts contained in a single word have the chance to expand, they will set before you flames spreading through houses and temples, the roar of crashing buildings and the indistinct uniform rumble produced by various sounds, the uncertain flight of some people, the last desperate embraces of others, the howling of infants and women, and the old people who have remained alive, unluckily for them, until that day; and then the devastation of things both sacred and profane, the milling around of those carrying off booty and coming back for more, and the prisoners, in chains, being pushed along, each one by his own torturer, and the mother trying not to let her child be taken away from her, and the struggle among the victors . . ."

Similarly, Dumarsais suggests the following extract from Racine's *Phèdre* as an example of hypotyposis:

Cependant sur le dos de la plaine liquide
S'élève à gros bouillons une montagne humide;
L'onde approche, se brise, et vomit à nos yeux,
Parmi des flots d'écume, un monstre furieux.
Son front large est armé de cornes menaçantes;
Tout son corps est couvert d'écailles jaunissantes;
Indomptable taureau, dragon impétueux,
Sa croupe se recourbe en replis tortueux . . .

Meanwhile on the surface of the ocean's plains
A watery mountain arises amidst great froth;
The wave approaches, breaks, and spews forth before
    our eyes,
Amidst the spray of foam, a furious monster;
Its broad forehead is armed with menacing horns,
All his body is covered with yellowish scales;
This indomitable bull, this aggressive dragon,
Has a croup that curves round in tortuous curls . . .

If we consider the four examples from Quintilian, we see that in the first all that is mentioned is a physical posture (and the reader is invited, as it were, to imagine the scene). The second describes a pose with a certain amount of spite; the solemnity of the red pallium is set against the vulgarity of that little woman ("*muliercula*"), leading the addressee to notice this clash. In the third passage what makes the description interesting is not only its greater precision and length but the unpleasantness of the things described (we must not forget that in the classical art of memory a monstrous or terrible image had more chance of being remembered by the speaker and therefore of being evoked at the right moment). The fourth example is not a specific instance, but it suggests what a detailed and moving description of an extended sequence of actions might be like, and I deliberately describe the dramatic sequence of these actions as if I were discussing a cinematic sequence.

In the case of the Racine passage we have something even more complex: the description of various phases of a natural event, but with continuous zoomorphic transformation of each of the wavy forms that are listed. It is difficult to resist the temptation, or the habit, of imagining them visually. It might seem irreverent to cite Walt Disney and Snow White's flight into the woods (though this irreverence would be lessened if we supposed that Walt Disney had poetic procedures of this very type in mind), but in reality both Racine and Walt Disney are simply following one of the most natural tendencies in human beings, namely, giving substance to shadows, or, rather, seeing threatening, animal forms in the shapeless darkness of nature in turmoil (and in this context Parret rightly sees hypotyposis as one of the figures that leads to the production of the sublime).

What I think we can say, however, is that in these examples we are faced with differing descriptive and narrative techniques, which have in common only the fact that the addressee draws a visual impression from them (if he wants to—in other words, if he wants to collaborate with the text). This means I can therefore say that hypotyposis does not exist as a specific rhetorical figure. Language allows us to describe faces, forms, positions, "scenes," and sequences of action, and it allows us to do this continually in everyday life (otherwise we could not even say, "Could you please go to the hardware store and get me something that looks like this"); all the more so, then, does it encourage us to do this for artistic reasons. However, it allows this to happen by way of a multiplicity of techniques, which are not reducible to a formula or rule, as can be the case with real tropes and rhetorical figures like synecdoche, hyperbaton, zeugma, and even—to some extent— metaphor.

All we need to do then is to proceed to a typology of techniques for representing or evoking space. Except that at this point we really need to ask ourselves what is meant by space—and we cannot avoid asking ourselves an analogous question about time.

There is Newtonian space and time, which exist as absolute entities, and Kantian space and time, which exist as pure intuitions and conditions that are *a priori* of experience. There is the Bergsonian contrast between clock time and the time of internal duration, and there is the measurable space of Cartesian geometry and the lived space of phenomenology. It is not a question of privileging one or the other, since language always allows us to speak of these things, and we can say without difficulty how many millions of miles we need to travel to reach Alpha Centauri or to make us undergo (or, rather, suffer) an interminable journey between Florence and Fiesole, not to mention a voyage around one's own room (in *Tristram Shandy* the discussion between two characters coming down a staircase takes up three chapters).

If we wanted to rewrite Lessing's *Laocoon* today (after the invention of new mimetic techniques like cinema), we would have to ask ourselves if a division between temporal arts and spatial arts still makes sense, and—if we regard such a division as still valid—ask how spatial arts can represent time and temporal arts represent space.

In the meantime, there can still be many reflections on how spatial arts represent space. The classic example of this is perspective, where a two-dimensional physical surface produces three-dimensionality as its proper content, and where a minimal portion of representational surface can express a vast expanse of space: this is realized by anyone who, after long contemplation of it in various reproductions, finally sees Piero della Francesca's *Flagellation* in the Ducal Palace at Urbino and is amazed at how such a small frame can contain what is perceived to be such a vast space.

I have dealt with the question as to how the arts of space represent time, or actually imply the time of their own contemplation, elsewhere.* Phenomenology is vast and requires first and foremost an analysis of the various relations between what Genette calls signifying spatiality and signified spatiality (and which for reasons that will become clear later I would prefer to refer to as spatiality of expression and spatiality of content). There are paintings that suggest a sort of freezing of the moment, like the Annunciation by Lotto, where Mary's gesture of surprise is caught in the moment a cat darts across the room, or the slash by Lucio Fontana, a snapshot of the lightning movement of the blade that has cut through the stretched canvas.

But when one thinks carefully about it, there is nothing unusual in the fact that a limited portion of space, which of itself is atemporal, can express an instant. The problem arises when you ask yourself how you can express a long period of time through portions of space. And you discover that, in order to express a long period of time you generally need a lot of space. There are stories in painting that represent a century-long succession of events through a series of frames, as happens with comic strips; and there are others that do so through the repeated visual presentation of the same characters in different hairstyles, situations, and ages; and these are all cases where an abundance of space is required to convey an abundance of time, and not only an abundance of signifying space, but also of the (semantic, not pragmatic) space that the beholder has to traverse. To grasp the flow of time in Piero's series of frescoes on the Finding of the True Cross in Arezzo you have to move, and not only with your eyes, but also with your feet, and you have to walk even more to follow the whole story narrated by the Bayeux tapestry. There are works that require a long time to circumnavigate, and a long period of attention to their minutest details, such as a Gothic

---

*See my "Il tempo dell'arte," in *Sugli specchi* (Milan: Bompiani, 1985), 115–24.

cathedral. A sculpture that appears as a little ivory cube can be experienced in a second of contemplation (even though I believe it should be touched and rotated in order to grasp all its facets), but a cube in which every side was of one million by one million kilometers has to be circumnavigated, maybe with the spaceship from *2001: A Space Odyssey*, otherwise one would not grasp its megagalactic sublimity.

If, then, to represent a lot of time one needs a lot of space, is it not the case (with the arts of time) that to represent a lot of space one needs a lot of time? Let us start by limiting this topic. We shall not be asking ourselves whether, for instance, music can represent space, even though intuitively we would reply yes. Even if we did not want to be extreme descriptivists, it is hard to deny that Dvořák's *New World Symphony* or Smetana's *Má Vlast* conjure up vast expanses, so much so that the conductor is tempted to conduct with expansive, smooth gestures, almost as if to suggest something "flowing," and that the length of these pieces contributes to the creation of that effect. Of course, certain kinds of music dictate a pirouette, others a leap, others a calm walk, and so there are rhythmic structures that determine or represent bodily movements with which we move through space—otherwise dance would not exist.

But let us limit our discussion to verbal discourse, and take up again the distinction between space of expression and space of content, emphasizing the fact that we shall have to deal not so much with the form of expression as with its substance.

We saw before that, however well intentioned Quintilian was, saying of two boxers that they stood upright on the tips of their toes does not strike us as a great hypotyposis, whereas describing the invasion and sack of a city event by event and moment by moment seems more visually evocative. But this latter description implies a certain number of pages (or at least of verses).

As a result, in speaking of spatial expression I would not consider those cases where, on the level of expression, something is said about space that, on the level of content, is not really about space but rather about something else, and it could even be about the flow of time, as happens in expressions such as "the party line," "it is a bleak outlook," "boundless culture," "he followed the discussion step by step," "he is on the wrong track," "in the middle of the night,"—see what Lakoff and Johnson write about these spatial metaphors.* I am thinking more of the substance of the expression, the quantity of which impinges on the spatiality expressed. I simply want to say that between mentioning a beautiful valley and describing it over one hundred pages, something should happen on the level of content; or, in other words, we ought to see something more of that valley.

Let us examine some techniques of verbal expression of space.

1. *Denoting.* This is the most simple, immediate, mechanical form, as when one states that there are twenty kilometers of distance between one place and another. Naturally it is up to the addressee, if s/he wants, to associate an image with the conceptual content just acquired (maybe the image of himself as overheated jogger, if the information is about an area devoid of transport), but one cannot say that the statement on its own does anything to force the addressee to picture that space for himself.

2. *Detailed Description.* Things are already different with a space that is *described,* as when we say that a square has a church to the right and an ancient palace to the left. Note that the simple mention of the respective positions of the two buildings would already be sufficient to make us recognize the piazza in question,

---

*In George Lakoff, and Mark Johnson, *Metaphors We Live By* (Chicago and London: University of Chicago Press, 1980).

and therefore we would have to say that every description of visible objects is of itself hypotypotic. But let us imagine that in the city where we are told this there are two squares with a church and a palace, and suddenly the force of the description as hypotyposis would diminish. We would then need to supply more details.

Here we come up against a problem of quantity: how many details do there need to be? Enough to encourage the addressee to build up an image in his mind, but not too many, because in that case the image would become impossible to build up. Take the case of this description in Robbe-Grillet's *The Voyeur:*

> The stone rim—a sharp, oblique edge, at the intersection of two perpendicular planes: the vertical wall that rose upright toward the quay and the flight of stairs that went up to the highest part of the pier—at its upper extremity (the high part of the pier) was extended in a horizontal line straight toward the quay.
>
> The quay, which the perspective effect pushed into the distance, sent out on both sides of this main line a group of parallel lines, which, with a precision that was further heightened by the morning light, delimited a series of long planes that were alternately horizontal and vertical: the upper plane of the massive parapet protecting the passage on the water side, its inner wall, the paving on the high part of the pier, and the unprotected side that plunged into the sea in the harbor. The two vertical surfaces were in shadow, the other two brightly lit by the sun: the upper floor of the parapet throughout its entire breadth, and the paved walkway, except for a narrow strip which was in darkness: the shadow projected by the parapet. In theory one should also have been able to see the mirror image of the whole construction in the harbor water, and on the surface, still within

the same system of parallel lines, the shadow projected by the high vertical wall going off straight toward the quay.

This passage (the description continues for almost two pages) is interesting because it says too much, and by saying too much it prevents the reader from building an image for himself (unless he is one of those few readers who manages to do so with considerable effort and intense concentration). This seems to point to the conclusion that for hypotyposis to exist, it must not say more than what leads the reader to collaborate with the text by filling empty spaces and adding details on his own initiative. In other words, hypotyposis does not so much have to make us see, as make us want to see. But where can one find a rule? In the case of Robbe-Grillet we could say that the passage fails deliberately in its attempt to make us see (an interestingly provocative act for a book entitled *The Voyeur* and belonging to the *école du regard*), because it does not offer a hook on which to hang any priority: everything is as important as everything else.

What does offering priority mean? It could mean emphasizing verbally, in a certain sense almost dictating, an emotional reaction ("in the center of the square there was something terrifying . . ."), or insisting on one detail at the expense of others.

There are countless examples of this, but I will restrict myself to a passage that has elicited thousands of attempts at translation into visual terms, from Revelation, chapter 4:

And lo, a throne stood in heaven, with one seated on the throne! And he who sat there appeared like jasper, and carnelian, and round the throne was a rainbow that looked like an emerald. Round the throne were twenty-four thrones, and seated on the thrones were twenty-four elders, clad in white garments, with golden crowns upon their heads. From the throne issue flashes of lightning, and voices and peals of thunder, and before the throne burn seven torches of fire, which are the seven spirits of God; and before the throne there is as it were a sea of glass, like crystal. And round the throne, on each side of the throne, are four living creatures . . .

This is hypotyposis if ever there was one. Yet the description does not include everything. It stops only at surface details; only the elders' clothes and crowns are mentioned, not their eyes or beards.

3. *Lists.* This is a technique that undoubtedly leads to the evocation of spatial images without establishing priorities. Three examples: one classical, or at least from late Latin, and two modern.

Here is the description of the city of Narbonne in Sidonius Apollinaris:

Salve Narbo, potens salubritate,
Urbe et rure simul bonus videri,
Muris, civibus, ambitu, tabernis,
Portis, porticibus, foro, theatro,
Delubris, capitoliis, monetis,
Thermis, arcubus, horreis, macellis,
Pratis, fontibus, insulis, salinis,
Stagnis, flumine, merce, ponte, ponto;
Unus qui venerere iure divos
Leneum, Cererem, Palem, Minervam
Spicis, palmite, pascuis, trapetis.

Hail, Narbonne, famous for your healthy air,
Both your town and your countryside are good to see,
As are your walls, citizens, periphery, shops,
Harbor, colonnades, forum, theater,
Shrines, capitols, banks,
Baths, arches, granaries, butchers,

Meadows, fountains, islands, salt flats,
Pools, river, merchandise, bridge, and sea;
The only town that can rightly worship the gods
Bacchus, Ceres, Pales, Minerva,
With your vine sprigs, corn ears, pasture land, and olive
     presses.

And here is a single paragraph from the description of the drawers in Leopold Bloom's kitchen, in the penultimate chapter of *Ulysses:*

What did the first drawer unlocked contain?
A Vere Foster's handwriting copybook, property of Milly (Millicent) Bloom, certain pages of which bore diagram drawings, marked *Papli,* which showed a large globular head with 5 hairs erect, 2 eyes in profile, the trunk full front with 3 large buttons, 1 triangular foot: 2 fading photographs of queen Alexandra of England and of Maud Branscombe, actress and professional beauty: a Yuletide card, bearing on it a pictorial representation of a parasitic plant, the legend *Mizpah,* the date Xmas 1892, the name of the senders: from Mr + Mrs M. Comerford, the versicle: *May this Yuletide bring to thee, Joy and peace and welcome glee:* a butt of red partly liquefied sealing wax, obtained from the stores department of Messrs Hely's, Ltd., 89, 90, and 91 Dame Street: a box containing the remainder of a gross of gilt "J" pennibs, obtained from same department of same firm: an old sandglass which rolled containing sand which rolled: a sealed prophecy (never unsealed) written by Leopold Bloom in 1886 concerning the consequences of the passing into law of William Ewart Gladstone's Home Rule bill of 1886 (never passed into law): a bazaar ticket, no 2004, of St. Kevin's Charity Fair, price 6d, 100 prizes . . .

And in this case the list continues for page after page. If we can say about the Narbonne passage that the presentation of architectural elements acts as a cinematic panning shot suggesting a shape (today we would say it suggests at least a skyline), for Joyce all that matters is the gargantuan abundance of irrelevant objects that opens up its unfathomable depths before our eyes, the labyrinthine richness of that drawer. Let us look at the description of another drawer, this one belonging to the old aunt in the "Othys" chapter of Nerval's *Sylvie:*

> She rummaged once more in the drawers. What delights! How everything smelled good, how all the bits and pieces shone and shimmered with lively colors! Two slightly damaged mother of pearl fans, Chinese porcelain boxes, an amber necklace and a thousand frills, among which shone out two little white woollen shoes with buckles encrusted with Irish diamonds.

We certainly see shining in the drawer those nice things of terrible taste that enchant the two young visitors, and we see them because priorities stand out—that is to say that some objects are emphasized at the expense of others. But then why do we also see Bloom's drawer, where no article has a privileged role? I would answer that Nerval wants us to see what is in the drawer, whereas Joyce wants us to see the unfathomability of the drawer. I do not know whether the reader manages to see Bloom's drawer better than Robbe-Grillet's pier, seeing that both are devoid of priorities. We can say, however, that Robbe-Grillet puts together objects that in themselves are not surprising, like a pier, a parapet, some surfaces and lines, whereas Joyce puts together things that are mutually incongruous and for that very reason surprising and unexpected. In some way (I presume) the reader has to prioritize a disordered ensemble of objects, or make some choices (perhaps by focusing on the sandglass), and by doing so collaborates in the task of making mental images.

4. *Accumulation.* Another technique (which was already suggested by Quintilian's third example) is the excited accumulation of events. The events have to be either incongruous or extraordinary. Naturally elements of rhythm intervene, and this is why the following hypotyposis from Rabelais (*Gargantua* I.27) lets us visualize the scene (whereas we would not be able to see the scene from a procedure that was merely one of listing, as in the wonderfully amusing list of "balls" in III.26 and 28, which is more enjoyable in phonic than in visual terms):

> With one lot he spilled their brains, with others he broke their arms and legs, and with a third he dislocated the neck bones, split their kidneys, slit their nose, burst their eyes, battered their jaws, shoved their teeth down their throats, shattered their shoulder blades, splintered their legs, dislocated their thigh bones, and plucked their limbs from their trunks.
>
> If any tried to hide among the thicker vine leaves, he broke the whole ridge of their back, breaking their spine like a dog's.
>
> If others tried to run and escape, he knocked his head away in pieces shattering his lamboidal joint. If any tried to climb up a tree, thinking he was safe, he impaled him through the arse with his stick [. . .]. Others he would stab beneath the ribs, wrecking their stomachs, and they died on the spot. Others he struck so fiercely on the navel that their tripes spilled out. And with others he pierced their bum-gut through their balls. It was, you must believe, the most gruesome spectacle ever seen [. . .]. Some died without speaking, others spoke without dying; and some died speaking, and spoke dying.

5. Description appealing to the addressee's personal experience. This technique requires that the addressee bring to the discourse something he has already seen and *suffered*. This activates not only preexisting cognitive schemes but also preexisting bodily experiences. I would suggest as a key example one of the many passages in Abbott's *Flatland:*

> Place a penny in the middle of one of your tables in Space; and leaning over it, look down upon it. It will appear a circle.
>
> But now, drawing back to the edge of the table, gradually lower your eye (thus bringing yourself more and more into the condition of the inhabitants of Flatland), and you will find the penny becoming more and more oval to your view; and at last when you have placed your eye exactly on the edge of the table (so that you are, as it were, actually a Flatland citizen) the penny will then have ceased to appear oval at all, and will have become, so far as you can see, a straight line.

Part of this technique involves the evocation of interoceptive and proprioceptive experiences on the part of the addressee. In other words, it makes the reader recall experiences in which he has suffered the *effort of proceeding through a space*. On this topic I would like to cite these two lines from Blaise Cendrars's *Prose du transsibérien* (by the way, this is a text that, since it has to describe a very long journey, uses many of the techniques I have already defined, from the list to minute description). At a certain point Cendrars reminds us that

> *Toutes les femmes que j'ai rencontrées se dressent aux horizons*
> *Avec les gestes piteux et les regards tristes des sémaphores sous la*
> *pluie . . .*
> (All the women I have met rise up on the horizons
> With the piteous gestures and sad looks of signals in the
> rain . . .)

If we bear in mind that in French "sémaphores" are not our city traffic signals (which in French are "feux rouges") but rather signals along the railroad tracks, those who have experienced trains proceeding slowly on misty nights will be able to evoke these ghostly shapes that slowly disappear in the drizzle, as though fading away, while one looks out of the window at the countryside immersed in darkness following the panting rhythm of the carriages (that carioca rhythm evoked by Montale in "*Addii, fischi nel buio*").

The interesting problem is, rather, how much these lines can be appreciated by those born in the age of high-speed trains, with their hermetically sealed windows (for which there is no longer even the trilingual notice banning us from leaning out). How does one react to a hypotyposis that summons up the memory of something that has never been seen? I should say the answer is *by pretending* to have seen it, and on the basis of the elements that the hypotyposic expression supplies us with. The two lines appear in a context that mentions a train traveling for days and days across endless plains, the signals (specifically named) in some way remind us of eyes twinkling in the dark, and the allusion to horizons makes us imagine them lost in a distance that the train's movement can only magnify second by second. . . . In any case, even those who only know today's express trains have seen through the window lights disappearing into the night. And suddenly the experience we have to remember becomes tentatively outlined: the hypotyposis can also *create* the memory it needs for it to work.

On the other hand, if it is actually true that those who have experienced their first kiss can easily savor a line like Dante's "*la bocca mi baciò tutto tremante*" (he kissed me on the mouth all trembling), would we say that those who read of a first kiss for the first time cannot pretend to have experienced it? If we try to deny this, then neither Paolo and Francesca's sin nor their trembling would be understandable, victims as they were (in turn) of a fine hypotyposis.

If this is what happens, then we can also record under this rubric the cases where hypotyposis requires us to imagine non-human experiences. Such is the case with the "fractalization of space visible only at an ant's pace," for which there is a wonderful example in Eliot's "The Love Song of J. Alfred Prufrock":

> The yellow fog that rubs its back upon the window-panes,
> The yellow smoke that rubs its muzzle on the
>   window-panes,
> Licked its tongue into the corners of the evening,
> Lingered upon the pools that stand in drains,
> Let fall upon its back the soot that falls from chimneys,
> Slipped by the terrace, made a sudden leap,
> And seeing that it was a soft October night,
> Curled once about the house, and fell asleep.

In this case, if the human traveler is moving too fast to realize what the walls and corners of the streets of London are like, the reader is asked to imagine at what speed fog might travel. This involves slowing down our pace, as it were, while reading, and following every crevice in the wall and edge of the window— exactly as would happen if we were asked to imagine how an ant travels through the curves of a fraction of space that we can cover, in an instant, with the sole of our foot.

It is not my intention to exhaust within the limits of such a brief paper the inexhaustible typologies of hypotyposis. I will suggest only some directions for research.

The different techniques of focalization could be analyzed. For instance, the excellent analysis by Joseph Frank of the agricultural fair and speeches in *Madame Bovary,* which he carried out in a genuinely pre-semiotic age, should be reread: the three levels of the square, the stage and the room are set up live, as it were, that is to say in a Griffith-style parallel montage, creating a visual effect through this emphasis on simultaneous speeches.* One would have to refer, of course, to the two battles of Waterloo, Stendhal's (seen by a protagonist, Fabrizio del Dongo, who is inside it, and who gets lost in the space he crosses haphazardly, while he loses the sense of the global space of the battle), and the one in *Les Misérables,* seen from on high by an omniscient Hugo, who analyzes the spaces Napoléon does not see. Elsewhere[†] I have spoken of the different points of view that gradually create the space in Manzoni's "*Quel ramo del lago di Como*" (That stretch of Lake Como)—where idiosyncratic syntax corroborates the play of points of view. It would be worthwhile following step by step the vision of the three trees during the carriage ride in *A l'ombre des jeunes filles en fleur,* in order to grasp a double phenomenon: a successive shifting of point of view and the interspersing of spatial description with other reflections that take time (in reading) and space (in writing) in order to make the sense of a journey real, and justify the slow, progressive change of visual angle.

We could continue, but it is worthwhile trying to say something in conclusion about what links these different manifestations of hypotyposis. We have already alluded to this at various stages, and all we need to do now is pull the threads together. Hypotyposis is not based on a semantic rule, as happens with tropes and rhetorical figures, a rule whereby—if you disregard it—you do not understand what is being said. When metonymy uses the container to stand for the content ("let's drink a glass"), if the addressee ignores the rule, he (pedantically) assumes that he is being invited to sip a solid object. If in using a simile or metaphor someone says that a girl is a little deer, an obtuse person who ignores the rule will note with amazement that the person named is not a

---

*See Joseph Frank, "Spatial form in modern literature," *Sewanee Review* (1945).
[†]"Lingering in the woods," in *Six Walks in the Fictional Woods* (Cambridge, MA and London: Harvard University Press, 1994), 49–73.

quadruped, nor has she horns on her forehead. But on the whole these misunderstandings do not take place, except in comic or surreal stories.

When, however, one is faced with any of the instances of hypotyposis cited up till now, the addressee can easily avoid collaborating and visualizing. He can merely grasp that he is being told that a city is being sacked, that a drawer is full of knickknacks, or that a certain Friar John was a giant-killer. We have even insinuated that in the case of Robbe-Grillet the reader can refuse, indeed may have to refuse, to see anything precise, because the author probably wanted to stimulate this refusal to activate an excess of visuals.

Hypotyposis is, then, a semantic-pragmatic phenomenon (besides, inasmuch as it is a figure of thought, like irony and similar figures, it requires complex textual strategies and can never be exemplified through brief quotations or formulas) and is a prime example of interpretative cooperation. It is not so much a representation as a technique for eliciting an effort to compose a visual representation (on the reader's part).

And indeed, why should we think that words "allow us to see," when they were invented precisely to speak of what is not before our eyes and what cannot be pointed at with a finger? The most words can do (since they produce emotional effects) is to lead us to imagine.

Hypotyposis uses words to make the addressee construct a visual representation. The proof of this is the kind of problems that arise in that exercise which is the opposite of ekphrasis (which is a verbal description of an image), and is the "translation," or visual materialization of what a verbal text allowed us to imagine. Let us go back to the description from Revelation I cited previously. The real problem for all the Mozarabic miniaturists (the illustrators of those splendid commentaries on Revelation known as the "Beati") was that of representing the four living creatures who are above and around the throne (in the Vulgate, which was the only version known to the illuminators, *"super thronum et circa thronum"*). How can these creatures be above and around the throne at the same time?

An examination of the solutions offered by the various "Beati" shows us how impossible the enterprise is, and gives rise to representations that do not "translate" the text satisfactorily. And this is because the miniaturists, having grown up using the Greco-Christian translation, thought that the prophet "saw" something similar to statues or paintings. But the culture of John the Apostle, like that of Ezekiel, from whose vision John drew inspiration, was a Hebraic culture, and moreover his was the imagination of a seer. Consequently, John was not describing pictures (or statues), but, if anything, dreams, and, if you like, films (those moving pictures that allow us to daydream, or in other words, visions adapted for the layman's state). In a vision that was cinematic in nature, the four creatures can rotate and appear at one moment above and before the throne, at another around it.*

But in this sense the Mozarabic miniaturist could not collaborate with the text, and in some sense, in his hands and in his mind, the hypotyposis failed to work. Proof therefore that there is no hypotyposis if the addressee does not play the game.

---

*See my "Jerusalem and the Temple as signs in medieval culture," in G. Manetti (ed.), *Knowledge through Signs* (Paris: Brepols, 1996), pp. 329–44.

Version of a paper given at the Centro di Studi Semiotici e Cognitivi at the University of San Marino on 29 September 1996, during a conference on the semiotics of space. I began my paper with a reference to Sandra Caviccioli's article "I sensi, lo spazio, gli umori. Micro-analisi di *In the Orchard di Virginia Woolf*" (in *VS* 57 [1990]), one of the finest analyses of space in literature. On that occasion the author was present in the room. Now that she is no longer with us, I would like to dedicate these reflections to her.

THE FLAWS IN THE FORM

I would like to reread a page from Luigi Pareyson's *Aesthetics*;* actually, it is less than a page, just a few lines from subsection 10 of the third section ("The Parts and the Whole") of chapter 3 ("Completeness of the Work of Art"). Subsection 10 is entitled "The essential nature of each part: structure, stopgaps, imperfections."

We know that one of the central preoccupations of Pareyson's *Aesthetics* was its polemic against Croce's idealism and against its most deleterious consequences in militant criticism. He aimed at reclaiming the character of totality in artistic form, and therefore refused to pick out in the work sporadic moments of "poetry," like flowers growing among the (however functional) brushwood of simple "structure." It is not really necessary, but it is useful to remind ourselves that "structure" in those days, and particularly in Italy, was something to avoid; it meant scaffolding, mechanical artifice that had nothing to do with moments of lyrical intuition, and at most stood out in a Hegelian sense as a negative

---

*I quote from the most recent edition of his *Estetica* (Milan: Bompiani, 1988), though this passage has remained unchanged since the first edition was published in 1954.

impulse, as conceptual residue, which at best served to let the moments of poetry shine like individual jewels. In his notes to the chapter Pareyson refers to Luigi Russo as a cautious champion of the "nonextraneity of structure in art," but the latter author (though he recognizes that there is a structure that is not pre-poetic, not a mere frame or skeleton on which to insert later poetic flowers, and sees structure "as though generated by the interior of the mind that has been moved to poetry") cannot avoid conceding that the mind so moved "catches its breath and rests in these havens of doctrine." So structure is absolved, but on the grounds that it does not harm the poetry, not because it too is poetry. Structure functions as a buoy to which the poetic swimmer clings: it is good that it is there, but only to let us catch our breath before we start again on the crawl of lyric effusion. As if to say that Dante, who could not see at every step "the sweet colors of the oriental sapphire," or Beatrice's "smiling eyes," took long rests by discoursing on theology and digressing on the composition of the heavens.

This concept of structure had nothing to do with the sense we would give to the term "structuralist" today; even though in this respect Pareyson's theory of the totality of form could be reread in a structuralist way, his inspiration came from organicist aesthetics of Kantian and Romantic origin, not through the post-Saussure axis.

However, by opposing so decisively the poetry/structure dichotomy with his notion of the totality of artistic form, Pareyson risked falling into an organicist rhetoric.

It was one thing to say that in the complete work (and in fact right from the first moment when the initial spark starts the creative process) *"tout se tient,"* and that therefore theory must affirm and interpretative activity pick out the organic design supporting it, the individual rule, the "forming form" that in some dark way precedes the work, directing it as it is created, and appearing as the result and revelation of the formed form. And quite another thing to celebrate this "unity-totality of the work" in tones that frankly, forty years on, seem to us to belong more to a rhetoric of the Beautiful than to a phenomenology of forms.

Just one example:

> This dynamic character of the unity-totality of the work of art can explain the relations that exist within it between the parts and the whole. In a work of art the parts have a dual kind of relationship: each part with the others, and each part with the whole. All the parts are connected among themselves in an indissoluble unity, so that each one is necessary and indispensable and has a specific and non-interchangeable place, so much so that the absence of any part would disrupt the unity and any variation would return it to disorder . . . Each part is set up as such by the whole, which itself has summoned up and arranged the parts of which it is made up: if changing parts leads to the dissolution of unity and disintegration of the whole, that is because the whole itself presides over the coherence of the parts among themselves and makes them work together to form the whole. In this sense the relations that the parts have among themselves do nothing but reflect the relation that each part has with the whole: the harmony of the parts forms the whole because the whole forms their unity (page 107).

Too neat. Here—as elsewhere—Pareyson seems to be seized by a Pythagorean raptus, and one day it might be worthwhile tracing the sources of his aesthetics that he does not own up to, by going back beyond Romanticism to Renaissance Neoplatonism, or Cusanus. Not to mention some readings of the mystics, with whom he was familiar even though he did not write about them.

Is it possible that a theorist so sensitive to the moment of actual reading of works of art could think of it as an experience so overwhelmingly totalizing, of almost Panic raptus, never disrupted by moments of perplexity or dissatisfaction, either on the part of the artist (who, when rereading, revising, or relistening to the work, may wish to correct himself) or on the part of the critic (who might be tempted to correct the artist)? The good interpreter, who has penetrated the work, is also he who, even at the peak of his enthusiasm for an author, says every now and again, "I don't like this," or even "I would have put it better" (then, perhaps out of modesty, he does not actually say anything, but is straining at the leash all the same). Yet Pareyson was the first to think of interpretation as an exercise that can also accentuate, attenuate, and put into perspective the work's various aspects, and therefore—out of loyalty to the spirit of the work—also correct it.

But it is immediately after writing the passage quoted above—and I chose that passage from the many I could have chosen precisely because of its closeness to the amazing "about-turn" I am about to discuss—that Pareyson confronts the problem of so-called inert moments, or "structure."

He confronts it in order to redeem structure, to make it part of the creative project, an essential, not a marginal or extraneous, moment: if "the whole emerges from the unity of its parts to produce something complete" there can be no trifling detail or irrelevant minutiae; and if in interpreting the work some parts are less important than others, this happens because in the organized form a distribution of functions takes place.

Pareyson is not saying—for this would be to read him as though he had written thirty years later, or had come from a different background—that *The Divine Comedy* is more beautiful for its theological construction than for its famous poetic pearls, which instead represent something accidental, not essential; but he certainly is saying that the Homeric structure underlying Joyce's *Ulysses* is as important in an aesthetic sense as Molly Bloom's soliloquy, which could not produce the effect it does were it not inserted into that structure, so that the reader must find in the monologue a whole host of infratextual quotations that necessarily refer back to other hints, apparently irrelevant and pointless, which have appeared over the course of the other chapters.

Pareyson does not express himself in these terms, of course. He writes, rather, that "the really perspicacious observation of a work . . . is aimed not so much at contemplating the detail in itself as at inserting it among other details . . . in order to examine its irreplaceability in that living nexus where it appears as essential to the whole as it is revelatory of it, and is ready to evoke all the other parts in the very act of being invoked by them."

And it is at this point that Pareyson realizes he has to come to terms not only with structure as framework but also with the irregularities, weaknesses, patches, mends, slips, drops in tension, and even actual faults that at times spoil the much-vaunted harmony and necessity of the structure.

Stopgaps, in fact. "Stopgap" ("*zeppa*" in Italian) is an inelegant word, like the flaw it alludes to, and in its sound "*zeppa*" conjures up cough, sneeze, regurgitation, and hiccup, whereas semantically it suggests a clumsy intrusion, an obvious repair job.*

And yet Pareyson, who is also an almost elevated writer, does not avoid this terminological stopgap when referring to an aesthetic stopgap. He uses it to describe works that appear "inconsistent and uneven, without thereby being open to the accusation of lacking poetry" (and we will allow this indulgence in the Crocean terminology to which he is so opposed; he means that certain works appear uneven and yet give an impression of great breadth and consistency of form), works in which the stopgaps function as crutches that are necessary for the whole work to proceed, they

---

*I have often wondered whether Pareyson's idea of the stopgap was inspired by some previous discussion. We know how devoid his *Estetica* is of notes, and his references are often generic. On this particular point, I have not found any reference or quotation in his notes. Taking a deconstructionist's privilege, and going against any sense of fidelity to the text, and therefore against all the teachings of my Maestro, I note that the dictionaries give also "*cuneo*" (wedge) as a definition of "*zeppa*," and I have decided to see in his choice of the latter nontechnical term an unconscious homage to his hometown (of Cuneo in Piedmont).

are bridges, bits of welding, "in which the artist works less carefully, less patiently or even with indifference, as though he were just getting through these bits, as though they were passages that, precisely because they are obligatory in order to move on, can be left to convention without prejudicing the whole" (p. 111).

Nevertheless, stopgaps do belong to the internal economy of the form, since the Whole requires them, even if only in a subordinate position. Let us deconstruct these metaphors (Pareyson's aesthetics abounds in metaphors, and if we read it without bearing this in mind we risk not noticing how it questions fundamental problems of organization of systems); let us forget a personalized Whole that requires something. Pareyson is telling us that the stopgap is an artifice that allows one part to be linked to another, and thus that it is necessary. If a door has to open gently or majestically it has to have a hinge, however mechanical its function may be. The bad architect, obsessed with aesthetics, gets irritated because a door has to revolve around a hinge, and redesigns the hinge so that it appears "beautiful" while carrying out its function; and often by so doing he manages to create a door that creaks, sticks, does not open, or opens badly. The good architect, on the other hand, wants the door to open in order to reveal other rooms, and he does not care whether, having redesigned everything in the building, when it comes to the hinge he has to resort to the eternal wisdom of the ironmonger.

The stopgap accepts its own banality, because without the speed that the banal allows us, it would slow up a passage that is crucial for the outcome of the work and its interpretation.

I would give as an example of stopgaps what contemporary theorists have called "turn ancillaries." These are the phrases found in novels after quoted speech:

"The murderer is the viscount," *pronounced* the police chief.
"I love you," he *said*.
"Some saint will help us," *replied* Lucia.

Apart from a few authors who take particular care in varying their "turn ancillaries" (choosing at different times between "he retorted," "quipped," "sneered," "added thoughtfully"—and I am not saying that these are the best), the others, from the greatest to the most banal novelist, use them just as they come, as it were, and those used by a great author like Manzoni are not in the end so different from those used by a writer of feuilletons like Carolina Invernizio. The fact is that "turn ancillaries" are stopgaps; they cannot be avoided, but nor can they be embellished very much, and the great writer is one who knows that when they are there, the reader tends to skip them; but if they were not there, the dialogue would become wearisome or incomprehensible.

But a stopgap is not just this. It can be a banal opening, which can be useful for finding a sublime ending. It was one night, at three in the morning, on the Colle dell'Infinito (the hill where Leopardi wrote "*L'infinito*") at Recanati, where the first words of one of the finest almost-sonnets of all time have been carved, that I realized that its opening, "*Sempre caro mi fu quest'ermo colle*" (This solitary hill has always been dear to me), is quite a banal line, which could have been written by any minor poet of the Romantic or other ages or movements. What can a hill be, in poetic "language," except "solitary"? And yet without that banal opening, the poem would not take off, and perhaps it needed to be banal, so that the Panic feeling of that shipwreck at the end, which is so memorable, could be felt.

I would go so far as to say, perhaps just to pursue my thesis, that a line like "*Nel mezzo del cammin di nostra vita*" (In the middle of the journey of our life) has the singsong dignity of a stopgap. If it were not followed by the rest of *The Divine Comedy*, we would not have attached much importance to it, perhaps we might have thought of it as just an idiom.

I am not saying that the opening phrase is always a stopgap. There are openings to some of Chopin's polonaises that are certainly not stopgaps. "*Quel ramo del lago di Como*" (That stretch of Lake Como) is not a stopgap; nor is "April is the cruellest month." But let us consider the end of *Romeo and Juliet* and then tell me whether it would not have ended better without the last sentence (in italics):

> A glooming peace this morning with it brings,
> The sun, for sorrow, will not show his head.
> Go hence to have more talk of these sad things;
> Some shall be pardon'd, and some punished:
> *For never was a story of more woe*
> *Than this of Juliet and her Romeo.*

However, if Shakespeare decided to conclude with this moralizing banality, it can only be because he wanted to allow the spectators to catch their breath before allowing them to leave in peace, after the bloodbath they had just witnessed. So it was right that there was a stopgap there.

"It was Leo who was the first to fall asleep" is not bad. But then Moravia adds: "Carla's unexpected, if inexperienced, assault on him had exhausted him." Come on, what can an adult who has been subjected to an adolescent's amorous assault be except "exhausted"? Does not that "unexpected, if inexperienced, assault" sound as if it had been taken from a judge's verdict? Nevertheless, without this rather clumsy but essential passage it would not be possible to begin chapter 10 of Moravia's *Gli indifferenti* (*The Time of Indifference*), where the sad truth is made evident that "*omne animal triste est post coitum.*"

There is no need to belabor the point: "Examples of this are so widespread as to embrace the whole history of the arts" (*Estetica*, p. 112). Certainly. Moreover, it is by arguing how stopgaps can be compensated for by the whole that Pareyson gradually moves on to talk of mutilations, of the action of time on things, of rubble, ruins, fragments, and the wastage that the work is subject to, and how despite all of this we can reconstitute its intimate legitimacy. A section that would not be clear unless we also saw the central value of the stopgap, and the appreciation for something that is not complete, because only if a work can be appreciated in spite of, and even because of, its imperfections can it be enjoyed in spite of (and perhaps because of) its weakness.

Thus, counterbalancing that kind of Platonic optimism that led Pareyson to celebrate form in its adamantine perfection, his remarks on stopgaps (inspired by concrete experiences of reading) lead his phenomenology of art back to more human dimensions.

If, however, we reexamine the problem of the stopgap in the light of Kant's doctrine of the reflecting judgment, it may become less marginal than it seems at first sight—both in the sense that the stopgap cannot be a marginal element in the work of art, and in the sense that the question of the stopgap is not so marginal in Pareyson's aesthetics. For Pareyson, the reference to Kant is obligatory: his theory of form as autonomous organism stems from his reflections on the third *Critique* and on the aesthetics of German idealism.

Let us review Kant's position: the recognition of organicity emerges in the reflecting judgment; the organicity of nature is postulated as an order that has to exist in things but which things by themselves do not exhibit; it has to be constructed, projected, *as if*. It is only because we cannot fail to see nature as an organism that we are then able to turn to art in the same spirit.

But a judgment of organicity will be, like all reflecting and teleological judgments, a hypothesis: nature is sampled through its primary patterns and is more and more subtly subjected to interpretative activity. This must be due to countless other influences, but the weight that interpretation assumes in Pareyson's philosophy is also due to Kantian aesthetics.

Interpretative activity involves (and this is a central point for Pareyson) a kind of "perspective." Now, in pronouncing verdicts on organicity in things of nature, one finds elements that seem to contradict the postulate of the perfection of form: namely, stopgaps. They remain as a record of evolution, elements that at first seem not to work together with the whole but to exist in a natural body like records of a failed attempt. In studying the work's form, and subsequently in categorizing it and inserting it into the architecture of genus and species, sometimes these elements are dropped, or kept in the shade while the beam of interpretative attention shifts to illuminate other elements it considers central.

One might wonder to what extent this criterion intervenes or not in the assignment of internal legitimacy to a work of art. The latter is given shape by the interpretative act, which sees it as a completed organism, and is stripped of apparently nonessential aspects, which are sacrificed in favor of others, and only in a further or parallel interpretation do these aspects come to assume a more prominent position. This is exemplified by the history of Dante criticism: theological elements that were seen by Romantic criticism as stopgaps (if they were defined as such) become fundamental in the light of a criticism that has injected greater familiarity with the medieval cultural world (dealing with a Dante that is reread not only after, say, Gilson, but also after Eliot), become the essential grain of the poetic architecture, just as much as the vaults and windows do in a Gothic cathedral. The perspective of Dante's cantica is thereby reversed: one discovers that Dante is sometimes more of a poet when he is talking of the planetary spheres and the flashes of light than when he is moved by the love affair of Paolo and Francesca.

The stopgap then becomes relative, surviving like a remnant of a stage of interpretation, and as such remains in reserve, ready to assume a different light in a new "reading," for which it will no longer be accidental.

We looked at the example of turn ancillaries: we accept them as stopgaps, and as stopgaps we "skim" them. That someone said, sneered, insinuated, or replied does not seem to us to be essential to the dialogue's progress or the narrative universe that it illuminates. They are almost casual support posts. Then, suddenly, for another reader these "points" (in the railway sense of the term) become fundamental, for good as well as for ill: if for some authors they are pure elements of a "gastronomic" strategy (at times the fact that someone "sighs" rather than "says" can produce effects that are actually pornographic), for others these interjectory mechanisms become instead an element of rhythm, an indicator of harshness or restraint, or of extraordinary inventiveness. The stopgap is then redeemed, and becomes a structural element; from essential but inelegant it becomes inessential but graceful, or even supremely necessary. The work as organism has been examined from a different point of view.

If this were the case, it would mean that in Pareyson's aesthetics a stopgap acts as more than a prudent corrective to the Platonic or Neoplatonic triumph of Form in all its metaphysical purity, and as a recognition of the material life of "forms," which are also accepted as impure and imperfect; it is also something that interpretation *sets aside,* keeping it as a latent opportunity or stimulus for later interpretations, a potential signal capable of calling the interpreter back to renewing with each reading his faithful commitment to the work's promises. Thus interpretation is reconfirmed as both free and faithful at the same time, capable of many indulgences as long as in the end it comes to rest in the recognition of a form, but is also capable of many changes of direction in order not to let the form rest in the condition that our reading has led it to provisionally.

And should it turn out that a stopgap can never, despite many rereadings, be redeemed at any cost (because it is genuinely evidence of a distraction or weakness), its very presence would be there to testify how and to what extent the interrogation of the work can be collaborative and *charitable,* can identify a pattern drawn even where it was only a sketch, a wish, an intention, left as a bequest to the infinite work of interpretation.

INTERTEXTUAL IRONY
AND LEVELS OF READING

I apologize if in the course of this talk I will have to quote, among my various examples, some that come from my own work as a storyteller as well, but I shall have to dwell on certain characteristics of so-called postmodern narrative, which some literary critics and theoreticians, in particular Brian McHale, Linda Hutcheon, and Remo Ceserani,* have found to be not only present in my fiction but also explicitly theorized in my *Reflections on "The Name of the Rose."* These features are metanarrative, dialogism (in Bakhtin's sense, in which, as I said in the *Reflections,* texts talk to one another), "double coding," and intertextual irony.

Although I do not yet know what exactly the postmodern is, nevertheless I have to admit that the above-mentioned characteristics are present in my novels. However, I would want to distinguish between them, because it often happens that these are understood as four aspects of the same textual strategy.

---

*Linda Hutcheon, "Eco's Echoes: Ironizing the Postmodern," in N. Bouchard and V. Pravadelli, eds., *Umberto Eco's Alternative* (New York: Peter Lang, 1998); Linda Hutcheon, *A Poetics of Postmodernism* (London: Routledge, 1988); Brian McHale, *Constructing Postmodernism* (London: Routledge, 1992); Remo Ceserani, "Eco's (Post)modernist fiction," in Bouchard and Pravadelli, 148 ff.

Metanarrative, inasmuch as it is a reflection that the text carries out on itself and its own nature, or the intrusion of the authorial voice reflecting on what it is narrating, and perhaps appealing to the reader to share its reflections, is much more ancient than the postmodern. Deep down, metanarrative in this sense is already present in Homer's "Sing, Muse . . . ," and—to come closer to our own time—is evident in Manzoni's reflections, for instance, on the suitability of talking about love in the novel. I admit that in the modern novel metanarrative strategy is present with greater insistence, and it has happened to me that, in order to highlight the reflection the text is carrying out on itself, I have turned to what I would call "artificial dialogism," namely, the fiction of a manuscript on which the narrating voice reflects, and tries to decipher and judge at the very moment when it is narrating (but as is all too clear, this strategy, too, was already present in Manzoni).

Even dialogism, especially in its most obvious form of "citationism," is neither a postmodern vice nor virtue; otherwise Bakhtin would never have been able to discuss it so far ahead of its time. In *Purgatorio* canto 26 Dante meets a poet who begins "freely to say:"

> *Tan m'abellis vostre cortes deman,*
> *qu'ieu no me puesc ni voill a vos cobrire.*
> *Ieu sui Arnaut, que plor e vau cantan . . .*

(So much does your courteous request please me,
that I cannot and do not want to conceal myself from you.
I am Arnaut, who weeps and goes on his way singing . . .)

Dante's contemporary reader would have recognized easily that this Arnaut was Arnaut Daniel, but only and precisely because he is brought on stage speaking Provençal (and with lines that, although invented by Dante, are modeled on the troubador tradition). The reader (whether modern or of that time) who is incapable of recognizing this kind of intertextual quotation is excluded from an understanding of the text.

Let us now come to so-called double coding. The man who coined the expression was Charles Jencks, for whom postmodern architecture

> speaks on at least two levels at once: to other architects and a concerned minority who care about specifically architectural meanings, and to the public at large, or the local inhabitants, who care about other issues concerned with comfort, traditional building and a way of life.* The postmodern building or work of art addresses simultaneously a minority, elite public, using "high" codes, and a mass public using popular codes.†

This idea can be understood in many ways. In architecture we all know examples of so-called postmodernism, which abound in quotations from the Renaissance or baroque, or some other epoch, blending "high" cultural models into an ensemble that nevertheless turns out to be pleasing and imaginative also for the popular user—often to the detriment of functionality and while reinstating the value of decoration and ornamentation. For instance, there are countless allusions to and components of extreme avant-gardism present in the Guggenheim Museum in Bilbao, which nevertheless also attracts visitors who have no knowledge of architectural history but who nonetheless say (as

---

*Charles A. Jencks, *The Language of Post-Modern Architecture* (Wisbech: Balding and Mansell, 1978), 6.
†Charles A. Jencks, *What Is Post-Modernism?* (London: Art and Design, 1986), 14–15. See also Charles A. Jencks, ed., *The Post-Modern Reader* (London: Academy Editions; New York: St. Martin's Press, 1992).

the statistics also show) they "like it." In any case, this element was also present in the music of the Beatles, which was also—and not accidentally—arranged in Purcell's style (in an unforgettable disk by Cathy Berberian) precisely because these melodies, so tuneful and pleasant, used cultured phrasing and echoes of other times, which are noticeable to the educated ear.

Examples of double coding can be found today in many advertisements, which are constructed like experimental texts that at one stage would have been understandable to only small groups of cineasts, and which nevertheless attract all types of spectators because of their various "popular" motifs, such as the allusion to erotic situations, the appeal of a well-known face, the rhythm of the editing, the musical accompaniment.

Many works of literature, because of their rediscovery of typical novel plots, have been appreciated even by the wider public, which ought to have been put off by avant-garde stylistic elements, such as the use of interior monologue, metanarrative play, the plurality of voices that are nested inside each other in the course of the narration, the unhinging of temporal sequences, leaps in stylistic register, intermingling of third- and first-person narration, and free indirect speech.

But this seems to mean only that one of the characteristics of so-called postmodernism is to provide stories that are capable of attracting a wide public even though they employ learned allusions and "arty" stylistic devices; in other words (in the most successful cases) if they can blend the two components in a nontraditional way. It is undoubtedly an interesting feature, and it is no accident that it has aroused perplexed attempts at explanations from theoreticians of the so-called quality best seller, a work that pleases *even though* it contains some artistic virtues and involves the reader in problems and procedures that were once the exclusive prerogative of high literature.

It has never been clear whether a quality best seller is to be understood as a popular novel that uses some "cultured" strategies, or as a "cultured" novel that for some mysterious reason becomes popular. In the first case the phenomenon should be explained in terms of a structural analysis of the work, concluding, for example, that its appeal to popular taste is due, say, to the reworking of a "plot," maybe a thriller plot, that hooks the reader and allows him to overcome the stylistic or structural difficulties. In the second case the phenomenon comes under the rubric of reception aesthetics, or, rather, reception sociology. One ought, for instance, to say that a quality best seller depends not on the poetics of the project but on a transformation of the reading public's tendencies, seeing that (i) one cannot underestimate the growth of a category of "popular" readers who, sated with "easy" and instantly consolatory texts, realize the fascination of works that challenge them to a more demanding though somehow more satisfying experience, and agree to reread them several times; and (ii) many readers, whom the publishing industry obstinately still considers "naive," have absorbed many of the techniques of contemporary literature through various channels, and consequently feel less embarrassed when faced with a quality best seller than some sociologists of literature.

In this sense the quality best seller appears to be a phenomenon that is as old as the world. Certainly *The Divine Comedy* was a quality best seller, if we are to give credence to the legends that say Dante took revenge on the blacksmith who sang his poetry badly (even if he did sing it badly, the fact is he sang it and therefore knew it). Shakespeare was also a quality best seller, judging by the size of the audience that followed him, even though they did not perhaps catch many of his subtleties and recycling of previous texts. Manzoni's *The Betrothed* was also a best seller, even though, with its at times essaylike qualities, it conceded very little to the tastes of those who had up until then fed themselves on gothic novels and popular romances—and yet it was the victim of countless pirated editions, and Manzoni was persuaded to accommodate popular tastes by personally supervising Gonin's illustrations for the 1840 edition. In fact, when you think carefully about it, the definition of quality best seller applies to all the great works that have come down to us in multiple manuscripts and printed editions on the wave of a success that has affected more than an elite readership, from the *Aeneid* to *Orlando Furioso* to *Pinocchio.* Consequently, this is not a unique phenomenon but a recurrent one in the history of art and literature, even if it must be accounted for in a different way in each individual age.

Now, in order to underline the differences between double coding and intertextual irony, allow me to reflect on my personal experience as a writer. *The Name of the Rose* begins by telling how the author came across an ancient manuscript. We are in full citationism here, since the topos of the rediscovered manuscript is of venerable antiquity, and as a direct consequence we immediately enter the area of double coding: if the reader wants to get access to the story as it is told, he has to accept some quite learned observations as well as a metanarrative technique raised to the nth degree, because not only is the author inventing out of the blue a text that he can dialogue with, but he is presenting it as a nineteenth-century, neo-Gothic version of the original manuscript, which went back to the end of the fourteenth century. The "popular" reader cannot enjoy the narrative that follows unless he has agreed to this game of Chinese boxes of sources, which confers on the story an aura of ambiguity stemming from the fact that the source is uncertain.

But, if you remember, the title on the page that talks about the manuscript is "Naturally, a Manuscript." That "Naturally" has various resonances, because on the one hand it is intended to stress that we are dealing with a literary topos, and on the other it lays bare an "anxiety of influence," since the reference is intended to be (at least for an Italian reader) to Manzoni, who begins his novel with a seventeenth-century manuscript. How many readers will have grasped or could grasp the various ironic resonances in that "Naturally"? And supposing they have not grasped them, will they still have access to the rest of the story without losing much of its flavor? So we see that that "Naturally" suggests what intertextual irony is.

Let us return to the various characteristics attributed to postmodern fiction. As far as metanarrative is concerned, it is impossible for the reader not to notice metanarrative observations. He might feel disturbed by them, he might ignore (or skip) them, but he notices they are there. The same goes for explicit citationism, as in the Dante example. The reader might not realize that Arnaut Daniel is speaking in his own poetic language, but he will notice that he is speaking in a language that is not that of the *Comedy,* and that therefore Dante is quoting something else, even if it is only the Provençal way of speaking.

When we come to double coding, we can have (and this tells us how many different profiles this notion can assume): (i) a reader who does not accept the mixture of cultured and popular styles and contents, and who therefore refuses to read it, precisely because he recognizes this mixture; (ii) a reader who feels at home precisely because he enjoys this process of alternating between difficulty and approachability, challenge and encouragement; and lastly (iii) a reader who perceives the entire text as a pleasant invitation and does not in the end realize the extent to which it draws on elite styles (so he enjoys the work, but misses its references).

It is only this third case that introduces us to the strategy of intertextual irony. Faced with that "Naturally," whoever appreciates its wink establishes a privileged relationship with the text (or the narrating voice); whoever does not continues to read all the same—and will be faced with two choices: either he will understand through his own capacities that the manuscript business must be a literary artifice (he manages to appreciate the game for the first time, thus "growing" as a competent reader), or, as many have done, he will write to the author asking whether that intriguing manuscript really does exist. But one thing should be made clear: in cases, for example, of double coding in architecture, the visitor might not notice that a colonnade with a tympanum is quoting from Greek architecture, but he nevertheless enjoys the harmony and ordered multiplicity of that construction. On the other hand, the reader who does not grasp my "Naturally" knows only that he is reading about a manuscript, but misses the reference and its playful irony.

A work can abound in quotations from other texts without necessarily being an instance of intertextual irony. Just to take one example, *The Waste Land* requires pages and pages of notes to identify its references not only to the world of literature but also to history and cultural anthropology, but Eliot deliberately provides the notes because he cannot imagine a naive reader who could miss every single reference and yet enjoy his text in a satisfactory manner. I would say that his notes are an integral part of the text. Of course, uncultured readers could limit their appreciation of the text to its rhythm, its sound, to the hint of ghostliness that appears on the level of content, with a vague knowledge that there is something else there, and enjoying the text like someone eavesdropping at a half-open door, glimpsing only hints of a promising epiphany. But for Eliot (I believe) these would be readers who have not yet grown up, not the Model Readers that he aimed at and wanted to form.

But cases of intertextual irony are different, and precisely because of this they characterize literary forms that, however erudite, can also enjoy popular success: the text can be read in a naive way, without appreciating the intertextual references, or it can be read in the full awareness of them, or at least with the conviction that one has to go looking for them. For an extreme example, let us imagine we had to read the *Don Quixote* that was rewritten by Borges's Pierre Menard (and that Menard's text can be interpreted differently from Cervantes's text, at least to the extent that Borges claimed). Whoever has not heard of Cervantes would enjoy a fascinating story, a series of mock-heroic adventures whose flavor comes across despite the not very modern Castilian in which they are written. But those who catch the constant reference to Cervantes's text will be able to appreciate not only the correspondences between the original and Menard's text but also the constant and inevitable irony of the latter.

Unlike more general cases of double coding, intertextual irony, by bringing into play the possibility of a double reading, does not invite all readers to the same party. It selects them, and privileges the more intertextually aware readers, but it does not exclude the less aware. If an author happens to introduce a character saying "*Paris à nous deux*," the naive reader does not identify the allusion to Balzac and yet can become passionately interested all the same in a character who is keen on challenges and boldness. The informed reader, on the other hand, "gets" the reference and savors its irony—not only the author's cultured wink, but also the effects of lowering the tone or changing the meaning (when the quotation is inserted into a context that is totally different from that of the source), the general allusion to the endless dialogue that goes on between texts.

If we had to explain the phenomenon of intertextual irony to a first-year university student, or at any rate to someone who is not in the know, we would perhaps have to tell him that, thanks to this citation strategy, a text presents two levels of reading. But if, instead of someone not in the know, we found ourselves facing someone who was a habitué of literary theory, we could be put on the spot by two possible questions.

First question: so then does "intertextual irony" not perhaps have something to do with the fact that a text can have not just two but four different levels of reading, namely, the literal, moral, allegorical, and anagogical levels, as is taught in Bible hermeneutics and as Dante claims for his own poem in the Letter to Cangrande?

Second question: but does "intertextual irony" not perhaps have something to do with the two model readers that textual semiotics, and in particular Eco, talk about, the first one known as the semantic reader and the second as the critical or aesthetic reader?

I will try to demonstrate that we are dealing with three quite distinct phenomena. But replying to these two apparently naive questions is not a pointless exercise, because as we shall see, we are facing a cluster of relationships that are not easy to disentangle.

Let us move to the first question, namely, to the theory of the multiple senses of a text. We do not need to think of the four senses of scripture; we just have to think of the moral meaning of fables: of course, a naive reader can interpret the fable of the wolf and the lamb as a quarrel among animals, but even if the author was not keen to tell us "*de te fabula narratur*" (the story is about you), it would be very difficult not to glimpse some parable in it, a universal moral lesson, just as happens with the parables in the Gospels themselves.

This joint presence of a literal and a moral sense informs all fiction, even fiction that is least concerned with educating its readers, as might be the case with a cheap police thriller: even from this kind of story the clever and sensitive reader could draw a series of moral teachings, such as that crime doesn't pay, that your deeds will find you out, that law and order are bound to triumph in the end, that human reason can succeed in unraveling the most complex mysteries.

It could even be said that in certain works the moral sense is so identical with the literal one as to constitute the only meaning. But even in so obviously moralizing a novel as *The Betrothed,* the risk of the reader getting only the story and missing the ethical lesson forces Manzoni to insert proverbial observations here and there, precisely in order that those who devour neo-Gothic plots of garish hue are not satisfied with the kidnaping of Lucia or the death of Don Rodrigo, and thereby risk the possibility of neglecting the message about Providence.

What is the real autonomy of these levels, when there is more than one of them? Can one read *The Divine Comedy* without grasping its anagogic message? I would say that that is what so much Romantic criticism did. Can one read the procession at the end of *Purgatorio* without apprehending its allegorical dimension? A good surrealist reading of it could do so. And as for *Paradiso*, Beatrice smiles and radiates so much that she would enchant any reader who ignores the upper levels of meaning, and some critics, inspired by criteria of pure lyricity, told us that we had to ignore these disturbing overlays of meaning in the poem as though they were totally unconnected and had to be removed.*

One could then say that those levels of reading that depend on overlays of sense can either be activated or not, depending on the historical epoch in question, and sometimes they become totally unfathomable, as can happen not only with texts from very ancient civilizations but, for instance, with many paintings of not so long ago, where—apart from those who are iconographers or iconologists—visitors to museums (and even critics who rely solely on the visual) enjoy Giorgione or Poussin without knowing what obscure mythologies their images refer to (though we are convinced that Panofksy enjoyed them even more, since he was able to read them at both levels, at the level of form and at the level of iconographical reference).

The answer to the second question is quite different. I have repeatedly built theories around the fact that a text (and particularly a text with an aesthetic aim, and in the present case a narrative text) tends to construct two Model Readers. It addresses in the first place a Model Reader of the first level, whom we will call the semantic reader, the reader who wants to know (and rightly so) how the story will end (whether Ahab will capture the whale, whether Leopold Bloom will meet Stephen Dedalus, after having accidentally crossed his path on a number of occasions in the

---

*For an idea of how misleading this practice has been, I refer to the essay in this same volume, "A Reading of the *Paradiso*" (above, pp. 16–22).

course of 16 June 1904, whether Pinocchio will become a real flesh-and-blood boy, or whether Proust's Narrator will manage to settle his accounts with Lost Time). But the text also addresses a Model Reader of the second level, whom we will call the semiotic or aesthetic reader, who asks himself what kind of reader that particular story was asking him to become, and wants to know how the Model Author who is instructing him step by step will proceed. To put it bluntly, the first-level model reader wants to know what happens, while the second-level model reader wants to know how what happens has been narrated. To find out how the story will end one usually just has to read the text once. To become a second-level model reader one has to read it several times, and some stories have to be read countless times.

There is no such thing as an exclusively second-level model reader; on the contrary, in order to become one, you have to have been a good first-level reader. Whoever has read *The Betrothed* and has not felt even the slightest shudder when Lucia sees L'Innominato appear in front of her cannot appreciate the way Manzoni's novel has been constructed. But it is certainly the case that you can be a first-level reader without ever reaching the second level, as happens with those who are equally enthused by *The Betrothed* and *Gargantua* without realizing that the latter is much richer in lexical terms than the former; or as happens with those who, not unreasonably, get bored reading *Hypnerotomachia Poliphili* because amid all those made-up words it is impossible to understand how things will turn out.

On close examination it is in the play between these two levels of reading that we can observe the two ways of understanding catharsis in Aristotle's *Poetics,* and in aesthetics in general: for we know that there is either a homeopathic or an allopathic interpretation of catharsis. In the first case catharsis stems from the fact that the spectator of a tragedy is genuinely seized by pity and terror, even to the point of paroxysm, so much so that in suffering these two passions he is purged of them, and emerges liberated by the tragic experience; in the second case the tragic text places us at a distance from the passion that is represented in it, through an almost Brechtian kind of estrangement, and we are liberated from passion not by experiencing it but by appreciating the way it is represented. You can easily see that for a homeopathic catharsis a first-level reader is sufficient (this is, after all, the kind of reader that cries when the cavalry arrives in a Western), whereas for an allopathic catharsis one needs a second-level reader—and this is what, perhaps erroneously, makes people attribute a greater degree of philosophical dignity, a more purified and purifying vision of art, to allopathic catharsis, whereas the homeopathic theory becomes linked to the celebration of Corybantism and the Eleusinian mysteries with their perfumes and drugs, or to the celebration of Saturday-night fever.

We should beware of understanding this distinction of levels as though on one side there were an easily satisfied reader, only interested in the story, and on the other a reader with an extremely refined palate, concerned above all with language. If that were so, we would have to read *The Count of Monte Cristo* on the first level, becoming totally enthralled by it, and maybe even shedding hot tears at every turn, and then on the second level we would have to realize, as is only right, that from a stylistic point of view it is very badly written, and to conclude therefore that it is a terrible novel. Instead, the miracle of works like *The Count of Monte Cristo* is that, while being very badly written, they are still masterpieces of fiction. Consequently the second-level reader is not only he who recognizes that the novel is badly written but also the one who is aware that, despite this, its narrative structure is perfect, the archetypes are all in the right place, the *coups-de-scène* judged to perfection, its breadth (though at times stretched to breaking point) almost Homeric in scope—so much so that to criticize *The Count of Monte Cristo* because of its language would be like criticizing Verdi's operas because his librettists, Francesco Maria Piave and Salvatore Cammarano, were not poets like Leopardi. The second-level reader is then also the person who real-izes how the work manages to function brilliantly at the first level.

However, it is certainly at this second level of critical reading that one is able to decide whether the text has two or more levels of meaning, whether it is worthwhile looking for an allegorical sense, or whether the tale is also saying something about the reader—and whether these different senses blend together in a solid, har-monious form or whether they can float about independently of one another. It is the second-level reader who will decide that it is difficult to decouple the literal from the moral sense in the fable of the wolf and the lamb (as though it were pointless without the moral sense to tell the story of that diatribe between animals). On the other hand, one can read with enjoyment and reverence the psalm "*In exitu Israel de Aegypto / domus Iacob de populo bar-baro / facta est Iudaea sanctificatio eius, / Israel potestas eius*" (When Israel went forth from Egypt, / the house of Jacob from a people of strange language, / Judah became his sanctuary, / Israel his do-minion), even without knowing that in anagogic terms the verses mean, among other things, that the sanctified soul will emerge from the enslavement of earthly corruption toward the freedom of eternal glory—and then the second-level reader will go and find out if the psalmist's text really did mean this as well.

There are certainly many analogies between the aesthetically and critically aware second-level reader and the reader who, faced with examples of intertextual irony, catches the references to the uni-verse of literature. But the two positions cannot be identical. Let us take some examples.

In the fable about the wolf and the lamb there are two senses (one literal, one moral), and certainly two readers: the first-level reader who understands not just the story (the literal sense) but also the moral, and the reader who recognizes the stylistic and narrative merits of Phaedrus as teller of fables. But there is no intertextual irony because Phaedrus is not quoting anyone—or if he does cite a previous fabulist, he simply copies him. Homer's Ulysses kills the suitors: just one meaning, but two readers—one who enjoys Ulysses' revenge and one who enjoys Homer's art—but no intertextual irony. In Joyce's *Ulysses* there are two meanings in the biblical-Dantesque mode (Bloom's story as an allegory of Ulysses' story), but it is very difficult not to notice that the story retraces the steps of Ulysses' wanderings, and if someone did not notice this, the title would offer him a clue. The two levels of reading still remain open, since one could read *Ulysses* just to know how the story ends—even though such a limited and limiting form of reading is highly improbable (in fact, it is exaggeratedly wasteful), and it would be advisable to stop the experiment after the first chapter and turn to more instantly rewarding stories. It is impossible to read *Finnegans Wake* except as a huge intertextual laboratory—unless you want to read it out loud to enjoy it as pure music. There are more than the four meanings of Holy Scripture here: they are infinite, or at least indefinite. The first-level reader follows the one or two possible readings of each single pun, then breathlessly comes to a halt, gets lost, moves to the second level to admire the cleverness of an unexpected and insoluble combination of etymologies and possible readings, gets lost again, and so on. *Finnegans Wake* does not help us to understand the distinctions we are talking about but, rather, puts them all into question, and confuses our ideas. But it does so without deceiving the naive reader by allowing him to proceed without noticing the game he is caught up in. Instead it grabs him by the throat and kicks him out the back door.

In attempting these definitions, one notices, I think, that the plurality of meanings is a phenomenon that is set up in a text even if the author was not thinking about it at all and has done nothing to encourage a reading on a multiplicity of levels. The worst hack telling stories of blood, horror, or death, or of sex and violence, cannot avoid leaving a moral sense fluctuating in the text, even if it is none other than the celebration of indifference toward evil, or of sex and violence as the only values worth pursuing.

The same can be said of the two levels of reading, the semantic and the aesthetic. In the end this possibility exists even for railway timetables. Two different timetables give me the same information on a semantic level, but I might value the first as better organized and easier to consult than the second, thus moving on to a judgment about their organization and functionality that looks more at the how than the what.

This does not happen with intertextual irony. Unless one goes looking for plagiarism or unconscious intertextual echoes, usually reading as a form of hunt-the-quotation exists in the form of a challenge between the reader and a text (leaving aside the author's intentions): the text somehow solicits the discovery of its secret dialogue with other texts.

As an author of novels that play very much on intertextual quotation, I am always happy for the reader to catch the reference, the wink; but, without calling the empirical author into question, whoever has recognized, let's say, in *The Island of the Day Before* nods in the direction of Jules Verne's *Mysterious Island* (for instance, the opening question about whether it was an island or a continent) must want other readers also to notice this allusion in the text.

Of course, if there is intertextual irony, it is because one must admit as legitimate even the reading of those who only want to follow the plot about a shipwreck and who do not know whether he has landed on an island or a continent. The duty of the aesthetic reader is to decide that even that first kind of reading is independent and legitimate, and that the text allows it. If in the same novel I introduce a double, I admit that there is a reader who will be amazed and excited by this situation, but I obviously am aspiring to a reader who realizes that the presence of a double is almost obligatory in a baroque novel.

When in *Foucault's Pendulum* the protagonist, Casaubon, spends his last night in Paris at the foot of the Eiffel Tower, he sees, from below, this construction as a monstrous being and becomes almost hypnotized by it. To write that passage I did two things: On the one hand, I spent some nights underneath the tower, trying to put myself at the center of its "paws" and to look at it from all possible angles, but always from the bottom upward. On the other hand, I looked up all the literary passages that had been written about the tower, especially while it was being built; these were mostly indignant, violent attacks on it, and what my protagonist sees and feels is a highly worked collage of a whole range of texts in both prose and verse. I was not anticipating that my reader could find all these quotations (and I myself am now unable to identify them and distinguish between them), but I certainly wanted the more subtle readers to sense the shadow of something *déjà vu*. At the same time I allowed the naive reader to live through the same sensations I had experienced at the foot of the tower, even though he did not know that they were bolstered with so much previous literature.

It is pointless concealing the fact that it is not the author but the text that privileges the intertextual reader over the naive one. Intertextual irony is a "classist" selector. You can have a snobbish reading of the Bible that is satisfied only by its literal sense, or at most appreciates the rhythmic beauty of the Hebrew text or of the Latin Vulgate (thus certainly bringing into play the aesthetic reader), but there cannot be a snobbish reading of an intertextually ironic text that ignores its dialogical element. Intertextual irony calls together the happy few—except that the more there are of these happy few, the happier they will be.

However, when a text unleashes the mechanism of intertextual irony, it has to expect that it will not produce just the allusions intended by the author, since the possibility of having a double reading depends on the breadth of the reader's own textual encyclopedia, and this encyclopedia varies from reader to reader. In a conference held in Louvain in 1999, Inge Lanslots made a number of very acute observations on the many allusions to Verne that run throughout *The Island of the Day Before,* and she was certainly right in this. In the course of her oral presentation she found references to another novel by Verne (that I was frankly unaware of) where many mechanical clocks are described, as in my novel. I did not mean to use the intentions of the empirical author as a parameter for validating interpretations of the text, but I had to reply that the reader ought to recognize the many quotations from baroque literature that are scattered throughout that text. Now the topos of mechanical clocks is typically baroque (just think of Lubrano's poems). It is difficult to ask a foreign critic who is not a specialist in Italian baroque literature to recognize one of its minor poets, and I admitted that her approach was not, so to speak, prohibited. If one goes hunting subterranean allusions, it is difficult to say whether the person that is right is the author who was unaware of them or the reader who has found them. However, I pointed out that recognizing an allusion to baroque literature went with the grain of the general characteristics of the text, whereas identifying an allusion to Verne, at that point, did not lead anywhere.

In any case, the discussion clearly convinced the speaker, because I cannot find any trace of her observation in the proceedings of that conference.*

There are other cases where it is much more difficult to keep a check on the reader's encyclopedia. In *Foucault's Pendulum* I named the hero Casaubon, and I was thinking of Isaac Casaubon, the man who stripped the *Corpus Hermeticum* of its mythical status with impeccable critical arguments. My ideal second-level reader, who has access to intertextual irony, could identify a certain analogy between what the great philologist understood and what my

---

*Franco Musarra, ed., *Eco in fabula* (Florence: Cesati, 2002).

character understands at the end of the novel. I was conscious of the fact that few readers would be able to recognize the allusion, and I believed that this was not essential in terms of textual strategy (in other words, one can read my novel and understand my Casaubon even without knowing about the historical Casaubon).

Before finishing my novel, I discovered by chance that Casaubon was also a character in *Middlemarch;* I had read this novel some time before, but that detail of nomenclature had left no trace in my memory. In certain cases the Model Author wants to ration interpretations that seem pointless to him, and I made an effort to eliminate a possible reference to George Eliot. Thus on page 63 there is the following dialogue between Belbo and Casaubon:

"By the way, what's your name?"
"Casaubon."
"Casaubon. Wasn't he a character in *Middlemarch?*"
"I don't know. There was also a Renaissance philologist by that name, but we are not related."

However, along came a clever reader, David Robey, who pointed out that, clearly not by chance, Eliot's Casaubon was writing a *Key to All Mythologies,* and I have to admit this does seem to fit my character. Later Linda Hutcheon devoted even more attention to this connection, and found other affinities between the Casaubons, which apparently increased the ironic-intertextual temperature of my novel.* As the empirical author I can say that this analogy had never even crossed my mind, but if the format of the encyclopedia of Hutcheon the reader is such as to allow her to see this intertextual relationship, and my text encourages it, then it must be said that the operation is objectively (in the sense of culturally and socially) possible.

---

*"Eco's Echoes: Ironizing the (Post)modern," op. cit., 171.

An analogous case is that of Foucault. My novel is entitled *Foucault's Pendulum* because the pendulum I talk about was invented by Léon Foucault. Had it been invented by Franklin, the title would have been *Franklin's Pendulum.* This time I was conscious right from the start that someone could sniff an allusion to Michel Foucault: my characters are obsessed by analogies and Foucault wrote about the four paradigms of similitude. As the empirical author, I was not very happy with this possible link because it seemed rather superficial. But the pendulum invented by Léon was the protagonist of my story, and I could not change the title, so I hoped that my Model Reader would not attempt a link with Michel. I was wrong: many readers did just that. Linda Hutcheon more than anyone else, and she actually identified precise correspondences between elements of the novel and the four figures of similitude listed by Michel Foucault in the chapter in his *The Order of Things* entitled "The Prose of the World." Needless to say, I had read *The Order of Things* when it came out in 1966, almost twenty years before starting to write my novel, and in the meantime I had come across the ghosts of analogy in the tradition of Renaissance and seventeenth-century Hermeticism, so that when I was writing I was thinking about these direct sources, or the deranged use of such sources in current texts on commercial occultism. Probably if the novel had been entitled *Franklin's Pendulum,* no one would have felt authorized to link the references to the theory of library classification to Michel Foucault; it would have been easier to think of Paracelsus. But I admit that the title of the book, or at any rate the name of the inventor of the eponymous pendulum, constituted too attractive a trail for a hunter of intertextual traces, and Linda Hutcheon was perfectly within her rights to find all she did find. And who knows whether, at least on the level of a psychoanalysis of the author, she is not in fact right, and that my interests in certain aspects of Hermeticism were stimulated by my early reading of Foucault (Michel).

Nevertheless, it would be interesting to establish whether my appeal to Foucault was a case of intertextual irony or simply one of unwitting influence. Up until now I have perhaps allowed people to think that intertextual irony depends on the author's intention, but I have theorized too much on the prevalence of *intentio operis* over *intentio auctoris* to allow myself to indulge in such naïveté. If a possible quotation appears in the text, and this quotation seems to go with the grain of the rest of the text (and other citations from it), the intentions of the empirical author count for little. The critic (or reader) is right, then, to talk of "citationism," and of the "textual echo" (I am using another of Linda Hutcheon's terms and am not playing on my own name) that the work encourages.

The fact is that once you start playing with intertextual irony it is difficult to resist the appeal of such echoes, even though some might be totally fortuitous, like the reference to Jules Verne's clocks. Linda Hutcheon, again, cites from page 378 of the American edition of *Foucault's Pendulum,* "The rule is simple: Suspect, only suspect," and finds an intertextual echo of E. M. Forster's "Connect, only connect." Acute critic that she is, she has the prudence to say that this "ironic play" exists in the English: for the Italian text (and it is not clear whether she had this to hand when she was writing) does not contain this intertextual reference since it says, "sospettare, sospettare sempre." The reference, which was certainly conscious, was inserted by the translator, Bill Weaver. We have to be honest, the English text does contain this echo, which means that translation can not only alter the play of intertextual irony, it can also enrich it.

In other instances you can come across the possibility of choosing between a reading that is squared and one that is cubed. In one passage from chapter 30 of the *Pendulum,* where the protagonists imagine that even the entire story told by the Gospels is an effect of an invention like that of the Plan they are hatching, Casaubon comments: "*Toi, apocryphe lecteur, mon semblable, mon frère.*" I do not recall what I was thinking about when I wrote this, but I probably would have been happy with the intertextual allusion to Baudelaire, which was already enriched by the allusion to the apocryphal Gospels. Linda Hutcheon, however, defines the phrase as "a parody of Baudelaire by Eliot" (in fact, if you remember, Eliot quotes this line from Baudelaire in *The Waste Land*), and certainly if this is so, it all becomes even richer. What are we to do? Divide readers into those who get as far as Baudelaire and those who come all the way up to Eliot? And what if there was a reader who found the "hypocrite lecteur" in Eliot, and remembered it, but did not know that Eliot was quoting Baudelaire?

Everyone noticed that *The Name of the Rose* begins with a quote from the Gospel according to Saint John ("In the beginning was the Word," etc.). But how many noticed that this can also be seen as a quote from the beginning of Pulci's *Morgante Maggiore,* which opens with a (very respectful) imitation of Saint John: "*In principio era il verbo appresso a Dio / ed era Iddio il verbo e il verbo lui. / Quest'era nel principio al parer mio / e nulla si può far senza costui*" (In the beginning the word was with God / and God was the Word and the Word was God. / This was in the beginning, it seems to me, / and we cannot do anything without Him)?

However, when you really think about it, how many readers did notice that my novel begins with a quotation from Saint John? I have found Japanese readers (and perhaps I did not need to go that far) who attributed those very virtuous thoughts to good old Adso, and yet despite this they did not miss the religious afflatus that animates the words of the young monk.

In fact, to be precise, intertextual irony is not, strictly speaking, a form of irony. Irony consists in saying not the opposite of the truth but the opposite of what one presumes the interlocutor thinks is true. It is ironic to define a stupid person as very intelligent, but only if the addressee knows that the person is stupid. If he does not know, then the irony is missed, and what one has is only false information. Thus irony becomes simply a lie when the addressee is not aware of the game.

On the other hand, in terms of intertextual irony, I can tell the story of a double without the addressee sensing the reference to the baroque topos, yet despite this the addressee will not have enjoyed any less this very respectable, literal story about a double. In *The Island of the Day Before* there are some *coups-de-scène* that are clearly modeled on Dumas, and my quotation of them is sometimes literal, but the reader who does not get the reference can still enjoy the *coups-de-scène,* even though in a naive fashion. Thus if I said previously that the game of intertextual irony is snobbish and aristocratic, I should correct myself, because it does not set up a "*conventio ad excludendum*" as regards the naive reader. It is like a banquet where the remains of the dinner served on the upper floor are distributed on the lower floor, but not the remains from the dinner table, rather the remains in the pot, and these are also set out nicely, and, since the naive reader thinks the feast is happening on only one floor, he will enjoy these for what they are worth (and, when all's said and done, they will be tasty and plentiful) without supposing that anyone has enjoyed more.

This is exactly what happens to the naive reader of Dante's sonnet "*Tanto gentile e tanto onesta pare,*" who does not know how much its language has changed from Dante's time to ours, and what were the philosophical postulates of Dante's poetry. He will enjoy an elegant declaration of love, and will derive great gain from it just the same, both emotional and intellectual gain. This shows that my culinary analogy was perhaps provocative, but it was not intended to place art and gastronomy on the same level.

And lastly, not even the most naive of readers can pass through the meshes of the text without entertaining the suspicion that sometimes (or often) it refers to something beyond itself. Here one sees then that intertextual irony not only is not a "*conventio ad excludendum,*" but a provocation and invitation to include, such that it can gradually transform the naive reader into a reader who begins to sense the perfume of so many other texts that have preceded the one he is reading.

Links between intertextual irony and biblical or Dantesque allegory? Some. Intertextual irony provides an intertextual second sense for readers who have been secularized and who no longer have any spiritual senses to look for in the text. The biblical and poetic second senses stemming from the theory of the four meanings allowed the text to flower vertically, each sense allowing us to approach ever closer to some Afterlife. The intertextual second sense is horizontal, labyrinthine, convoluted, and infinite, running from text to text—with no other promise than the continual murmuring of intertextuality. Intertextual irony presupposes an absolute immanentism. It provides revelations to those who have lost the sense of transcendence.

However, I would not take too seriously anyone who started to moralize about this or drew the conclusion that intertextual irony is the aesthetics of the godless. It is a technique that can be activated even by a work that then aims at inspiring spiritual second senses, or one that presents itself as a high moral lesson, or is capable of talking about death and the infinite. Remo Ceserani has kindly pointed out that my presumed postmodernism is not without a sense of melancholy and pessimism.* This is a sign that intertextual irony does not presuppose at every turn a carefree carnival of dialogism. But it is certainly true that the text, to the extent that it is tormented, asks its reader to be aware of the rumble of intertextuality that has preceded our torments, and that author and reader also know how to unite in the mystic body of worldly Scriptures.

---

*"*Eco e il postmoderno consapevole*," in *Raccontare il postmoderno* (Turin: Bollati Boringhieri, 1997), 180–200.

Revised version of a lecture given in Forlí, Italy, in February 1999.

THE *POETICS* AND US

Allow me, as an Italian, to approach the question of Aristotle's *Poetics* in the form of a confession by a child of this century. Italian culture produced the great Renaissance commentators on Aristotle, and in the baroque period it was Emanuele Tesauro who, with his *Cannocchiale aristotelico,* re-presented to the world of post-Galilean physics Aristotle's poetic theories as the sole key to approaching the human sciences. But at the very beginning of the following century this same Italian culture was enriched by Vico's *New Science,* the work that questioned every Aristotelian precept in order to posit a language and poetry that develop outside any rules. By doing so, Vico unwittingly opened the door— while in France, from Boileau to Batteux, from Le Bossu to Dubos, and right down to the *Encyclopédie,* writers were still looking to set down the rules of tragedy with the rules of taste— to a philosophy, a linguistics, and an aesthetics of the unpredictable freedom of the Spirit.

This is not the genteel, classical French *Esprit* but romantic, Hegelian *Geist,* which emerges through history only to become history itself. Thus, from nineteenth-century Idealism to Croce, Italian culture was dominated over the course of a hundred years by the rejection of all rhetoric and all poetics. Under an Idealist aesthetics that read all language as founded from the outset on aesthetic creativity, the phenomenon of poetry could be described no longer as the deviation from a preexisting norm but rather as a new dawn. The few pages devoted by Croce to Aristotle show irredeemable prejudices, which resulted in a formally impeccable syllogism: aesthetics began with Baumgarten's idea of a *"scientia cognitionis sensitivae, gnoseologia inferior"* (a science of sensory cognition, a lower gnoseology); Aristotle was unable to read Baumgarten, and thus Aristotle had nothing to say on aesthetics.

I remember the shivers I experienced as a young man, feeling as marginalized as a young homosexual in Victorian society, when I discovered that the Anglo-Saxon tradition had continued to take Aristotle's poetics seriously, and without interruption.

I was not amazed to find traces of Aristotle in Dryden or Hobbes, in Reynolds or Dr. Johnson, not to mention the references to the *Poetics,* however vague and even at times polemical, that I found in Wordsworth or Coleridge; but I was struck by the readings of poets and critics who were contemporaries of Croce but who gave me the outline of a culture for which Aristotle was still a model, a point of reference.

One of the classics of American critical theory, Richards's *Principles of Literary Criticism* (1924) opens with a reference to Aristotle; if Wellek and Warren's *Theory of Literature* (1942) managed to blend the principles of Anglo-Saxon criticism with the work of the Russian formalists and of the structuralists in Prague, it was because they referred to Aristotle in almost every chapter. In the 1940s the masters of the New Criticism measured themselves against Aristotle. I discovered the Chicago school, which defined itself unreservedly as neo-Aristotelian, a critic of contemporary theater like Francis Fergusson (*The Idea of a Theater,* 1949), who used the notions of plot and action and interpreted *Macbeth* as an imitation of an action, and Northrop Frye, who played with the Aristotelian notion of *mythos* in his *Anatomy of Criticism* (1957).

But we need only cite the influence of the *Poetics* on a writer like Joyce. He not only speaks about it in the 1903 *Paris Notebook,* written during his visits to the Bibliothèque Sainte Geneviève, but in 1904 writes a short ironic poem on catharsis. He tells Stuart Gilbert that the Aeolus episode in *Ulysses* is based on Aristotle's *Rhetoric.* In a letter to his brother Stanislaus of 9 March 1903, he criticizes Synge for not being Aristotelian enough for his tastes. In a letter to Pound of 9 April 1917, he says of *Ulysses*: "I am doing it, as Aristotle would say—by different means in different parts." Lastly, the theory of literary genres in the *Portrait* is of clear Aristotelian origin. In that work Stephen Dedalus works out a definition of pity and terror, deploring the fact that Aristotle had not provided one in the *Poetics* and ignoring the fact that he had, however, done so in the *Rhetoric.* Through a kind of miraculous elective affinity, the definitions Joyce invents are very similar to those in the *Rhetoric*—but he studied with the Jesuits, and along with a secondhand version of Saint Thomas he must also have come across a thirdhand account of Aristotle. To say nothing of the English-speaking cultural environment in which he lived, about whose Aristotelian interests we have already spoken.

I believe, however, that I underwent my most decisive Aristotelian experience reading Edgar Allan Poe's *Philosophy of Composition,* where he analyzes, word by word, structure by structure, the birth, technique, and raison d'être of his poem "The Raven." In this text Aristotle is never named, but his model is ever present, even in the use of some key terms.

Poe's project consisted in showing how the effect of "an intense and pure elevation of soul" (Beauty) is achieved by careful organization of structures, and in showing how "the work proceeded step by step, to its completion with the precision and rigid consequence of a mathematical problem," while still keeping track of a unity of impression (which is in physical terms the unit of time that corresponds to one reading of the text), and of place, and of emotional tone.

The extraordinary thing about this text is that its author explains the rule whereby he managed to convey the impression of spontaneity, and this message, which goes against any aesthetics of ineffability, is the same as that transmitted by the *Poetics.* This Aristotelian lesson is also found later in Pseudo-Longinus's *On the Sublime,* which is usually seen as a celebration of the aesthetic "je ne sais quoi." *On the Sublime* certainly wants to tell us about a poetic effect that is based not on rational or moral persuasion but, rather, on a feeling of wonder that is produced as a kind of ecstasy and *coup de foudre.* But right from the first page of the treatise, the anonymous author tells us he does not want just to define the object of his discourse but also to tell us the strokes of artifice by which it can be produced. Hence, in the second part of the work, we find a minute analysis of the rhetorical strategies to be adopted in order to achieve, through definable procedures, this indefinable effect.

Poe proceeds in the same way, except that *The Philosophy of Composition* is a fascinating and ambiguous text: is it a set of rules for other poets, or is it an implicit theory of the art in general, extrapolated from a personal experience of writing, by a writer who positions himself as a critical reader of his own work?

The fertile ambiguity of this text was noticed by Kenneth Burke, who approached Poe's text in explicitly Aristotelian terms. If there is a discipline called Poetics, it will have nothing to do with a criticism seen as commercial advice to the reader, or a distribution of approval or disapproval. It will have to deal with one of the dimensions of language, and in that sense it will be the proper object of the critic, just as poetry is the object of the poet. "An approach to the poem in terms of Poetics is an approach in

terms of the poem's nature as a kind (a literary species or mode)."*
In this sense Burke's definition comes close to that given by the
Prague school, for whom poetics is the discipline that explains
the "literariness" of literature, which is to say that it explains why
a literary work can be defined as such.

Burke is well aware that defining literary processes and the
rules of genre can lead, as has happened, to the transformation of
a descriptive into a normative science. Nevertheless, poetics cannot escape its duty to formulate rules that are implicit in the
poet's practice, even if the artist is not conscious of them.

Poe, on the other hand, was conscious of them and consequently worked as a "*philosophus additus artifici*" (philosopher as
well as an artist). Perhaps he did so "*après-coup,*" and while he
wrote he may have been unaware of what he was doing, but as a
reader of his own work he later understood why "The Raven"
produces the effect it does and why we say it is a good poem. The
analysis carried out by Poe the author could have been done by a
reader like Jakobson. Thus, while trying to define a compositional practice of which his poem was an example, Poe identified
strategies characterizing artistic procedure in general.

Poe's essay is Aristotelian in the principles that inspired it, in
its aims, results, and ambiguities. Lubomir Doležel wondered
whether Aristotle's *Poetics* is a work of criticism (i.e., one that
aims at the evaluation of the work it discusses) or of poetics,
which aims, as we saw, at defining the conditions of literariness.[†]
Doležel, quoting Frye, reminds us that the *Poetics* highlights an
intelligible structure of knowledge that is neither poetry itself nor
the experience of poetry (harking back to some distinctions that

---

*"Poetics in particular, language in general," in *Poetry* (1961); later in *Language as Symbolic
Action: Essays on Life, Literature, Method* (Berkeley and Los Angeles: University of California
Press, 1966), 32.
†"Aristotelian Poetics as a Science of Literature," 1984, now "Aristotle: Poetics and Criti-
cism," in *Occidental Poetics: Tradition and Progress* (Lincoln: University of Nebraska Press,
1990), 11–32.

appeared in the *Metaphysics*) and considers it as a productive science, which aims at knowledge in order to create objects.

In this sense Poetics does not interpret individual works, to which it turns only as a repertoire of examples. But in pursuing this aim Poetics becomes entangled in a paradox; in trying to capture the essence of poetry it misses its most essential feature, namely, its uniqueness and the variability of its manifestations.

Doležel thus observes that Aristotle's *Poetics* is at one and the same time the founding text both of literary theory and of literary criticism in the West, and this comes about precisely because of its inherent contradiction. It establishes a metalanguage of criticism, and allows judgments founded on the knowledge this metalanguage supplies. But this result is achieved at a certain price. Every Poetics that proposes ideal structures, and chooses to ignore the particularities specific to individual works, is always in the end a theory of the works that the theorist judges to be best. Thus even Aristotle's *Poetics* has (allow me to paraphrase Popper) its own "influencing aesthetics," and Aristotle betrays his own critical preferences every time he chooses an example.

According to Gerald Frank Else, only a tenth of all Greek tragedies meet the structures posited by Aristotle.[*] In a vicious circle, an intuitive critical judgment has preceded and determined the choice of the corpus it will use to work out the general principles that justify the judgment in critical terms. Doležel points out that Else's statement is also based on a critical prejudice, but his argument holds in any case, since it highlights the presence of the vicious circle that has flawed the entire history of poetics and criticism.

We thus find ourselves facing not an opposition (as was long thought) between a normative poetics and an aesthetics that operates on such a level of generality as never to be compromised by the reality of particular works (Aquinas's "Beauty is the splendor of the Transcendentals brought together" is an aesthetic definition

---

[*]*Aristotle's Poetics* (Cambridge, MA, and London: Harvard University Press, 1957).

that allows us to justify both *Oedipus Rex* and a good adventure story) but, rather, the oscillation between a descriptive theory and a critical practice that presuppose each other in turn.

Aristotle speaks to us not only of abstract criteria such as order and measure, verisimilitude or necessity, or organic balance (*Poetics* 1450b 21 ff.) but also of that criterion which will negate every purely formalistic reading of the *Poetics*. The fundamental element in tragedy is plot, and plot is the imitation of an action whose aim, the *telos,* is the effect that it produces, the *ergon.* And this *ergon* is *catharsis.* A tragedy will be beautiful—or will work well—if it is able to effect purification from passions. Thus the cathartic effect is a kind of coronation of a tragic work, and this resides in the tragedy not as a written or acted discourse but as a discourse that is received.

The *Poetics* represents the first appearance of an aesthetics of reception, but it presents some unresolved problems of every reader-oriented theory.

We know that catharsis can be interpreted in two ways, and both interpretations are upheld by that enigmatic expression appearing at 1449b 27–28: tragedy accomplishes "*ten ton toiouton pathematon catharsin*" (the catharsis of such passions).

The first interpretation is that Aristotle is thinking of a purification that releases *us* through the intense experience of *our own* passions—as would seem to be suggested by the *Politics* (which, however, unfortunately refers to the *Poetics* for an explanation that is never given in either of the two works), and therefore the purification must be understood in traditional medical terms, as a homeopathic action, a liberation of the spectator through the identification with the characters' passions—and it is imposed on us as an experience we cannot avoid. Tragedy is, in this view, a corybantic, psychagogic machine (if some detachment were possible, this would be produced solely by comedy, but we know too little about what Aristotle meant by comedy).

The second interpretation understands catharsis in an allopathic sense, as a purification undergone *by the passions themselves,* inasmuch as they are "beautifully" represented and seen from afar as the passions of others, through the cold gaze of a spectator who becomes a pure, disembodied eye—and who enjoys not the passions he experiences but the text that puts them onstage.

Radicalizing this conflict of interpretations, we might say that in one interpretation it leads to a Dionysiac aesthetic, in the other to an Apollonian aesthetic. And, in more banal terms, on one side we have an aesthetics of the discotheque and pulp fiction (and I will talk later about how to read the *Poetics* as a theory of mass-media emotions), and on the other an aesthetics seen as a moment of serene and detached contemplation, where art shows us the splendor of truth.

This ambiguity is due to the very sources Aristotle was drawing on. The Pythagoreans "had appropriate chants for the passions of the soul, some for weaknesses and others for angers, through which, by exciting and raising the passions in just measure, they would be returned to a courageous virtue" (Iamblichus, *Life of Pythagoras*). And Pythagoras used poetic texts such as Homer, dithyrambs, threnodies, and laments for cathartic purposes. It is reasonable to assume that Aristotle meant a purification that comes about through an act of free vision of the miraculous organization of the great phenomenon that is tragedy, and at the same time he was fascinated by the psychagogic powers his own culture spoke about.

There are other fertile ambiguities in the *Poetics.* Aristotle is an Alexandrian who has partly lost the religious spirit that characterized the fifth century B.C. He works a little bit like a contemporary Western ethnologist trying to track down universal constants in the tales of savages, which fascinate him but which he does not understand except from the outside. So then we come up with another, very modern reading of Aristotle, one that Aristotle himself encourages, pretending to talk about tragedy whereas in reality he is providing us with a semiotics of narrativity. The tragic spectacle includes story, characters, diction, thought, spectacle, and music, but "the most important of these elements is the composition of the actions . . . For the end of tragedy is the story and the facts" (1450a 15–23).

I agree with Ricoeur when he says that in the *Poetics* narration founded on plot, this ability to compose a story, *he ton pragmaton systasis,* becomes a kind of common genus of which the epic is a species.* The genre that the *Poetics* discusses is the representation of an action (*pragma*) through a plot (*mythos*), and epic diegesis and dramatic mimesis are only species of this genre.

Now the theory of plot is what has perhaps most profoundly influenced our century. The first theory of narrativity emerges with the Russian formalists, who propose on the one hand the distinction between *fabula* and *sjužet,* and on the other hand the deconstruction of the fabula into a series of narrative motifs and functions. It is hard to find direct references to Aristotle in the works of Šklovsky, Veselovskij or Propp, but in the first study of the Russian formalists, by Victor Erlich (*Russian Formalism,* 1954)† the debt of the Formalists to the Aristotelian tradition was clearly shown—even though Erlich pointed out correctly that the Formalist notions of *fabula* and *sjužet* are not strictly coterminous with those of *pragma* and *mythos*. Similarly, one could say that Aristotle's narrative functions are less numerous than those of Propp. But the principle is the same, without a doubt, and this was noticed by the first structuralist critics at the beginning of the 1960s (but it would be unfair not to mention the "Dramatic Situations" of Polti and Souriau, vague descen-

---

* *Time and Narrative,* vol. 1, trans. Kathleen McLaughlin and David Pellauer (Chicago and London: University of Chicago Press, 1984), 2.

† See his *Russian Formalism: History-Doctrine,* now in its 4th edition (The Hague and New York: Mouton, 1980).

dants of Gozzi—and therefore of an eighteenth-century Italian who had not forgotten Aristotle).

"The narratives of the world are numberless," wrote Roland Barthes in his "Introduction à l'analyse structurale des récits."* "It is thus legitimate that, far from abandoning any idea of dealing with narrative on the grounds of its universality, there should have been (from Aristotle on) a periodic interest in narrative form and it is normal that the newly developing structuralism should make this form one of its first concerns." In the same issue of *Communications* in which Barthes's essay was first published (vol. 8, 1966), Genette's contribution, "Frontières du récit," was based on a reading of Aristotle, as was the first articulation of Bremond's semiology of the story, which could be seen as a meticulous systematization of the formal structures suggested by Aristotle. (Curiously, Todorov, who would show in his other works that he knew Aristotle very well, would base his *Grammaire du Décameron* on a purely grammatical basis.)

I am not saying that a theory of plot and narrativity emerges only in our century.† But it is curious that contemporary culture

---

*See Barthes, "Introduction to the Structuralist Analysis of Narratives"), in Susan Sontag, ed., *A Barthes Reader* (London: Jonathan Cape, 1982), 251–95 (251–52).

†On the contrary, the cultures that have produced the novel have always produced theories of plot. Going back to the rejection of Aristotle that characterized Italian culture after the seventeenth century, I do not want to stick my neck out by deciding what the cause or effect was, but it is certainly true that for centuries Italian culture did not produce either good novels or good theories of plot. Although it was a great culture for storytelling in the form of the novella, starting with Boccaccio, Italian literature produced novels much later than other cultures. We have quite a vast tradition of baroque novels, but without any peaks of excellence (even though at that time Aristotle was still being followed), and then nothing of interest until the nineteenth century, where, however, there are few Italian titles one would rank alongside the Dickenses, Balzacs, and Tolstoys. It is true that the novel is the product of bourgeois culture and that Italy had a burgeoning bourgeoisie in Boccaccio's time, but it did not have a modern bourgeoisie until much later than the rest of Europe. But whether this was cause or effect, it did not have theories of plot either. It is for this reason that Italy (which today has excellent writers of detective fiction, and also had two or three such authors in the period before the Second World War) was not a land where the detective story emerged or developed; for the detective story is nothing but the *Poetics* boiled down to its essential coordinates, a sequence of events (*pragmata*) whose wires have been crossed, and the plot tells us how the detective unravels them.

returned to this "strong" aspect of the *Poetics* at the very time when, as many see it, the form of the novel was entering a period of crisis.

However, to tell and listen to stories is a biological function. One cannot easily escape the fascination of plots in their raw state. If Joyce avoids the rules of Attic tragedy, he does not escape the Aristotelian idea of narration. He may put it into crisis, but he recognizes it. The nonadventures of Leopold and Molly Bloom are comprehensible to us because they are patterned on the backdrop of our memories of the adventures of Tom Jones or Télémaque. Even the Nouveau Roman's refusal to make us feel pity or terror becomes exciting against the background of our conviction that a story should arouse these passions in us. Biology strikes back: when literature refused to give us plots, we went to look for them in films or newspaper reports.

There is, then, another reason why our age has been fascinated by the theory of plot. The fact is that we have convinced ourselves that the model of the pair fabula/narrative discourse, *pragma* and *mythos,* serves not only to explain the literary genre that in English is called fiction. Every discourse has a deep structure that is narrative or can be developed in narrative terms. I could cite Greimas's analysis of Dumézil's introduction to his *Naissance d'archanges,** where the scientific text manifests a polemical structure that emerges in the shape of academic *coups-de-scène,* struggles against opponents, victories and defeats. In *The Role of the Reader* (Bloomington: Indiana University Press, 1981) I tried to show how one can find a story even beneath the (apparently plotless) text that opens Spinoza's *Ethics:* "*Per causam sui intelligo id cujus essentia involvit existentiam; sive id cujus natura non potest concipi nisi existens*" (By cause of itself, I understand that whose essence involves existence, or that whose nature cannot be conceived except as existing).

---

*"Des accidents dans les sciences dites humaines," in *Du Sens II* (Paris: Seuil, 1983).

There are at least two inset *fabulae* here. One concerns a grammatically implicit agent (*ego*) who carries out the action of understanding or signifying and by so doing moves from confusion to a clearer knowledge of God. Let's remember that if *"intelligo"* is interpreted as "I understand" or "I recognize," then God remains an object that is not modified by the action, but if one translates that verb as "I want to signify" or "I want to say," then the agent sets up, through the act of self-definition, his object of discourse (he makes it exist as cultural object).

However, this object, with its own attributes, is the subject of another story. It is a subject that performs an action through which, through the fact of being, it exists. It seems that nothing happens in this adventure about the nature of God, since there is no temporal interval between the actualization of his being and the actualization of his existence (in fact, neither of these ever moves from some preceding potential to the act, because they have always been there), nor does his existence, when it comes, change his essence. Certainly this is an extreme case, where both action and the passing of time are at zero degrees (which equals infinity), and God acts always in his self-manifestation, uninterruptedly and forever producing the fact that he exists through the simple fact that he is. It is not much for an adventure story, but it is enough for the essential conditions of a *fabula* to emerge. There is no *coup-de-scène*, perhaps, but this depends on the reader's sensitivity. The Model Reader of a story like this is a mystic or a metaphysics expert, a textual cooperator who is able to feel the most intense emotions at this nonstory whose exceptional nature never ceases to strike him like a thunderbolt. Even the *Amor Dei Intellectualis* is a burning passion, and one feels a stupefied and continual sense of surprise in recognizing the presence of Necessity.

If, then, our age discovers that every philosophical or scientific discourse can also be read as a narrative, this may be happening now because, more than in any other epoch, science and philosophy (perhaps even to deal with the crisis of the novel) present themselves (it has been said) as grand narratives. This does not mean—as happens for some people—that by being narratives they do not have to be judged in terms of their truth. They simply want to express some truth by using a structure that is attractive in a narrative sense. And if then the great philosophical narratives do not seem sufficient, we have seen that instead of going to look for truth in the philosophers of the past, much contemporary philosophy has gone to look for it in Proust or Kafka, Joyce or Mann. Thus it is not so much that philosophers have given up pursuing the truth as that art and literature have also taken on that function. But these are marginal observations, and Aristotle does not come into them.

The *Poetics* has many faces. One cannot have a fertile book without it also producing contradictory results. Among my first discoveries of the modernity of Aristotle, I remember a book by Mortimer Adler, who had worked out an aesthetics of film based on Aristotelian principles. In his *Art and Prudence* he gave the following definition: "A film is a representation of a completed action, of a certain length, using a combination of images, sound effects, music and other things."* Perhaps this definition was a bit scholastic (Adler was a Thomist who also inspired Marshall McLuhan), but the idea that although the *Poetics* was not capable of defining "high" literature, it was still of use as a perfect theory of popular literature and art was upheld by other authors as well.[†]

I do not accept the idea that the *Poetics* cannot define "high" art, but it is certainly the case that, with its insistence on the laws of plot, it is particularly suited to describing the strategies of the

---

*(New York: Longman, 1937).

[†]See, for instance, Robert Langbaum, "Aristotle and modern literature," *Journal of Aesthetics and Art Criticism* (September 1956).

mass media. The *Poetics* is certainly the theory of, among others things, the John Ford–style Western—and not because Aristotle was a prophet but because whoever wants to put on stage or screen an action using plot (which is what a Western does without any clutter) cannot do other than follow what Aristotle had perceived. If telling stories is a biological function, Aristotle had already understood all that was needed from this biology of narrativity.

The mass media are not alien to our biological tendencies; on the contrary, the media could be accused of being human, all too human. The problem, if it exists, lies in the question whether the pity and terror they provoke genuinely lead to a catharsis; but if one understands catharsis in its homeopathically minimalist sense (have a good cry and you'll feel better), they are, in this minimalist state, applied *Poetics*.

One could even say that if we stick to Aristotelian ideas for the construction of a *mythos* that will produce an effective *ergon*, we can only fall into mass-media syndrome. Coming back to Poe, if we read only the pages that he devotes to the production of emotions which he saw as his aim, we would think we were dealing with a screenwriter for *Dallas*. Since he wanted to write a poem that would produce an impression of melancholy ("since Melancholy is the most legitimate of all the poetic tones") in a little over one hundred lines, he wondered which was the most depressing of all melancholic subjects, and concluded that it was death, and that the most melancholy death was that of a beautiful woman, "unquestionably the most poetical topic in the world."

If Poe had stuck only to these principles, he would have written *Love Story.* Luckily he knew that if plot is the dominant element in every story, it must however be tempered with other elements. He avoided the mass-media trap (albeit an antelitteram one) because he had other formal principles. Hence his calculation of the number of lines, his analysis of the musicality of the word "Nevermore," and the deliberate visual contrast between Pallas's white breast and the blackness of the raven, and everything that makes "The Raven" a poetic composition and not a horror film.

But we are still dealing with Aristotle. Poe calculated an appropriate and organic mixture of lexis, opsis, dianoia, ethos, melos. That is how he put flesh on the bare bones of a *mythos*. The mass media can make us cry, and offer us consolation, but they usually do not allow us to purify ourselves while enjoying a "great creation" that has been well structured. When they do do this, and for me the Ford of *Stagecoach* certainly does do this, then they really do achieve the ideals of the *Poetics*.

We come to the last ambiguity. The *Poetics* is the first work to develop a theory of metaphor. Ricoeur (quoting Derrida on this topic, who says that in Aristotle the defined is implicated in the person who defines) observes that, in order to explain metaphor, Aristotle created a metaphor, borrowing it from the order of movement.* In fact, the Aristotelian theory confronts us with the fundamental problem of all philosophies of language, namely, whether metaphor is a departure from an underlying literalness or the birthplace of every degree zero of writing.

Although it is true that I remain faithful to a theory of interpretation that, when dealing with written texts, must presuppose a literal degree zero from which metaphor is the departure that must be interpreted, it is also true that if we look at things from the glottogonic point of view (whether at the origins of language, as Vico wanted, or at the origins of every text that comes into being), we must take account of the moment when creativity can

---

* *The Rule of Metaphor: Multi-disciplinary Studies of the Creation of Meaning in Language,* trans. Robert Czerny, with Kathleen McLaughlin and John Costello (London: Routledge and Kegan Paul, 1978), I.2.

emerge, for it does so only at the cost of a metaphorical vagueness that names an object that is as yet unknown or unnamed.

The cognitive power of metaphor on which Aristotle insisted—though this was in the *Rhetoric,* not the *Poetics*—becomes manifest either when it puts something new before our eyes, working on preexisting language, or when it invites us to discover the rules of a future language. But the final Aristotelian legacy, the heretical currents of Chomskyan linguistics, and George Lakoff in particular, present us today with the problem of a more radical nature—even though this radicalism was already present in Vico: the problem is not so much seeing what the creative metaphor does with a language that is already established, as seeing how the already established language can be understood only by accepting, in the dictionary that explains it, the presence of vagueness, fuzziness, and metaphorical bricolage.*

It is not by chance that Lakoff is one of those authors who have begun to elaborate, on the fragments of a semantics where definition was based on atomic properties, a semantics in which definition is represented in the form of a sequence of actions.

One of the pioneers of this tendency (who recognized his Aristotelian debts) was Kenneth Burke with his Grammar, Rhetoric, and Symbolism of Motives, where philosophy and literature, and language, were analyzed in "dramatic" form, through a combined game using Act, Scene, Agent, Agency, Purpose.

Not to mention Greimas, who makes no effort to conceal the fact that a theory of narrativity presides over semantic understanding—I am thinking of that Case Grammar that works on a semantic structure in terms of Agent, Counter-Agent, Goal,

---

*George Lakoff and Mark Johnson, *Metaphors We Live By* (Chicago and London: University of Chicago Press, 1980). See also George Lakoff, *Women, Fire and Dangerous Things* (Chicago and London: University of Chicago Press, 1987).

Instrument, etc. (Fillmore, Bierwisch),* and of many models used in Frames Theory and in Artificial Intelligence. Dominique Noguez has recently published an amusing hoax (in which I am both hero and victim) on the Semiology of the Umbrella. He did not know that reality is stranger than fiction and that one of the models in artificial intelligence is that of Charniak, who, in order to explain to a computer how to interpret the sentences where the word "umbrella" appears, supplies a narrative description of what one does with an umbrella, how one handles it, how it is made, and what purpose it serves.† The concept of umbrella is boiled down to a network of actions.

Aristotle did not manage to match his theory of action with that of definition, because, imprisoned by his own categories, he thought there were substances that preceded every action they allowed or had to undergo. We had to wait for the crisis of the concept of substance to rediscover a semantics implicit not in his works on logic but in those on ethics, poetics, and rhetoric, and to think that even the definition of essences could be articulated in terms of underlying actions.

And yet Aristotle could have developed a suggestion from Plato's *Cratylus*. We know that that work presents the myth of the Nomotheta, or "name giver," a sort of Adam of Greek philosophy. But the problem, which went back to before Plato, was whether the names given by the Nomotheta were provided according to convention (*nomos*) or because they were motivated by the nature of the things (*physis*). The question as to which of the two solutions Socrates (and through him Plato) opted for has generated and still generates endless pages of commentary on the

---

*Charles Fillmore, "The Case for Case," in E. Bach et al., eds., *Universals in Linguistic Theory* (New York: Holt, 1968); Manfred Bierwisch, "On Classifying Semantic Features," in D. D. Steinberg and L. A. Jakobovits, eds., *Semantics* (Cambridge: Cambridge University Press, 1971).

†Eugene Charniak, "A Partial Taxonomy of Knowledge about Actions," *Institute for Semantic and Cognitive Studies. Castagnola. Working Papers* 13 (1975).

Cratylus. But whatever the answer, every time he seems to adhere to the theory of "motivation," Plato speaks of cases where the words represent not the thing in itself but, rather, a source or result of an action. The strange difference between the nominative and genitive in Zeus/Dios is due to the fact that the original name expressed an action, "di'hon zen" (he through whom life is given). Similarly, it is said that "anthropos" can be reduced to "he who is capable of reconsidering what he has seen," inasmuch as the difference between man and animals is that man does not just perceive but can reason and reflect on what he has perceived. We are tempted to take Plato's etymology seriously when we remember that Thomas Aquinas, when considering the classical definition of man as a mortal and rational animal, maintained that specific differences such as "rationality" (which distinguishes man from every other species of living thing) are not atomistic accidents but names we give to sequences of actions and behaviors through which we recognize that there is a rationality in a certain creature that is not perceptible in other ways. Human rationality is inferred from symptoms, so to speak, like talking and expressing thoughts. We know our faculties *"ex ipsorum actuum qualitate,"* from the quality of the actions of which the faculties are origin and cause.*

According to one of Peirce's examples, lithium is not defined merely by its position in a periodic table of elements nor by its atomic number but through the description of the operations that must be carried out in order to produce a sample of it.† If the Nomotheta had known and named lithium, he would therefore have invented an expression that could, like a hook, capture a whole series of accounts of sequences of actions. He would have seen, say, tigers not as individuals embodying "tigerness" but rather as animals able to develop certain behaviors, interacting

---

Summa Theol. I. 79.8; *Contra Gentiles,* 4.46.
† *Collected Papers,* 2. 330.

with other animals and in a particular environment—and this story would have been inseparable from its own protagonist.

With these reflections I have perhaps strayed too far from Aristotle, but I was still on the track of his suggestions about action.

In any case, the conference was devoted to contemporary strategies of *appropriation* of antiquity, and every act of appropriation implies a certain amount of violence. Just as I am convinced that Kant said the most interesting things on our cognitive processes not in the *Critique of Pure Reason* (where he was speaking in fact of cognition) but in his *Critique of Judgment* (where he seems to be discussing art), in the same way why should we not go and look for a modern theory of knowledge not (or at least not only) in Aristotle's *Analytics* but also in the *Poetics* and *Rhetoric?*

Abbreviated version of a paper presented at the conference "Les Stratégies contemporaines d'appropriation de l'Antiquité," held at the Sorbonne in October 1990. The proceedings were published as *Nos grecs et leurs modernes,* ed. Barbara Cassin (Paris: Seuil, 1992).

THE AMERICAN MYTH IN
THREE ANTI-AMERICAN GENERATIONS

The extract that follows is taken from *l'Unità*, 3 August 1947, at the start of the cold war. I remind you that *l'Unità* was the official daily paper of the Italian Communist Party, which was at that time heavily committed to celebrating the triumphs and virtues of the Soviet Union and to criticizing the vices of America's capitalist culture:

> Around 1930, when Fascism began to be "the hope of the world," some young Italians happened to discover America in American books, an America that was thoughtful and barbaric, happy and quarrelsome, dissolute, fertile, laden with all the world's pasts, and at the same time young and innocent. For a few years these young men read, translated, and wrote with a joy of discovery and rebellion that made official Fascist culture indignant, but their success was such that it forced the regime to tolerate it in order to save face. . . . For many people the encounter with Caldwell, Steinbeck, Saroyan, and even with old Sinclair Lewis opened up the first chink of freedom, the first suspicion that not everything in the world's culture came down to the

Fasces. . . . At this point American culture became something very serious and precious for us, a sort of enormous laboratory where with a different kind of freedom and different methods people pursued the same goal of creating a taste, a style, a modern world that the best among us were seeking, perhaps with less immediacy but with just as much stubborn determination. . . . We noticed, during those years of study, that America was not *another* place, a *new* start in history, but just the giant theater where everyone's drama was played out with greater openness. . . . At that time American culture allowed us to see our own dramas being worked out as though on a giant screen. . . . We could not take part openly in the drama, in the tale, in the problem, so we studied American culture a little bit like we study past centuries, Elizabethan theater, or the poetry of the *dolce stil novo*.

The author of this article, Cesare Pavese, was already a famous writer, a translator of Melville and other American writers, and a Communist. In 1953, in the introduction to a posthumous collection of Pavese's essays (he had committed suicide), Italo Calvino, who was then a member of the Communist Party (which he left at the time of the Hungarian crisis), expressed the feeling of left-wing intellectuals toward the United States in these terms:

America. Periods of discontent have often witnessed the birth of a literary myth that sets up a country as a term of comparison, as in Tacitus's or Mme de Staël's re-creation of Germany. Often the country discovered is only a land of utopia, a social allegory that has barely anything in common with the real country; but despite this it is just as useful, indeed the aspects that are emphasized are the very ones the situation needs. . . . And this America invented by writers, hot with the blood of different races, smoky with factory chimneys and with well-watered fields, rebellious against church hypocrisies, shouting with strikes and masses in revolt, really did become a complex symbol of all the ferments and realities of the time, a mixture of America, Russia, and Italy, along with a taste of primitive lands—an unresolved synthesis of everything Fascism tried to deny and exclude.

How could it have come about that this ambiguous symbol, or, rather, this contradictory civilization, was able to fascinate a generation of intellectuals that had grown up in the Fascist period, when schools and mass propaganda only celebrated the pomp of Romanitas and condemned the so-called Jewish demoplutocracies? How could it have happened that the young generation of the 1930s and '40s went beyond official stereotypes and created a sort of alternative education for themselves, their own flow of counterpropaganda against the regime?

I remind you that this second day of our conference is dedicated to "The image of the United States in Italian education." If by "education" we mean the official school curriculum, I cannot see why this topic should interest us. Italian students should know that New York is on the East Coast, and that Oklahoma is a state and not just a musical by Rodgers and Hammerstein. But if by "education" we mean what the Greeks called *"paideia,"* our task becomes more exciting. *"Paideia"* was not just the transmission of knowledge: it was the ensemble of social techniques through which young men were initiated into adult life after an ideal education. To achieve this *"paideia"* was to become a mature personality, a man, someone who is *"kaloskagathos,"* beautiful because good and good because beautiful. In Latin *"paideia"* was translated as *"humanitas,"* which the Germans translate, I believe, as *"Bildung,"* which is in turn more than just *"Kultur."*

In ancient times *"paideia"* was transmitted through philosophical conversation and a homosexual relationship. In modern times we use prescribed texts and school lessons. But recently *"paideia"* has also become involved with mass communication.

Not only in the sense that the circulation of books is a feature of mass communication, but also because choosing one's own curriculum in the jungle of the mass media can constitute an instance of constructing one's own *"humanitas."* What I mean is that Woody Allen has something to do with *"paideia,"* while John Travolta does not: but we must not be so dogmatic. If I think about my own growth in *"humanitas,"* I would have to put on the list of my Spiritual Sources *The Imitation of Christ, No No Nanette*, Dostoyevsky, and Donald Duck. No place for Nietzsche or Elvis Presley. I agree with Joyce that "music hall, not poetry is a criticism of life." Ripeness is all.

It is with this idea of education in mind that I would like to chart in broad terms the history of three generations of Italians who, for different historical and political reasons, somehow considered themselves, or ought to have considered themselves, anti-American; and who, in some way, on their own, working against or indeed even in support of their anti-American ideology, created an American Myth.

The first character in my story signed the articles he wrote in the 1930s as "Tito Silvio Mursino." This was an anagram of Vittorio Mussolini, Il Duce's son. Vittorio belonged to a group of young Turks fascinated by cinema as an art, an industry, a way of life. Vittorio was not content with being the son of the Boss, though this would have been enough to guarantee him the favors of many actresses: he wanted to be the pioneer of the Americanization of Italian cinema.

In his journal *Cinema* he criticized the European cinematographic tradition and asserted that the Italian public identified emotionally only with the archetypes of American cinema. He talked of cinema in terms of the "star system," with a certain frankness and without any aesthetic concerns. He genuinely loved and admired Mary Pickford and Tom Mix, just as his father admired Julius Caesar and Trajan. For him American films were the people's literature. And Oreste del Buono, in the *Almanacco Bom-*

piani 1980, noted that Vittorio was somehow, albeit unwittingly and in a different key, repeating Gramsci's theory of a "national-popular art," except that he went to find the roots of "national-popular" in the area between Sunset Boulevard and Malibu.

Vittorio was not an intellectual, nor even a great business-man. His trip to the USA to establish a link between the two cinematographic industries ended up as a fiasco: political gaffes, sabotage by the Italian authorities themselves (his father looked on the initiative with tremendous skepticism), irony from the American press. Al Roach said to him that after all he was a decent guy, why didn't he change his name?

However, let us reread some of Vittorio Mussolini's statements:

> Is it perhaps heresy to state that the spirit, mentality and temperament of Italian youth, despite the logical, natural and inevitable differences in another people, are closer to those of the young people across the Atlantic than to the youth of Russia, Germany, Spain and France? Moreover, the American public loves films with broad horizons, is sensitive to real problems, is attracted by the childish but happy sense of adventure, and if this youthfulness is given to them by not having centuries of history, culture, systems and philosophical laws behind them, it is certainly much closer to our bold generation than to those of many old countries in Europe.

This was written in 1936. And this model of America remained valid until 1942, when the Americans became official enemies. But even in the case of the most violent wartime propaganda, the most hated enemies were the English, not the Americans. The radio propagandist Mario Appelius coined the slogan "*Dio stramaledica gli Inglesi!*" (God double-damn the English!), but I do not recall an anti-American slogan that was as virulent and widely broadcast as this. In any case, popular sensibilities were certainly not anti-American. But perhaps the most interesting indication of this widespread feeling is to be found in the writings of young Fascist intellectuals who wrote for the journal *Primato*. *Primato* came out between 1940 and 1943, with one of the most contradictory figures of the Fascist regime as editor: Giuseppe Bottai. A liberal-fascist and anti-Semite, he was also an Anglophile who was regarded with suspicion by his German allies; he even authored an educational-reform program that was inspired in part by John Dewey. He was a supporter of avant-garde art but an enemy of the vulgar classicism that was official Fascist art, an aristocratic champion of human inequalities but opposed to intervention in the Spanish civil war. Bottai tried to gather the best young intellectuals of the time around *Primato,* filling the pages of the journal with the maximum amount of dissent that was compatible with the situation. Among the young contributors to *Primato* we find not only representatives of liberal anti-Fascism (Montale, Brancati, Paci, Contini, Praz) but also the best of what would become future Communist culture (Vittorini, Alicata, Argan, Banfi, Della Volpe, Guttuso, Luporini, Pavese, Pintor, Pratolini, Zavattini).

It is striking to notice that, in February 1941, a brilliant young intellectual like Giaime Pintor could publish in the journal an article on the robotization of German soldiers, warning that Europe would never return to freedom so long as it was dominated by the dark shadow of German flags. Giaime Pintor had been brought up under Fascism, and day by day, article after article, he developed a lucid and courageous critique of the European dictatorships, writing in 1943, a few months before he died during the Resistance war, an article that he was unable to publish at the time:

> Germany has gradually presented itself in our reflections as the natural antithesis of this world and by extension of this world's mirror in Europe. No people is closer to the Americans in the youthfulness of its blood and the openness of its

desires, yet no people celebrates its own legend with such different words. Here too the roads of corruption and of purity are perilously close; but a constant folly drags the Germans off course and overwhelms them in inhuman and difficult exploits.

On either side there are forces capable of altering the course of our experience, of throwing us into a corner like useless scrap, or of leading us to safety on any shore at all. But America will win this war because its initial élan is following truer forces, because it believes that its goal is easy and right. "Keep smiling": this peace slogan came from America with a whole complement of edifying tunes, when Europe was an empty shopwindow and the austerity of behavior imposed on totalitarian countries revealed only the desperate and bitter face of Fascist reaction. The extreme simplicity of American optimism at that time might have enraged all those who were persuaded of the duty to wear mourning as a sign of humanity, and those who placed pride for their dead before the well-being of those who were alive. But the great pride of America in her children today will be the awareness that they have run up the steepest road in history, that they have avoided the dangers and ambushes latent in a development that has been almost without any holdup. Enrichment and bureaucratic corruption, gangsters and crises, all this has become part of a body that is developing. And this is the only history of America: a people that is growing, compensating with their constant enthusiasm for the mistakes they have made, and offering rescue from future dangers with their goodwill. The most hostile forces— illness and poverty—could meet on American soil, but the outcome of these risks and fears was always a positive mood, reiterating each time the exaltation of man.

The stupidity of one phrase hangs over America: a materialist culture. A culture of producers: this is the pride of a race that has not sacrificed its own strength to ideological ambitions and has not fallen into the easy trap of "spiritual values." It has made technology its own way of life, has felt new affections emerge from the daily practice of collective work, and new legends arise from the horizons it has conquered. Whatever Romantic critics might think, such a profoundly revolutionary experience has not ended in silence; and while in Europe after the last war people took up the themes of Decadence or formulas like surrealism that were devoid of a future, America expressed itself in a new narrative and in a new language: it invented the cinema.

Many feel they know about American cinema, and their impressions combine those ambivalent feelings of attraction and disgust that have been described as one of our most incurable complexes as Europeans, but which no one has shed light on with the necessary vigor. Now that an enforced abstinence has cured us of its excess of publicity and of the disgust produced by habit, one can perhaps go back to the significance of that educational moment and recognize in American cinema the greatest message our generation has ever received.

Pintor was extraneous to the aristocratic dismissals of mass media that would become typical of the postwar European Left. Nowadays we might say he was closer to Benjamin than to Adorno.

Cinema is thus seen as a revolutionary weapon abolishing all political frontiers. But even on the aesthetic front American cinema teaches us to look at the world with fresh, innocent eyes, and has fulfilled Baudelaire's prayer by showing us "how wonderful and poetic we are, with our polished shoes and bourgeois ties." Today, Pintor reminded us, Germany is perpetuating the rhetoric of "the past." America, on the other hand, does not have any cemeteries to safeguard, her mission is the destruction of idols, while the utopia of the new man, at that stage still a mere pronouncement in Marxist ideology, can be achieved wherever man learns not to surrender to mysticism and nostalgia, whether in America or in Russia.

> Much of what we said about America may be naive and inexact, much may have to do with topics extraneous to the historical phenomenon of the USA and its present shape. But it matters little: *because, even if that continent did not exist, our words would not lose their meaning. This America has no need of Columbus, it has been discovered inside ourselves, it is the land that one sets out for with the same hope and confidence as the first emigrants and as all who are determined to defend the dignity of the human condition even though it cost much labor and error.*

With the image of this universal America in his heart, Giaime Pintor joined the British army in Naples and died trying to cross the German lines to organize the partisan resistance in Lazio. Where did this image of America come from? Pintor and Vittorio Mussolini, from opposite sides of the barricade, tell us that the myth came via cinema. But novels and stories had also played a role in its spread and its inspiration. And at the origin of this dissemination we find two writers, Elio Vittorini and Cesare Pavese. Both had grown up under Fascism: Vittorini tried his luck with *Primato,* Pavese had already been condemned to internal exile in 1935. Both were fascinated by the myth of America. Both would become Communists.

Vittorini collaborated with the publisher Bompiani, who had already in the 1930s started to publish Steinbeck, Caldwell, Cain, and other American writers, though *Primato* was constantly blocked by the Ministry of Popular Culture (the Minculpop), as is documented in a series of official letters (masterpieces of unintentional humor) that ban or threaten to confiscate this book or that because it expresses a nonheroic vision of life, or represents characters of inferior race, or portrays in too crude a language behavior that does not correspond to the Fascist and Roman ideal of morality. Pavese too worked as a translator, almost clandestinely, since he could not obtain proper permits, having been condemned as an anti-Fascist.

In 1941 Vittorini prepared for Bompiani *Americana,* an anthology of over one thousand pages, with texts by authors from Washington Irving to Thornton Wilder and Saroyan via O. Henry and Gertrude Stein, all translated by young writers with names like Alberto Moravia, Carlo Linati, Guido Piovene, Eugenio Montale, and Cesare Pavese.

From today's perspective the collection was quite comprehensive, perhaps a bit too enthusiastic, and certainly unbalanced: it undervalues Fitzgerald, overestimates Saroyan, and contains authors like John Fante, who would not retain such a prominent position in literary chronicles. This anthology was meant to be not a history of American literature, however, but rather the construction of an allegory, a kind of *Divine Comedy* where Paradise and Inferno were one.

Vittorini had already written in 1938 (in *Letteratura* volume 5) that American literature was a world literature with a single language, and that being American was the same as not being American, as being free from local traditions, and open to the common culture of humanity.

In *Americana* the first description of the United States is almost Homeric, with its images of plains and railways, snowy mountains and endless landscapes stretching from coast to coast. There was a lithographic innocence about it, a bit like Currier and Ives, an epic based not on any direct evidence but on pure intertextual fantasy. In it we find the same freedom with which Vittorini had translated and would translate his own American authors, all written in "Vittorini-speak," where an intense creativity pushed philological precision into second place. But the America that Vittorini draws here is a prehistoric land shaken by earthquakes and continental drift, where instead of dinosaurs and mammoths what dominates is the gigantic outline of Jonathan Edwards waking Rip van Winkle and challenging him to an epic duel with Edgar Allan Poe, who is riding on Moby-Dick. Even his critical judgments are metaphors and hyperboles:

> Melville is Poe's adjective and Hawthorne's noun. He tells us that purity is ferocity. Purity is a tiger . . . Billy Budd hanged. He is an adjective. But in the way that happiness is an adjective of life. Or as despair is an adjective of life.

> America as *chanson de geste*. Pound and the blacks singing the blues.

> America is today (*because of the new legend that is taking shape*) a kind of new fabulous Orient, and man appears in it, at different times, as an exquisite uniqueness, whether he is Philippine, Chinese, Slav, or Kurd, because he is substantially always the same: the lyrical "I," the protagonist of creation.

It was a multimedia book. Not just a book of literary excerpts and critical link passages, but also a superb anthology of photographs. Images taken by the photographers of the New Deal, who worked for the Works Progress Administration. I emphasize the photographic documentation because I learned about young people of the time who were culturally and politically regenerated by the impact of those very images: looking at them, they had the feeling of a different reality, a different rhetoric, or, rather, an antirhetoric. But the Minculpop could not accept *Americana*. The first edition, of 1942, was confiscated. It had to be republished without Vittorini's passages, but with a new preface by Emilio Cecchi, one that was more academic and more prudent, less enthusiastic and more critical, more "literary."

But even this emasculated version of *Americana* circulated and produced a new culture. Even without the pages written by Vittorini, the very structure of the anthology acted like a speech. The montage was the message. The very (highly debatable) way the American writers were translated produced a new sense of language. In 1953 Vittorini would say that he had influenced young people not by what he had translated but by how he had translated.

Already as far back as 1932, Pavese, writing about O. Henry, had said that America, like Italy, was a culture of dialects. But unlike Italy, in America the dialects had won out against the language of the ruling class, and American literature had transformed English into a new popular language. I remember that Pavese had turned to Piedmontese dialect for translating certain passages in Faulkner. One of his ideas was that there was an affinity between the Midwest and Piedmont. Once more this is Gramsci's "national-popular" notion, except that now, instead of rinsing his language in the Arno, as Manzoni had said, the writer rinsed it in the Mississippi.

We are talking of a case not of simple pidginization but rather of the creolization of a language.

Thus the generation that had read Pavese and Vittorini fought the partisan war, often in the Communist brigades, celebrating the October revolution and the charismatic figure of the people's Little Father, but remaining at the same time fascinated and obsessed by an America that was hope, renewal, progress, and revolution.

Vittorini and Pavese were adults by the end of the war, nearly forty. The second generation of my outline, on the other hand, contained youngsters born in the 1930s. Many of them entered adult life, at the end of the war, as Marxists.

Their Marxism was not like Vittorini's or Pavese's, which was totally identified with the Liberation struggle and their hatred of Fascist dictatorships, more a sense of universal brotherhood than a precise ideology. For this second generation Marxism involved experience of political organization and philosophical commit-ment. This generation's ideal was the Soviet Union, its aesthetic was socialist realism, its myth the working class. Politically op-posed to America as an economic and political system, they did sympathize with certain aspects of American social history, with that "genuine America" that was characterized by the first pio-neers and the early anarchist opposition movement. The "social-ist" America of Jack London and Dos Passos.

It was for this very reason that, even in the fiercest moments of the McCarthy campaign, official Marxist culture never com-pletely denied the spirit of *Americana,* even when Vittorini left the party because of his ideological dissent from its leader, Palmiro Togliatti.

However, what interests us is a different facet of this second generation, which could live both inside and outside the two Marx-ist parties of the time, the Socialist Party and the Communist Party, and any definition of it would end up being so vague and impre-cise that I am forced to indulge in a bit of fictional license. I will construct a fictitious character I will call Roberto. Among the members of the class that he is meant to represent, there will have been 90 percent Robertos and 10 percent Robertos. Mine will be 100 percent Roberto. Perhaps among the members of the Central Committee of the Italian Communist Party there were not many Robertos; but Roberto inhabited more the territory outside the party, the territory of cultural activities, publishing houses, cine-mas, newspapers, concerts, and it was in this very sense that he was culturally highly influential.

Roberto could have been born between 1926 and 1931. Ed-ucated along Fascist lines, his first act of rebellion (subconscious rebellion, of course) was his reading of comics (badly) translated from American. Flash Gordon against Ming was for him the first image of the fight against tyranny. *The Phantom* may have been a colonialist, but instead of imposing Western models on the natives of the jungle in Bengali, he tried to preserve the wise, ancient traditions of the Bandar. Mickey Mouse the journalist fighting against corrupt politicians for the survival of his newspaper was Roberto's first lesson in the freedom of the press. In 1942 the government forbade speech bubbles and a few months later suppressed all American characters; Mickey Mouse or Topolino was replaced by Toffolino, a human, not an animal character, in order to preserve the purity of the race. Roberto began secretly collecting the pieces he had once read, a bland and painful protest.

In 1939 Ringo from *Stagecoach* was the idol of a generation. Ringo fought not for an ideology or a fatherland but for himself and a prostitute. He was antirhetorical and therefore anti-Fascist. Also anti-Fascist were Fred Astaire and Ginger Rogers, because they were opposed to Luciano Serra the pilot, the character in the imperialist Fascist film that Vittorio Mussolini had also helped make. The human model to whom Roberto turned was an appropriate mix of Sam Spade, Ishmael, Edward G. Robinson, Chaplin, and Mandrake. I imagine that for an American, even in a period of mass nostalgia, there would be nothing that would link Jimmy Durante, the Gary Cooper of *For Whom the Bell Tolls,* the James Cagney of *Yankee Doodle Dandy* and the crew of the *Pequod.* But for Roberto and his friends there was a thread that united all these experiences: these were all people who were happy to live and unhappy to die, and they constituted the rhetorical counterpoint to the Fascist Superman who celebrated Sister Death and went toward his own destruction holding two grenades and with a flower in his mouth, as the Fascist song said.

Roberto and his generation also had their own music: jazz. Not just because it was avant-garde music, which they never felt was different from that of Stravinsky or Bartók, but also because it was degenerate music, produced by blacks in the brothels. Roberto became antiracist for the first time because of his love of Louis Armstrong.

With these models in mind Roberto somehow joined the partisans in 1944 at a very young age. After the war he was either a member or a fellow traveler of a left-wing party. He respected Stalin, was against the American invasion of Korea, and protested against the execution of the Rosenbergs. He left the party at the time of the Hungarian crisis. He was firmly convinced that Truman was a Fascist and that Al Capp's Li'l Abner was a left-wing hero, a relation of the down-and-outs of *Tortilla Flat.* He loved Eisenstein but was firmly convinced that cinematic realism was also there in *Little Caesar.* He adored Hammett and felt betrayed when the hard-boiled novel came under the aegis of the McCarthyite Spillane. He thought that a northwest passage for socialism with a human face was on *The Road to Zanzibar* with Bing Crosby, Bob Hope, and Dorothy Lamour. He rediscovered and popularized the epic of the New Deal, he loved Sacco, Vanzetti, and Ben Shahn, before the 1960s (when they became famous again in America) he knew the folk songs and protest ballads of the American anarchist tradition, and in the evening listened with his friends to Pete Seeger, Woodie Guthrie, Alan Lomax, Tom Jodd, and the Kingston Trio. He had been initiated into the myth of *Americana,* but now his bedside book was Alfred Kazin's *On Native Grounds.*

This is why when the generation of '68 launched its challenge, perhaps even against men like Roberto, America was already a way of life, even though none of those youngsters had read *Americana.* And I am not talking about jeans or chewing gum, the America that dominated Europe as the model for the consumer society: I am still talking about the myth that had emerged in the 1940s, which was somehow still operational deep down. Of course, for those young people America as a Power was the enemy, the world's policeman, the foe to be defeated in Vietnam as much as in Latin America. But that generation's front was by now on four sides: their enemies were capitalist America, the Soviet Union that had betrayed Lenin, the Italian Communist Party that had betrayed the revolution, and lastly, the Christian Democrat establishment. But if America was an enemy as a government and as the model for a capitalist society, there was also an attitude of rediscovery and recovery of America as a people, as a melting pot of races in revolt. They no longer had in mind the image of the Marxist American of the 1930s, the man in the Lincoln Brigades in Spain, the "premature anti-Fascist" reader of the *Partisan Review.* Rather, they identified a labyrinthine camp in which there was a mixture of oppositions between old and young, black and white, recent immigrants and established ethnic groups, silent majorities and vocal minorities. They did not see any substantial difference between Kennedy and Nixon, but they identified with the Berkeley campus, Angela Davis, Joan Baez, and the early Bob Dylan.

It is difficult to define the nature of their American myth: they somehow used and recycled bits of American reality, the Puertoricans, underground culture, Zen, not so much comics as Comix, and so not Felix the Cat but Fritz the Kat, not Walt Disney but Crumbs. They loved Charlie Brown, Humphrey Bogart, John Cage. I am not charting the profile of any particular political movement between 1968 and '77. Maybe I am drawing an x-ray image, revealing something that continued to live underneath the Maoist, Leninist, or Che Guevarist surface. I know I am photographing something that was there, because this something exploded in and after 1977. The student revolt of that time resembled more a black ghetto uprising than the storming of the Winter Palace. And I suspect that the secret, clearly subconscious model for the Red Brigades was the Manson family.

I certainly cannot speak of the present generation with the same Olympian detachment with which I discussed the 1930s generation. I am trying to identify, in the confusion of the present, the model for the American image-myth. Something invented like previous ones, the product of creolization.

America is no longer a dream, since you can get there at low cost with a budget airline.

The new Roberto was perhaps a member of a Marxist-Leninist group in 1968, threw the odd Molotov cocktail at an American consulate in 1970, some cobblestones at the police in 1972, and at the window of a Communist bookshop in 1977. In 1978, after avoiding the temptation to join a terrorist group, he saved some money and flew to California, perhaps becoming an ecological revolutionary or a revolutionary ecologist. For him America has become not the image of future renewal but a place to lick his wounds and console himself after his dream was shattered (or prematurely reported dead). America is no longer an alternative ideology, it is the end of ideology. He got his visa easily, because in fact he was never enrolled in any of the parties of the genuine Left. If Pavese and Vittorini were still alive, they would not have been able to get one, because they, the authors of our American dream, would have had to reply "Yes" on the consulate form asking whether you have ever been a member of a party that wants to subvert American society. American bureaucracy is not a dream; if anything, it is a nightmare.

Is there a moral in this story of mine? None, and several. To understand the Italian attitude toward America, and in particular the attitude of anti-American Italians, you must also remember *Americana* and all that happened in those years, when left-wing Italians dreamed of Comrade Sam and, pointing their finger toward his image, would say: "I want you."

Originally written as a paper for a conference held at Columbia University in January 1980 on "The Image of America in Italy and the Image of Italy in America." The original paper was for an American audience, hence the abundance of information on several Italian figures, from Vittorio Mussolini to Vittorini.

THE POWER OF FALSEHOOD

In his *Quaestio Quodlibetalis* XII.14, Saint Thomas Aquinas replies to the question "Utrum veritas sit fortior inter vinum et regem et mulierem," in other words, whether the power of truth is more potent, more persuasive, and more constricting than the authority of a king, the influence of wine, or the fascination of a woman.

The reply given by Aquinas—who respected the king, did not disdain, I believe, the odd glass of good wine at his table, and had proved that he could resist the temptations of women by chasing with a burning brand the naked courtesan whom his brothers had introduced into his bedroom to persuade him to become a Benedictine and not dishonor the family by donning the mendicant habit of the Dominicans—was, as usual, subtle and complex: wine, rulers, women, and truth are not comparable because "*non sunt unius generis*" (they are not of one genus). But if one considers them "*per comparationem ad aliquem effectum*" (by comparing them in their effects), they all can move the human heart to some course of action. Wine acts on our corporeal aspect, "*quod facit per temulentiam loqui*" (since it makes us speak through drink), while our animal-sensitive nature can be swayed by "*delectatio venerea*" (erotic pleasure), or in other words by a woman (Thomas could not conceive of sexual impulses on the other side that could legitimately move a woman, but we cannot expect Thomas to be Heloise). As for the practical intellect, it is obvious that the king's wishes, or the rule of law, has power over it. But the only force that moves the speculative intellect is truth. And since "*vires corporales subiciuntur viribus animalibus, vires animales intellectualibus, et intellectuales practicae speculativis . . . ideo simpliciter veritas dignior est et excellentior et fortior*" (bodily power is subject to animal powers, and our animal powers are inferior to intellectual strength, and practical intellectual strength is second to speculative intellectual power . . . then it is clear that truth is worthier, more excellent, and stronger).

Such then is the power of truth. But experience teaches us that truth often takes a long time to prevail, and the acceptance of truth costs blood and tears. Might it not happen that something dubious shows similar force, whereby it would be legitimate to talk of the power of the falsehood?

To show that the falsehood (not necessarily in the form of a lie, but certainly in the form of an error) has been the engine behind many historical events, I would have to appeal to a criterion of truth. But if I chose this in too dogmatic a manner, my discourse would run the risk of ending the very moment it began.

If one maintained that all myths, all revelations in every religion, were nothing but lies, then, since belief in gods, of whatever kind, has shaped human history, we could only conclude that we have been living for millennia under the rule of falsehood.

However, we would then be guilty not only of banal euhemerism: the fact is that this same skeptical argument would appear singularly related to its opposite argument about the importance of faith. If you believe in any revealed religion, you have to admit that if Christ is the Son of God, then he is not the Messiah that Jerusalem is still waiting for, and if Mohammed is Allah's prophet, then it is an error to make sacrifices to the Plumed Serpent. If you are a follower of the most enlightened and indulgent theism, ready to believe at the same time in the Communion of Saints and the Great Wheel of the Tao, then you will reject as the fruit of error the massacre of infidels and heretics. If you are a worshipper of Satan, you will think the Sermon on the Mount puerile. If you are a radical atheist, no faith will be anything but a mistake. Consequently, since in the course of history many have acted in the belief of something that someone else did not believe in, we are obliged to admit that for each of us, in different measure, History has been largely a Theater of Illusions.

Let us stick, then, to a less contentious notion of truth and falsehood, even though it is philosophically contestable—but we all know that if we listened to philosophers everything would be contested, and we would never get anywhere. Let us stick to the criterion of scientific or historical truth that has been accepted by Western culture; in other words, to the criterion whereby we all accept that Julius Caesar was killed on the Ides of March, that on 20 September 1870 the troops of the young kingdom of Savoy entered Rome by the breach of Porta Pia, that sulphuric acid is H_2SO_4, or that the dolphin is a mammal.

Naturally each of these notions is liable to revision on the basis of new discoveries: but for the time being they are recorded in the Encyclopedia, and until proved otherwise we believe it to be a factual truth that the chemical composition of water is H_2O (and some philosophers believe that this truth must hold true in all possible worlds).

At this point we can say that in the course of history it has been the case that credit has been given to beliefs and assertions that today's Encyclopedia says are *factually* false; and such credit as to conquer the wise, cause the birth and collapse of empires, inspire poets (who are not always witnesses to truth), push human beings to heroic sacrifices, intolerance, massacres, or the search for truth. If that is so, how can we not assert that the power of falsehood exists?

The almost canonical example is that of Ptolemy's hypothesis. Today we know that for centuries humanity accepted a false representation of the universe. It tried all possible tricks to make good the falsity of the image, it invented epicycles and deferents, in the end it tried with Tycho Brahe to have all the planets move around the sun provided that it continued to move around the earth. It was on the basis of this image that not just Dante Alighieri acted, which is not significant, but also the Phoenician navigators, Saint Brendan, Erik the Red, and Christopher Columbus (and one of the above was the first to reach America). Moreover, but on the basis of a false hypothesis, man managed to divide up the globe into parallels and meridian degrees, as we still do, only changing the first meridian from the Canaries to Greenwich.

The example of Ptolemy, which by association triggers the memory of Galileo's unfortunate story, seems deliberately created to lead one to think that my history of falsehood and its power, in its secular boldness, only concerns cases where a dogmatic thought has refused to accept the light of truth. But let us consider a story of the opposite hue, the story of another false opinion, patiently constructed by modern secular thinking to defame religious thought.

Try an experiment, and ask an ordinary person what Christopher Columbus was aiming to prove when he wanted to reach the East by sailing to the West, and what the learned men of Salamanca obstinately denied in order to stop his voyage. The reply, in most cases, will be that Columbus thought the earth was round, while the wise men of Salamanca held that it was flat and that after a short while the three caravels would plunge into the cosmic abyss.

Nineteenth-century lay thought, irritated by the fact that the church had not accepted the heliocentric hypothesis, attributed the idea that the earth was flat to the whole of Christian thought (patristic and scholastic). Nineteenth-century positivism and anticlericalism went to town with this cliché, which, as Jeffrey Burton Russell has shown, was reinforced during the battle fought by the supporters of Darwin's ideas against all forms of fundamentalism.* It was a question of proving that just as the churches had been wrong about the roundness of the earth, so they could be mistaken about the origin of species.

They then exploited the fact that a fourth-century Christian author like Lactantius (in his *Institutiones Divinae*), who had no choice but to regard as correct many biblical passages in which the universe was described as being modeled on the Tabernacle, and therefore as a quadrangle, was opposed to pagan theories of the roundness of the earth, also because he could not accept the idea that the antipodes existed where men would have to walk with their heads upside down . . .

Finally it was discovered that a sixth-century Byzantine geographer, Cosmas Indicopleustes, in his *Topographia Christiana*, had maintained that the cosmos was rectangular, with an arch that curved over the flat floor of the earth (once more the archetype was the Tabernacle). In an authoritative book, *History of the Planetary Systems from Thales to Kepler* by J. L. E. Dreyer, it was admitted that Cosmas was not an official representative of the church, but a lot of space was given to his theory.† Although E. J. Dijksterhuis concedes in *The Mechanization of the World Picture* that Lactantius and Cosmas must not be considered representative of the scientific culture of the church fathers, he asserts that Cosmas's theory became the prevailing opinion for many centuries to come.‡

The fact is that Lactantius was left to stew in his own juice by early and medieval Christian culture, and Cosmas's text, written in Greek, and therefore in a language that the medieval Christian

---

Inventing the Flat Earth (New York: Praeger, 1991).
†(Cambridge: Cambridge University Press, 1906).
‡(Oxford: Oxford University Press, 1961).

had forgotten, was made known to the Western world only in 1706, in Montfaucon's *Collectio Nova Patrum et Scriptorum Graecorum*. No medieval author knew Cosmas, and he was regarded as an authority of the "dark ages" only after his work had been published in English in 1897!

Ptolemy knew, of course, that the earth was round; otherwise he would not have been able to divide it into 360 meridian degrees. Eratosthenes knew it as well, since in the third century B.C. he had calculated the length of the Equator in broadly accurate terms. In fact, Pythagoras, Parmenides, Eudoxus, Plato, Aristotle, Euclid, Aristarchus, Archimedes all knew of it—and it turns out that the only people who did not believe it were two materialist philosophers, Leucippus and Democritus.

Macrobius and Martianus Capella were also well aware that the earth was round. As for the church fathers, they had to cope with the biblical text that mentioned the damned tabernacle shape, but Augustine, even though he did not hold strong opinions on the matter, knew the views of the ancients, and agreed that sacred scripture spoke in metaphors. His position is rather a different one, one quite common in Patristic thought: since it is not by knowing the shape of the earth that one's soul is saved, the question appeared to him to be of little interest. At a certain point Isidore of Seville (who was no model of scientific accuracy) calculates that the length of the equator was eighty thousand stadia. Could he have thought the earth was flat?

Even a first-year high-school student can easily deduce that if Dante enters the cone of Hell and comes out the other side to see unfamiliar stars at the foot of Mount Purgatory, this means that he knew perfectly well that the earth was round. But let's forget about Dante, since we tend to think he can do no wrong. The fact is that the same opinion was held by Origen and Ambrose, and in the Scholastic period many writers—such as Albertus Magnus and Thomas Aquinas, Roger Bacon, John of Holyrood, Pierre d'Ailly, Giles of Rome, Nicole d'Oresme, and John

Buridan, to name but a few—spoke and thought of the earth as spherical.

What, then, was the question at issue in Columbus's time? It was that the learned men of Salamanca had made more precise calculations than his, and believed that the totally spherical earth was bigger than our Genoese mariner thought, and therefore that he was mad to try to circumnavigate the globe and arrive in the East by sailing West. Columbus, though, inspired by sacred fire, and a good sailor, if a hopeless astronomer, thought the earth was smaller than it was. Naturally neither he nor the wise men of Salamanca suspected that another continent lay between Europe and Asia. So you see how complicated the question is, and how narrow are the bounds between truth and error, right and wrong. The doctors of Salamanca, though they were right, made a mistake; and Columbus, though wrong, pursued his error with determination and was right—through serendipity.

Yet have a look at Andrew Dickson White's *History of the Warfare of Science with Theology in Christendom.** It is true that in these two thick volumes he aims to list all the cases where religious thought retarded the development of science, but since he is an informed man, he cannot conceal the fact that Augustine, Albertus Magnus, and Aquinas knew very well that the earth was round. Nevertheless, he claims that in order to maintain this they had to fight against the dominant theological view. But the dominant theological view was represented precisely by Augustine, Albertus, and Aquinas, who consequently did not have to fight against anyone.

Once more it is Russell who reminds us that a serious work like that by F. S. Marvin, which appeared in 1921 in *Studies in the History and in the Method of the Sciences,* repeats that "[t]he

---

*(New York: Appleton, 1896).

maps of Ptolemy . . . were forgotten in the West for a thousand years,"* and that in a manual written in 1988 (A. Holt-Jensen, *Geography: History and Concepts*) it is claimed that the medieval church taught that the earth was a flat disk with Jerusalem at the center; and even Daniel Boorstin, in his popular *Discoverers* of 1983, states that from the fourth to the fourteenth century Christianity suppressed the notion that the earth was round.

How did the idea spread that the Middle Ages considered the earth a flat disk? We saw that Isidore of Seville calculated the length of the equator, yet in the actual manuscripts of his work there is a diagram that inspired many representations of our planet, the so-called T-map.

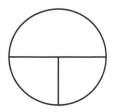

The structure of the T-map is very simple: Given that the circle represents the planet earth, three lines forming a T separate an upper semicircle from two lower quarter circles. The upper portion represents Asia, upper because according to legend the earthly paradise was in Asia; the horizontal bar represents on one side the Black Sea, on the other the Nile, while the vertical line represents the Mediterranean, so the quarter circle on the left is Europe, and the one on the right is Africa. All around is the large circle of the ocean.

Could it have been that these maps signified that the earth was a flat circle?

---

*F. S. Marvin, "Science and the Unity of Mankind," in Charles Singer, ed., *Studies in the History and Method of the Sciences* (2 vols.; Oxford: Oxford University Press, 1921), II, 344–58 (352).

In a manuscript from the *Liber Floridus* by Lambert of Saint-Omer, from the twelfth century, the emperor holds a circle in his hand, on which is drawn a T-map. It is not by accident that this map appears as a regal symbol in the hands of an emperor. It has a symbolic rather than a geographical value. With a little bit of goodwill one could interpret it not as a circle but as the schematic representation of a terrestrial globe, as happens in other images.

However, the impression of a circle is given by the maps illustrating the commentaries on the Apocalypse by Beatus of Liébana, a text written in the eighth century but which, illustrated by Mozarabic miniaturists in subsequent centuries, had a wide influence on the art in Romanesque abbeys and Gothic cathedrals, and T-maps are found in countless illuminated manuscripts.

How was it possible that people who believed that the earth was round made maps where what one saw was a flat earth? The first answer is that this is just what we also do. Criticizing the flatness of these maps would be like criticizing the flatness of one of today's atlases. This was simply a naive and conventional form of cartographic projection. However, there are other factors we have to bear in mind.

The Middle Ages was a period of great travels, but with the roads in disrepair, forests to traverse, and stretches of sea to cross relying on any sailor who was around, there was no chance of drawing adequate maps. They were purely schematic, like the *Instructions for Pilgrims* at Santiago de Compostela, and they said more or less: "If you want to go from Rome to Jerusalem proceed southward and then ask as you go along." Let us try to think of a railway map as found in any railway timetable that you buy from a newsstand. Nobody could extrapolate from that series of crisscrosses, which in themselves are clear enough if you want to take a train from Milan to Livorno (and realize that you have to go via Genoa), the exact shape of Italy. The exact shape of Italy is not of any interest to someone who has to go to the station.

The Romans had charted a series of roads connecting every city in the known world; these roads were represented in what is called Peutinger's map (named after the person who rediscovered it in the fifteenth century). The map shows with great precision every road of the time, but it places them roughly along two stretches of land, the upper one representing Europe and the lower one Africa, so that the Mediterranean appears as a little stream. We are in exactly the same position as with the railway timetable map. The shape of the continents is not of any interest, only the information that there is a road that allows you to go from Marseille to Genoa. And yet the Romans, from the Punic wars onward, had crisscrossed the Mediterranean and knew very well that it was not the little stream that was shown on the map.

For the rest, medieval journeys were imaginary. The Middle Ages produced encyclopedias, called *Imagines Mundi,* that tried more to satisfy the taste for marvels, telling of distant and inaccessible countries, and these were all from books written by people who had never seen the places they wrote about, since the force of tradition counted more than actual experience. Various maps of the world of the time aim not to represent the shape of the earth but to list the cities and peoples that could be seen there. Furthermore, symbolic representation counted more than empirical representation, and often what preoccupied the illuminator was putting Jerusalem at the center of the earth, not how to get to Jerusalem. Last point: medieval maps did not have any scientific function but met the demand for marvels that came from the public, I mean in the same way that today glossy magazines show us the existence of flying saucers and on TV they tell us that the Pyramids were built by an extraterrestrial civilization. Even in the *Nuremberg Chronicle,* which was actually written in 1493, or in Ortelius's atlases in the next century, maps represented mysterious monsters that were thought to inhabit those countries the maps themselves already showed in acceptable cartographic terms.

Perhaps the Middle Ages were cartographically naive, but many modern historians have been even more naive and have not known how to interpret their criteria for mapmaking.

Another fake that changed the history of the world? The Donation of Constantine. Nowadays, thanks to Lorenzo Valla, we know that the *Constitutum* was not authentic. And yet without the profound belief in that document's authenticity, European history would have run a different course: no investiture struggles, no struggle to the death for the Holy Roman Empire, no papal temporal power, but also no Sistine Chapel—which is painted after the Donation has been proved false, but it can be painted because it was believed to be authentic for centuries.

In the second half of the twelfth century a letter arrived in the West telling how in the Far East, beyond the areas occupied by the Muslims, beyond the lands that the Crusaders had tried to remove from the dominion of the infidels, but which had come back under Saracen control, there flourished a Christian kingdom, governed by the fabled Prester John, or Presbyter Johannes, "*rex potentia et virtute dei et domini nostri Iesu Christi*" (a king by the power and virtue of our lord Jesus Christ). The letter began by saying:

> You must know and firmly believe that I, Prester John, am the lord of lords, and in all riches that exist under the heavens, in virtue and in power I outdo all the kings of the earth. Seventy-two kings pay us tribute. I am a devout Christian and I protect and support with alms everywhere true Christians governed by the sovereignty of my Clemency [. . .].
>
> Our sovereignty extends to the three Indias: from India Major, where rests the body of Thomas the Apostle, our dominions extend toward the desert, pushing toward the borders of the Orient before bending back toward the West as

far as deserted Babylon, beside the Tower of Babel [. . .] In our dominions there are born and live elephants, dromedaries, camels, hippopotamuses, crocodiles, [. . .] panthers, wild asses, white and red lions, bears, and white blackbirds, deaf cicadas, griffins, tigers, jackals, hyenas, wild bulls, centaurs, wild men, horned men, fauns, satyrs and their female equivalents, pygmies, cynocephali, giants forty cubits tall, one-eyed men, cyclops, a bird called the phoenix, and almost every kind of animal that lives under heaven's vault [. . .] In one of our provinces there is a river called the Indus. This river, which flows from Paradise, extends its meandering course through different channels throughout the whole province and in it are found natural stones, emeralds, sapphires, carbuncles, topazes, chrysolites, onyxes, beryls, amethysts, sardonyxes, and many other precious gems [. . .].

In the furthermost regions of our land [. . .] we have an island [. . .] where all year round, twice a week, God rains manna in great abundance, which is gathered and eaten by the peoples who live on no other food but this. For they do not plow, nor sow, nor reap, nor move the earth in any way to extract its richest fruit [. . .]. All these people, who live only on divine food, live for five hundred years. Yet when they reach the age of a hundred, they are rejuvenated and regain their strength by drinking thrice the water from a fountain which springs up at the root of a tree that grows in that place [. . .] None of those among us are liars [. . .] Among us there is no one who is an adulterer. No vice has any power with us.*

Translated and paraphrased several times in the course of the following centuries (up until the seventeenth century), and existing

---

*See, also for what follows, Gioia Zaganelli, *La lettera del Prete Gianni* (Parma: Pratiche, 1990).

in various languages and versions, the letter played a decisive role in the expansion of the Christian West toward the Orient. The notion that there could be a Christian kingdom beyond the Muslim territories legitimized all their expansionist and exploratory undertakings. Prester John would be spoken about by Giovanni Pian del Carpine, William of Rubrouck, and Marco Polo. Halfway through the fourteenth century Prester John's kingdom would move from a vague Orient to Ethiopia when Portuguese navigators began their African adventure. Contacts with Prester John would be attempted by Henry IV of England, the duc du Berry, and Pope Eugenius IV. At Bologna, when Charles V was crowned, there would still be discussion of Prester John as a possible ally for the reconquest of the Holy Sepulchre.

How did Prester John's letter come about, and what was its aim? Perhaps it was a document of anti-Byzantine propaganda, produced in Frederick I's scriptoria, but the problem concerns not so much its origins (this period abounded in forgeries of all types)* as its reception. This geographical fantasy served to bolster a political project. In other words, the ghost evoked by some scribe with a flair for forgeries (a highly prized literary genre at the time) acted as an alibi for the expansion of the Christian world toward Africa and Asia, and friendly support for the white man's burden.

Another invention that was rich in historical implications was that of the Rosicrucian confraternity. Many scholars have discussed the climate of extraordinary spiritual renewal that emerged at the dawn of the seventeenth century, when the idea of a Golden Century gathered pace. This climate of expectation pervaded both Catholic and Protestant areas in different forms (in an interplay of mutual influences): plans for ideal republics come

---

*See Umberto Eco, "Fakes and Forgeries," in *The Limits of Interpretation* (Bloomington: Indiana University Press, 1990), 174–202.

forward—from Campanella's *Città del sole* to Johann Valentin Andreae's Christianopolis, as well as hopes of a universal monarchy and a general renewal of morals and religious sensibility—at the very time when Europe, in the period around the Thirty Years' War, was raging with national conflicts, religious hatreds, and the rise of *raison d'état*.

In 1614 a manifesto appeared, entitled *Fama Fraternitatis R. C.,* in which the mysterious Rosicrucian confraternity revealed its existence, and gave notice of its own history and its mythical founder, Christian Rosencreutz—who had apparently lived in the fifteenth century and learned secret revelations from Arabic and Jewish sages in the course of his wanderings in the Orient. In 1615 there appeared, alongside the *Fama,* which was in German, a second manifesto, in Latin, *Confessio Fraternitatis Roseae Crucis. Ad Eruditos Europae.* The first manifesto hopes that there might arise in Europe too a society in possession of gold, silver, and jewels in abundance, which would distribute these to the kings to satisfy their needs and legitimate aims, a society that would teach the rulers to learn everything that God has allowed man to know and help them with their deliberations.

Amid alchemical metaphors and more or less messianic invocations, both manifestos insist on the secret nature of the confraternity and on the fact that their members cannot reveal its real nature ("our edifice—even though a hundred thousand people should see it—will be forever intangible, indestructible, and hidden from the sinful world"). Consequently, the final appeal of the *Fama,* to all the learned men of Europe, to make contact with those who had drawn up the manifesto, might appear even more ambiguous: "Even though we have not for the moment revealed our names, nor when we meet, nevertheless we will certainly get to know everyone's opinion, in whatever language it is expressed; and whoever makes his name known to us can confer with one of us either viva voce or, should there be some impediment to that, in writing."

Almost at once, people from all corners of Europe began to write appeals to the Rosicrucians. Nobody claimed to know them, no one said he was a Rosicrucian, everyone tried somehow to let it be understood that they were entirely in agreement with its program. Julius Sperber, Robert Fludd, and Michael Maier all speak to the invisible Rosicrucians: Maier, in his *Themis Aurea* (1618), maintains that the confraternity really does exist, even though he admits that he is too humble a person to have ever belonged to them. But as Frances Yates observed, the usual behavior of Rosicrucian writers was to claim not only that they were not Rosicrucians but that they had never even met a member of the confraternity.*

For a start, Johann Valentin Andreae and all his friends in the Tübingen circle, who were immediately suspected of being the authors of the manifestos, spent their lives either denying the fact or playing it down as a literary game, a youthful folly. Moreover, not only is there no historical evidence of the existence of the Rosicrucians, but by definition there cannot be. Still today, the official documents of the AMORC (*"Anticus et Mysticus Ordo Rosae Crucis,"* whose temple, rich in Egyptian iconography, can be visited in San José, California) state that the original texts legitimizing the order certainly do exist but for obvious reasons will remain secret and locked up in inaccessible archives.

We are interested not so much in today's Rosicrucians, however, who are just part of folklore, as in the historical ones. From the earliest appearance of the first two manifestos critical pamphlets began to be published, attacking the confraternity with accusations of various kinds, in particular those of being forgers and charlatans. In 1623 there appeared in Paris anonymous notices announcing the arrival of the Rosicrucians in the city, and this announcement unleashed fierce polemics, in both Catholic

---

* *The Rosicrucian Enlightenment* (London: Routledge, 2000).

and libertine circles; the common rumor that the Rosicrucians were devil worshippers was expressed in an anonymous *Effroyables Pactions faites entre le diable et les prétendus invisibles* (Terrifying Pacts Made between the Devil and the So-Called Invisible Ones), also of 1623. Even Descartes, who during a journey to Germany had tried—it is said—to contact them (unsuccessfully, of course), was suspected on his return to Paris of belonging to the confraternity, and he got out of the predicament with a masterstroke: since the common legend had it that the Rosicrucians were invisible, he made his appearance at many public occasions and thus defused the rumors that surrounded him, according to Baillet in his *Vie de Monsieur Descartes*. A certain Neuhaus published, first in German, then in French in 1623, an *Advertissement pieux et utile des frères de la Rose-Croix* (Pious and Useful Advertisement of the Brothers of the Rosy-Cross), which asked if there were any Rosicrucians, who they were, where they took their name from, and why they revealed themselves to the public; and it concluded with the extraordinary argument that "since they change and turn their names into anagrams, and conceal their age, and come here without revealing their identity, there is no Logician who can deny that they must of necessity exist."

This tells us that it only required someone to make an appeal for the spiritual reform of humanity for the most paradoxical reactions to be unleashed, as though everyone were waiting for some decisive event.

Jorge Luis Borges, in his "'Tlön, Uqbar, Orbis Tertius,'" writes of an improbable country, described in an unfindable encyclopedia. From the researches into this country it emerges, through vague clues based on texts that plagiarize each other, that in fact what is being talked about is an entire planet, "with its own architectures and wars, with the terror of its mythologies and the sound of its languages, with its emperors and seas, its minerals and birds, its fishes, its algebra and its fire, and its theological and metaphysical controversies." This entity is the creation of "a secret society of astronomers, engineers, metaphysicians, poets, chemists, moralists, painters, geometers . . . under the guidance of an obscure man of genius."

We are here faced with a typical Borges invention: the invention of an invention. Yet Borges's readers know that he never invented anything; his most improbable stories come from his rereading of history. In fact, at a certain point Borges says that one of his sources was a work by Johann Valentin Andreae, which (though Borges got this information secondhand from De Quincey) "described the imaginary community of the Rosicrucians; a community that others later genuinely founded from the example of what he had imagined."

In fact the Rosicrucian story produced historical developments of considerable significance. Symbolic Masonry, a transformation of actual masonry (which had real confraternities of artisans, who had preserved over the course of the centuries the terms and ceremonies of the ancient builders of cathedrals), emerges in the eighteenth century thanks to some English gentlemen. With Anderson's Constitutions, symbolic Masonry tried to legitimize itself by maintaining the antiquity of its origins, which they claimed went back to the Temple of Solomon. In subsequent years, through the efforts of Ramsay, who created so-called Scottish Masonry, what is worked into this foundation myth is the relationship between the builders of the Temple and the Templars, whose secret tradition apparently reaches modern Masonry through the mediation of the Rosicrucians.

If in early Masonry the Rosicrucian theme introduces elements of mysticism and the occult into an organization that is by now a rival to throne and altar, at the beginning of the nineteenth century it will be in defense of throne and altar that the Rosicrucian and Templar myth will be taken up again in order to combat the spirit of the Enlightenment.

Already before the French Revolution people discussed the myth of secret societies and the fact that there existed Unknown

Superiors who guided the destiny of the world. In 1789 the marquis de Luchet (in his *Essai sur le secte des Illuminés*) warned: "in the bosom of the thickest darkness a society of new beings has been formed, who know each other without ever having been seen. . . . This society takes from the Jesuit rule its blind obedience, from Masonry its trials and external ceremonies, and from the Templars its subterranean echoes and incredible daring."

Between 1789 and 1798, as a response to the French Revolution, the Abbé Barruel wrote his *Mémoires pour servir à l'histoire de jacobinisme,* apparently a historical work but one that could however be read as a serial novel. After being destroyed by Philippe le Bel, the Templars turned into a secret society to destroy the monarchy and the papacy. In the eighteenth century they got hold of Masonry to create a sort of academy whose diabolical members included Voltaire, Turgot, Condorcet, Diderot, and D'Alembert—and it was from this group that Jacobinism was born. But the Jacobins themselves were in turn controlled by an even more secret society, the Bavarian Illuminati, who were regicides by vocation. The French Revolution was the final outcome of this conspiracy.

It did not matter that there were profound differences between secular, enlightened Masonry and the Masonry of the Illuminati, which was occultist and related to the Templars, nor that the Templar myth had already been exploded by one of its brothers and fellow travelers, who would later take another road: I am referring to Joseph de Maistre. . . . No, it did not matter, it was too good a story.

Barruel's book contained no reference to the Jews. But in 1806 Barruel received a letter from a certain Captain Simonini, who reminded him that both the Mani and the Old Man of the Mountains of Muslim memory (the Templars were suspected of being in league with the latter) were Jews (and you can see that here the network of occult ancestry becomes dizzying). Masonry then had been founded by the Jews, who had infiltrated all secret societies.

Barruel did not take up this rumor publicly, and in any case it did not produce any interesting effects until the middle of the century, when the Jesuits began to worry about the anticlerical originators of the Risorgimento, such as Garibaldi, who were affiliated with Masonry. The idea of showing that the Carbonari were emissaries of a Judeo-Masonic plot appeared to be useful as a polemic.

But still in the nineteenth century, the anticlerical supporters in turn tried to defame the Jesuits, to show that the latter were doing nothing other than plotting against the good of humanity. More than some "serious" authors (from Michelet and Quinet to Garibaldi and Gioberti), the writer who made this motif popular was a novelist, Eugène Sue. In *The Wandering Jew,* the evil Monsieur Rodin, the quintessence of Jesuit skulduggery, clearly appears as a replica of the Unknown Superiors of both Masonic and clerical memory. Monsieur Rodin reappears on the scene in Sue's last novel, *The Mysteries of the People,* where the notorious Jesuit plot is exposed down to the last detail. Rudolph of Gerolstein, who has migrated from *The Mysteries of Paris* to this novel, denounces the Jesuit plot, warning "with what cunning this infernal plot has been organized, and what terrifying outrages, what horrendous slavery, what despotic destiny it meant for Europe. . . ."

After Sue's novels came out, a certain Monsieur Joly wrote a pamphlet of liberal inspiration in 1864, directed against Napoléon III: in it Machiavelli, who stands for the cynical dictator, converses with Montesquieu. The Jesuit plot described by Sue is now attributed by Joly to Napoléon III.

In 1868 Hermann Goedsche, who had published other clearly libelous pamphlets, wrote a popular novel, *Biarritz,* under the pseudonym Sir John Retcliffe, in which he describes an occult ceremony in the cemetery in Prague. Goedsche is simply copying a scene from Dumas's *Joseph Balsamo* (1849), which describes the meeting between Cagliostro, head of the Unknown

Superiors, and other Illuminati, when they are all plotting the affair of the Queen's necklace. But instead of Cagliostro and company, Goedsche has representatives of the twelve tribes of Israel appear at a meeting, as they prepare to take over the world. Five years later the same story will be taken up in a Russian work (*The Jews, Masters of the World*), where it is treated as if it were real history. In 1881 *Le Contemporain* reprints the same story, claiming that it comes from a reliable source, the English diplomat Sir John Readcliff. In 1896 François Bournand uses the story of the Grand Rabbi again (but this time he is called John Readclitt) in his book *Les Juifs, nos contemporains*. From this point onward, the Masonic meeting invented by Dumas, blended with the Jesuit plot invented by Sue and attributed by Joly to Napoléon III, becomes the real speech made by the Great Rabbi, which then resurfaces in various forms and in various places.

There now comes on the scene Pëter Ivanovic Rakovskij, a Russian already suspected of contacts with groups of revolutionaries and nihilists, who later (having duly repented of his past) would become involved with the Black Centurions, a terrorist organization of the extreme Right, and then turn informer before becoming head of the czar's political police (the Okhrana). Now Rakovskij, to help his political protector (Count Sergej Witte), who had been worried by an opponent of his, Elie de Cyon, had Cyon's house searched and found a pamphlet in which Cyon had copied Joly's text against Napoléon III, but attributed Machiavelli's ideas to Witte. Rakovskij, fiercely anti-Semitic—this was happening at the time of the Dreyfus affair—takes that text, cancels all references to Witte, and attributes the ideas to the Jews. One cannot be called Cyon, even with a C (rather than an S), without evoking a Jewish conspiracy.

The text altered by Rakovskij probably constituted the primary source for the *Protocols of the Elders of Zion*. It betrays its novelistic source since it is not really credible, except in a novel by Sue, that the "baddies" should express their wicked plans in such an open and shameless way. The Elders openly declare that they have "a vaulting ambition, an all-consuming greed, a ruthless desire for revenge and an intense hatred." They want to abolish the freedom of the press but encourage libertinism. They criticize Liberalism but uphold the idea of capitalist multinationals. To stir up revolution in every country, they intend to exacerbate social inequalities. They want to build subways so as to bomb big cities. They want to abolish the study of the classics and ancient history but to encourage sport and visual communication in order to turn the working classes into imbeciles . . .

It was easy to identify a document produced in nineteenth-century France in the *Protocols*, because it abounds in references to problems in French society at the time, but it was also easy to spot many very famous popular novels among its sources. Alas, the story—once more—was so convincing in narrative terms that it was taken seriously.

The rest of this story is History. An itinerant monk, Sergej Nilus, in order to further his "Rasputinian" ambitions, and obsessed with the Antichrist, printed and commented on the *Protocols*. After this the text travels across Europe until it comes into Hitler's hands. . . .*

We have explored some false ideas that have made history, and about which everyone has more or less heard. But there are other crazed ideas we have forgotten about.

From 1925 onward publicity was given in Nazi circles to the theory of an Austrian pseudoscientist, Hans Hörbiger, a theory called WEL, that is, *Welteislehre*, the theory of eternal ice. It had

---

*I know that I took up this story both in *Foucault's Pendulum* and in *Six Walks in the Fictional Woods*, but it is always worth repeating, and unfortunately the story can never be retold often enough. As always, the evidence derives largely, apart from my own personal researches into the "roman feuilleton," from Norman Cohn, *Warrant for Genocide: The Myth of the Jewish World Conspiracy and the Protocols of the Elders of Zion* (London: Serif, 1996), and from that inexhaustible source of anti-Semitic arguments, Nesta Webster, *Secret Societies and Subversive Movements* (London: Boswell, 1924).

enjoyed the favor of men such as Rosenberg and Himmler. But with Hitler's rise to power Hörbiger was taken seriously even in some scientific circles—for instance, by a scholar like Lenard, who had discovered x-rays along with Roentgen.

According to the theory of eternal ice (expounded as early as 1913 by Philip Fauth in his *Glacial-Kosmogonie*), the cosmos is the theater of an eternal struggle between ice and fire, which produces not an evolution but an alternation of cycles, or of epochs.* There was once an enormous mass at a very high temperature, millions of times bigger than the sun, which collided with an immense accumulation of cosmic ice. The mass of ice penetrated this incandescent body, and after working inside it as vapor for hundreds of millions of years, it caused the whole thing to explode. Various fragments were projected both into icy space and into an intermediate zone where they became the solar system. The moon, Mars, Jupiter, and Saturn are made of ice, and the Milky Way is a chain of ice that traditional astronomy has viewed as stars; but in fact these are photographic tricks. Sunspots are produced by blocks of ice detaching themselves from Jupiter.

Now the force of the original explosion is decreasing, and every planet completes not an elliptical revolution, as official science erroneously believes, but something approximating an (imperceptible) spiral around the bigger planet that attracts it. At the end of the cycle through which we are living, the moon will come closer and closer to the earth, gradually making the waters of the oceans rise, submerging the tropics, and allowing only the tallest mountains to emerge, while the cosmic rays will become more and more powerful and cause genetic mutations. Finally the moon will explode, turning into a mixture of ice, water, and gas, which in the end will plummet down onto the earth's globe. Because of complicated events due to the influence of Mars, the earth too will turn into a sphere of ice and in the end will be

---

*Philip Fauth, *Hörbigers Glacial-Kosmogonie* (Kaiserslautern: Hermann Kayser Verlag, 1913).

reabsorbed by the sun. Then there will be a new explosion and a new beginning, just as in the past the earth had already had and then reabsorbed another three satellites.

This cosmogony presupposed a sort of Eternal Return that went back to very ancient myths and epics. Once more, what today's Nazis call the wisdom of Tradition was in this way set up against the false knowledge of liberal Jewish science. Furthermore, a glacial cosmogony seemed very Nordic and Aryan. In *The Morning of the Magicians* Pauwels and Bergier attribute to this profound belief in the glacial origins of the cosmos the confidence, encouraged by Hitler, that his troops would be able to cope very well in the frosts of Russian territory.* But they also maintain that the need to prove how cosmic ice would react had slowed down the experiments on the V-1s. Still in 1952, a certain Elmar Brugg published a book in honor of Hörbiger, whom he hailed as the twentieth-century Copernicus, claiming that the theory of eternal ice explained the profound links between earthly events and cosmic forces, and concluding that the silence of democratic-Jewish science about Hörbiger was a typical example of the conspiracy of mediocrities.

The cultivators of magical-Hermetic and neo-Templar sciences operating around the Nazi Party—for instance, the adepts of the *Thule Gesellschaft* founded by Rudolf von Sebottendorf—is a phenomenon that has been widely studied.† Apparently in Nazi circles they also paid attention to another theory, which posits that the earth is empty and we live not on its outside, on its eternal, convex crust, but inside it, on the internal concave surface. This theory was articulated at the beginning of the nineteenth century by a certain Captain J. Cleves Symmes of Ohio,

---

*Louis Pauwels and Jacques Bergier, *The Morning of the Magicians,* trans. Rollo Myers (London: Souvenir, 2001), II, 5–7.
†See, for instance, Nicholas Goodrick-Clarke, *The Occult Roots of Nazism* (Wellingborough: Aquarian Press, 1985), or René Alleau, *Hitler et les sociétes sécrètes* (Paris: Grasset, 1969).

who wrote to various scientific societies: "To the whole world: I declare the earth is hollow, habitable within; containing a number of solid concentric spheres; one within the other, and that it is open at the pole twelve or sixteen degrees." A wooden model of his universe is still preserved in the Academy of Natural Sciences in Philadelphia.

The theory was taken up again in the second half of the century by Cyrus Reed Teed, who specified that what we think is the sky is a mass of gas filling the inside of the globe, with some zones of brilliant light. The sun, the moon, and the stars are not, he said, celestial globes, but rather visual effects caused by various phenomena.

After the First World War the theory was introduced into Germany by Peter Bender, and then by Karl Neupert, who founded the *Hohlweltlehre* (hollow-earth theory) movement. According to some sources, the theory was taken seriously in the upper echelons of the German hierarchy, and in some quarters of the German navy it was held that the hollow-earth theory would allow them to establish more accurately the positions of British ships, because if they used infrared rays, the curve of the earth would not obscure their observation.* It is even said that some shots with the V-1s missed their targets precisely because they calculated their trajectory on the hypothesis of a concave, not a convex, earth's surface. Here—if this is true—we can see the historical, even providential usefulness of deranged astronomical theories.

But it is easy to say that the Nazis were mad and that they are all dead, apart from good old Martin Borman, who is always said to be in hiding somewhere. The fact is that if you go on the Internet and ask any search engine to find sites dealing with Hollow Earth, you will find that there are still very many followers of the

---

*For instance, Gerard Kniper, of the Mount Palomar observatory, in an article that came out in *Popular Astronomy* in 1946, and Willy Ley, who had worked on the V-1 in Germany, in his article "Pseudoscience in Naziland," in *Astounding Science Fiction* 39 (1947).

theory. And it is no use saying that the sites (and the books they publicize) have been created by some cunning old foxes counting on a public of idiots and/or devotees of New Age ideas. The social and cultural problem is not the cunning foxes, but the idiots, who are clearly still legion.*

What unites all the stories I have mentioned, and what made them so persuasive and credible?

The Donation of Constantine was probably created not as a deliberate forgery but as a rhetorical exercise that people only began to take seriously later.

The Rosicrucian manifestos were, at least according to their presumed authors, an erudite game and, if not a joke, at least a literary exercise that could be categorized under the genre of utopias.

Prester John's letter was certainly a deliberate fake, but equally certainly it did not intend to produce the effects it in fact created.

Cosmas Indicopleustes was guilty of fundamentalism, a pardonable weakness considering the times in which he lived, but as we have seen, no one really took him seriously, and his text was maliciously exhumed as an "authoritative" work only more than a thousand years later.

The *Protocols* emerge initially on their own, through an accumulation of novelistic themes that gradually kindle the imagination of a few fanatics and become transformed en route.

---

*In 1926 Admiral Byrd flew over the North Pole and in 1929 over the South Pole without sighting any hole giving access to the center of the earth, but a huge literature has arisen on Byrd's flights (just search for "Byrd" on the Internet), where various bizarre spirits interpret his findings in exactly the opposite sense, seeing them as proof that the access holes exist. This is also because, if you photograph these zones during the day, you notice a dark zone that is the portion of the Arctic Circle that is never shone on by the sun during the winter months. Those who want maps showing the polar conduits leading to the center of the Earth should look at sites like *www.v-j-enterprises.com/holearth.html* or *www.ourhollowearth. com/Polar Opn.htm*. Those who want to penetrate more deeply into the hollow earth's archipelago can visit countless sites, among which I will cite only *www.healthresearcharchbooks. com/categories/hollowearth.html* and hohle-erde.de/body_l-he.htme. Of course, you can't believe everything you read.

And yet each one of these stories had an advantage: they appeared convincing in narrative terms, more so than day-to-day or historical reality, which is much more complex and incredible, and they seemed to provide a good explanation for something that otherwise was more difficult to understand.

Let us turn again to Ptolemy's account. We now know that Ptolemy's hypothesis was scientifically false. And yet, if our intelligence is now Copernican, our perception is still Ptolemaic: we not only see the sun rising in the East and traveling across the sky throughout the hours of daylight, but we behave as though the sun went around us and we stayed still. And we say: "the sun rises, is high in the sky, is going down, sets. . . ." Even a professor of astronomy speaks, thinks, and perceives this way: Ptolemaically.

Why did the story of the Donation of Constantine have to be disproved? It guaranteed a continuity of power after the collapse of the empire, it perpetuated an idea of Latinity, it indicated a guide, a point of reference amid the flames and slaughters perpetrated by the many suitors who were competing for the nuptials of Europe. . . .

Why reject Cosmas's account? In other respects he was a careful traveler, a diligent gatherer of geographical and historical curiosities, and in any case his theory of the flat earth—at least from a narrative point of view—was not entirely improbable. The earth was a huge rectangle bounded by four immense walls upholding two layers of the heavenly vault: on the first shone the stars, and on the intervening layer, or insole, lived the Blessed. Astronomical phenomena were explained by the presence of a very high mountain to the north, which by hiding the sun created night, and by coming between the sun and the light produced eclipses. . . .

As has been observed, even Teed's hollow-earth theory was difficult to refute for nineteenth-century mathematicians, because it was possible to project the convex surface of the earth onto a concave surface without noticing too many discrepancies.

Why reject the story of the Rosicrucians if it answered the need for religious harmony? And why discount the story of the *Protocols* if it managed to explain so many historical events with its conspiracy myth? As Karl Popper has reminded us, "The conspiracy theory of society . . . is akin to Homer's theory of society. Homer conceived the power of the gods in such a way that whatever happened in the plain before Troy was only a reflection of the various conspiracies on Olympus. The conspiracy theory of society . . . comes from abandoning God and then asking: 'Who is in his place?' His place is then filled by various powerful men and groups—sinister pressure groups, who are to be blamed for having planned the great depression and all the evils from which we suffer."*

Why consider it absurd to believe in conspiracies and plots, when they are used even today to explain the failure of our actions, or the fact that events have taken a different turn from the one we wanted?

False stories are above all stories, and stories, like myths, are always persuasive. And how many other false stories could we discuss . . . ? For instance, the myth of the Southern Land, that immense continent that was meant to run along the whole of the polar ice cap and subtropical Antarctica. The firm belief in the existence of this land (certified by countless geographical maps showing the globe wrapped, to the south, by a substantial sort of land support) encouraged navigators for three centuries and from various countries to attempt to explore the southern seas and Antarctica itself.

What can we say about El Dorado and the fountain of eternal youth, which inspired mad and courageous heroes to explore the two Americas? Of the impulse given to the new science of

---

* *Conjectures and Refutations: The Growth of Scientific Knowledge* (London and Henley: Routledge and Kegan Paul, 1976), 123.

chemistry by the hallucinations caused by the specter of the philosopher's stone? Of the story of phlogiston, the account of cosmic ether?

Let us forget for a moment that some of these false tales have produced positive effects and others have produced horror and shame. All of them have created something, for good or ill. Nothing is inexplicable about their success. What constitutes the problem is, rather, how we have managed to replace these with other stories that we consider true today. In my essay on fakes and forgeries, written some years ago, I concluded that there certainly exist tools, either empirical or conjectural, to prove that something is a fake, but that every judgment on the question presupposes the existence of an original that is authentic and true, against which the forgery is compared; however, the real cognitive problem consists not only in proving that something is a forgery but in proving that the authentic object is just that: authentic.

And yet this obvious consideration must not lead us to conclude that there is no criterion of truth, and that stories said to be false are the same as those that we consider today to be true, just because both belong to the literary genre of narrative fiction. There is a practice of verification that is based on slow, collective, public work done by what Charles Sanders Peirce called the Community. It is through our human faith in the work of this community that we can say, with a certain degree of tranquillity, that the *Constitutum Constantini* was a forgery, that the earth moves around the sun, and that Saint Thomas Aquinas at least knew that the earth was round.

At most, recognizing that our history has been shaped by many stories that we now regard as false must make us cautious, and always ready to call into question the very stories that we now hold as true, since the criterion of wisdom of the community is based on constant wariness about the fallibility of our knowledge.

Some years ago there appeared in France a book by Jean-François Gautier, entitled *L'Univers existe-t-il?** Does the universe exist? Good question. And what if the universe were just a concept like cosmic ether, phlogiston, or the conspiracy by the elders of Zion?

Gautier's arguments are philosophically sensible. The idea of the universe as the totality of the cosmos is an idea that comes from the most ancient cosmographies, cosmologies, and cosmogonies. But can we possibly describe, as if we could see it from above, something inside which we are contained, of which we form a part, and which we cannot leave? Can we provide a descriptive geometry of the universe when there is no space outside it onto which to project it? Can we speak of the beginning of the universe when a temporal notion like that of a beginning must refer to the parameters of a clock, whereas at most the universe is its own clock and cannot be referred to anything that is external to it? Can we say with Eddington that "hundreds of thousands of stars make up a galaxy; hundreds of thousands of galaxies make up the universe," when, as Gautier observes, although a galaxy is an object that can be observed, the universe is not, and therefore one is establishing an unwarranted analogy between two incommensurate entities? Can one postulate the universe in order to then study with empirical instruments this postulate as if it were an object? Can a singular object (certainly the most singular of all objects) exist that has as its characteristic that of being just a law? And if the story of the big bang were just a story as fantastic as the Gnostic tale that claimed that the universe was born from the mistake made by an unskillful Demiurge?

Basically this critique of the notion of the universe is like the Kantian critique of the notion of World.

---

*(Arles: Actes Sud, 1994).

Since for some people the suspicion that the sun does not go around the earth seemed at a certain moment in history just as foolish and execrable as the suspicion that the universe does not exist, it is useful to keep our mind free and fresh for the moment when the community of men of science decrees that the idea of the universe was an illusion, just like the flat earth and the Rosicrucians.

Deep down, the first duty of the Community is to be on the alert in order to be able to rewrite the encyclopedia every day.

Expanded version of the inaugural lecture for the academic year 1994–95 at the University of Bologna.

HOW I WRITE

THE BEGINNINGS, REMOTE.

I am a rather anomalous example of a fiction writer. For I began to write stories and novels between the ages of eight and fifteen, then I stopped, only to start again when I was on the verge of fifty. Before this explosion of mature impudence, I spent more than thirty years of presumed modesty. I said "presumed," and I need to explain this. Let us proceed in the proper order, namely, as is my wont in novels, by going back in time.

When I began to write I would take a notebook and write the first page. The title would have a Salgari flavor, because his works were one of my sources (along with those of Verne, Boussenard, Jacolliot, and the years 1911–21 of the *Giornale illustrato dei viaggi e delle avventure di terra e di mare* [Illustrated Journal of Travels and Adventures on Land and Sea], discovered in a trunk in the basement). So they had titles like *Gli scorridori del Labrador* (The Pirates of Labrador) or *Lo sciabecco fantasma* (The Phantom Ship). Then at the bottom I would write the name of the publisher, which was Tipografia Matenna, a daring hybrid of "*Matita*" (Pencil) and "*Penna*" (Pen). I then proceeded to insert an illustra-

302

tion every ten pages, like those by Della Valle or Amato for Salgari's books.

The choice of illustration determined the story I would then have to write. I would write only a few pages of the first chapter. I wrote in block letters, without allowing myself any changes, in order to do things correctly from the publishing point of view. Needless to say, I would abandon the enterprise after a few pages. Thus I was, at that time, the author of only great unfinished novels.

Of this output (which was lost during a move) I have retained only one finished work, of indeterminate genre. For I was given a huge kind of notebook as a present, its pages faintly marked with horizontal lines and big purple margins. That gave me the idea of writing (the title page bears the date of 1942, followed by Year XXI of the Fascist Regime, as was the custom, and indeed the requirement) *In nome del "Calendario"* (In the Name of "Calendar"), the diary of a magician, Pirimpimpino, who passed himself off as the discoverer, colonizer, and reformer of an island in the Glacial Arctic Ocean called the Acorn, whose inhabitants adored the god "Calendar." Every day this Pirimpimpino would note down, and with great documentary pedantry, the deeds and (what I would call today) socioanthropological structures of his people, interspersing these diary jottings with literary exercises. I have found in it a "Futurist short story," which goes like this: "Luigi was a good man, that was why, once he had kissed the hares' plates, he went to the Lateran to buy the present perfect [. . .]. But en route he fell into a mountain and died. A shining example of heroism and philanthropy, he was mourned by the telegraph poles."

For the rest the narrator described (and drew) the island he ruled, its woods, lakes, coasts, and mountainous regions, dwelled on his own social reforms, his people's rites and myths, introduced his own ministers, and spoke of wars and pestilences. . . . The text alternated with drawings, and the story (which did not follow the rules of any genre) turned into an encyclopedia—and with hindsight one can see how the child's boldness presaged the adult's weaknesses.

Until the point where, no longer knowing what to make happen to the king and his island, I ended the tale on page 29, saying: "I will go on a long voyage. . . . Perhaps I will not even come back; just one small confession: in the early days I declared myself to be a wizard. This is not true: I am only called Pirimpimpino. Forgive me."

After these experiments I decided that I would have to go over to comics, and I did produce some. If photocopiers had existed at that time, I would have distributed them widely; instead, in order to make up for my limitations as amanuensis, I proposed that my school friends give me a number of pages from their squared paper notebooks, which amounted to the number of pages for the volume, plus some more as compensation for my expenses in ink and labor, promising to produce several copies of the same adventure. I drew up all the contracts without realizing how laborious it was to copy the same story ten times. In the end I had to give the notebooks back, humiliated by my failure, not as an author, but as a publisher.

At middle school I wrote narratives because by that time "essays" (where there was no choice of subject) had been replaced by "chronicles" (where we had to recount "a slice of life," but there was an element of choice). I excelled in humorous sketches. My favorite author then was P. G. Wodehouse. I still have my masterpiece: a description of how I prepared, after many experiments, to demonstrate to neighbors and relatives a technological wonder, namely, one of the first unbreakable glasses; I dropped it triumphantly on the ground, where, of course, it smashed into pieces.

Between 1944 and 1945 I turned to epic, with a parody of *The Divine Comedy* and a series of portraits of the gods of Olympus, all portrayed in the style of that dark period, when we were coping with rationing, blackouts, and Rabagliati's songs.

Finally in my first two years of high school, I wrote an "Illustrated Life of Euterpe Clips" (with illustrations), and at that stage my literary models were the novels of Giovanni Mosca and Giovanni Guareschi. In my final years there I wrote some stories with more serious literary ambitions. I would say that at that time the dominant tone was a magic realism à la Bontempelli. For a long time, I would get up early and plan to rewrite "The Concert," which contained an interesting narrative idea. A certain Mario Tobia, a failed composer, gathered together all the mediums of the world to produce onstage, in the form of ectoplasms, the greatest musicians of the past, to play his "Conradino of Swabia." Beethoven conducting, Liszt on the piano, Paganini on the violin, and so on. Just one contemporary, Louis Robertson, on the trumpet. There was quite a good description of how gradually the mediums were unable to keep their creatures alive, and the great composers of the past slowly dissolved, amid the whines and dissonances of dying instruments, leaving on its own up there, shrill, magical and unopposed, Robertson's trumpet.

I ought to leave to my faithful readers (all twenty-four of them, I would say, in order not to compete with the Great Manzoni's twenty-five readers, since I want to outdo him only in modesty) the job of recognizing how both episodes were exploited forty years later in *Foucault's Pendulum*.

I also wrote some "Ancient Stories of the Young Universe," whose protagonists were the earth and the other planets, just after the birth of the galaxies, as they were seized by reciprocal passions and jealousies: in one story, Venus fell in love with the Sun and with a huge effort managed to remove herself from her own orbit to go and annihilate herself in the incandescent mass of her beloved. My little, unaware Cosmicomics.

At sixteen my love for poetry began. I devoured the Hermetic poets, but my own taste was more for Cardarelli and the classicism of those who wrote for *La Ronda*. I no longer know whether it was the need for poetry (and the contemporary discovery of Chopin) that caused the flowering of my first, platonic, and unspoken love, or vice versa. In either case, the mixture was disastrous, and not even the most tender and narcissistic of nostalgias would allow me to revisit those efforts now without feeling deep and thoroughly deserved shame. But a severe critical sternness must have emerged from that experience: that was what drove me, in the space of a few years, to decide that my poetry had the same functional origin and the same formal configuration as teenage acne. Hence the resolution (kept for over thirty years) to abandon so-called creative writing, and to limit myself to philosophical reflection and the writing of essays.

The Essayist and the Fiction Writer

This was a decision that I have never regretted for thirty years or more. What I mean is that I was not one of those who are condemned to write about science while burning with desire to write about art. I felt totally fulfilled doing what I was doing, and what's more, I looked with a touch of Platonic disdain at poets, prisoners of their own lies, imitators of imitations, unable to attain that vision of the hypercelestial Idea with which I—as a philosopher—believed I had chaste, peaceful, and daily intercourse.

In reality, I now realize, I was satisfying my passion for narrative, without noticing it, in three different ways. First of all, through a constant exercise of oral narrativity (I missed enormously our young children when they grew up, because I could no longer tell them stories). Second, by playing with literary parodies and pastiches of various types (a period documented in my *Misreadings* [New York: Harcourt, 1993], written in the late fifties and early sixties. And third, by making a narrative out of every critical essay. I have to explain this point because I think it is essential for understanding both my activity as an essayist and my (subsequent) future as a narrator.

When I was examined for my graduating thesis on the problem of aesthetics in Thomas Aquinas, I was struck by one of the criticisms of the second examiner (Augusto Guzzo, who, however, later published my thesis as it was): he told me that what I had actually done was to rehearse the various phases of my research as if it were an inquiry, noting the false leads and the hypotheses that I later rejected, whereas the mature scholar digests these experiences and then offers his readers (in the final version) only the conclusions. I recognized that this was true of my thesis, but I did not feel it to be a limitation. On the contrary, it was precisely then that I was convinced that all research must be "narrated" in this way. And I think I have done so in all my subsequent works of nonfiction.

As a result, I could refrain peacefully from writing stories because in fact I was satisfying my passion for narrative in another way; and when I would later write stories, they could not be anything other than the account of a piece of research (only in narrative this is called a Quest).

WHERE DID I START FROM?

Between the ages of forty-six and forty-eight I wrote my first novel, *The Name of the Rose.* I do not intend to discuss the (how shall I say, existential?) motives that led me to write a first novel: they were numerous, probably cumulative, and I believe the fact that I felt a desire to write a novel is motivation enough.

One of the questions that the editor of this volume has put to the writers she has contacted is: What are the phases one goes through in the genesis of a text? The question blithely implies that writing goes through phases. Usually naive interviewers hover between two mutually contradictory convictions: one, that a text we call creative develops almost instantaneously in the mystic heat of inspirational raptus; or the other, that the writer has followed a recipe, a kind of secret set of rules that they would like to see revealed.

There is no set of rules, or, rather, there are many, varied and flexible rules; and there is no hot magma of inspiration. But it is true that there is a sort of initial idea and that there are very precise phases in a process that develops only gradually.

My three novels stemmed from a seminal idea that was little more than an image: that was what seized me and made me want to go on. *The Name of the Rose* was born when I was struck by an image of the murder of a monk in a library. When I wrote in the *Reflections on "The Name of the Rose"* that "I wanted to poison a monk," this provocative formula was taken literally, unleashing a series of follow-up questions on why I wanted to commit this crime. But I did not want to poison a monk at all (and indeed have never done so): I was fascinated by the image of a monk who was poisoned while reading a book in the library. I do not know whether I was under the influence of the traditional poetics of the English detective novel, where the murder has to be committed in a vicarage. Perhaps I was following up certain emotions I had felt at sixteen, during a retreat in a Benedictine monastery, where I walked through Gothic and Romanesque cloisters and then went into a dark library where, open on a lectern, I found the *Acta Sanctorum,* and there I learned that there was not just one Blessed Umberto, as I had been led to believe, with a feast day on 4 March, but also a Saint Umberto, a bishop, whose feast was celebrated on 6 September and who had converted a lion in a forest. But one can see that at that point, while I was leafing through that folio volume open vertically in front of me, in supreme silence, amid shafts of light entering through opaque windows that were almost grooved into the walls and ended in pointed arches, I had experienced a moment of upheaval.

I don't know. But the fact is that that image, of the monk murdered while reading, demanded at a certain point that I construct something else around it. The rest came bit by bit, in order to make sense of that image, including the decision to set the story in the Middle Ages. Initially I thought it should take place in our own time; then I decided that, since I knew and loved the medieval period, it was worthwhile making it the backdrop of my story. All the rest came on its own, gradually, as I read, looked at images, reopened cupboards where there was a twenty-five-year-old pile of filing cards on the Middle Ages, which had been filled out for completely different purposes.

With *Foucault's Pendulum* things were more complicated. I had to go and look for the seminal image—or, rather, the two seminal images, as we shall see—like a psychoanalyst gradually extracting the patient's secret from some disconnected memories and fragments of dreams. Initially I felt only one anxiety: I've written a novel—I said to myself—the first novel in my life, and perhaps the last, because I have the feeling that I put into it all the things that I liked or found intriguing, along with everything that, even indirectly, I could say about myself. Is there anything else that is truly my own that I could narrate? And into my mind came two images.

The first was that of the pendulum, which I had seen for the first time thirty years previously in Paris, and it had made a huge impression on me. I am not saying that I forgot about it over the years. On the contrary, at one point in the sixties I was asked by a film-director friend of mine to write a script for a film. I don't want to talk about this, since subsequently it was used to make a terrible film that had nothing to do with my original idea, and luckily I managed to ensure that my name did not appear anywhere on it—not to mention the fact that I was paid just a token fee. But in that script there was a scene that took place in a cavern at the center of which hung a pendulum, and someone was clinging to it as he whirled through the darkness.

The second image that imposed itself on me was that of myself playing a trumpet at a funeral of partisans. A true story, which, besides, I had never stopped telling. Not often, but always in situations of great intimacy: late at night, having the last whiskey in a welcoming bar, or during a walk along the water, when I felt that a woman, either opposite or beside me, was just waiting for a good story in order to say "How wonderful" and take my hand. A true story around which other memories clustered, and a story I found beautiful.

That was it, the pendulum and that story in the cemetery on a sunlit morning. I felt that I could tell a story around those two things. There was just one problem: how to get from the pendulum to the trumpet? The reply to this question took me eight years, and became the novel.

Similarly, with *The Island of the Day Before* I started from two very strong images that had surfaced in instant reply to the question: if I were to write a third novel, what could it be about? I've spoken too much about monasteries and museums, I said to myself, too much, that is, about places of culture: I should try to write about nature. Nature and nothing else. And how would I be forced to see nature and nothing else? By placing a shipwrecked man on a deserted island.

Then, at the same time, but for totally independent reasons, I bought one of those world-time watches, where a middle ring rotates in the opposite direction to the hands in order to make local time line up with a series of places written on the outer ring. These kinds of watches have a sign indicating the international dateline. That this line exists, we all know, if for no other reason than having read *Around the World in Eighty Days*, but it is not something we think about every day. This provided a flash of inspiration: my man had to be west of that line and see an island to the east, an island distant in both space and time. It was a short step from here to deciding that he must actually be not on the island but opposite it.

At the outset, since my watch showed, at this fated point, the Aleutian Islands, I could see no good reason for placing someone there to do something. Where was he? Stuck on an oil-rig platform? Moreover, as I will make clear shortly, I only write about places I have been to, and the idea of going to such cold places, looking for an oil-rig platform, did not exactly fascinate me.

Then, as I continued to leaf through the atlas, I discovered that the line also passed through the Fijian archipelago. Fiji, Samoa, the Solomon Islands . . . At this point other memories intervened, other trails opened up. I read a few things, and then I was in the middle of the seventeenth century, the century when exploration voyages to the Pacific began to proliferate. This stirred the memory of many aspects of my old research on baroque culture. That then led to the idea that the man could be shipwrecked on a deserted ship, a kind of ghost ship . . . And off I went. By that stage, I would say, the novel could walk on its own two feet.

FIRST OF ALL, CONSTRUCT A WORLD

But *where* does a novel walk to? Here is the second problem that I consider fundamental for a poetics of narrative. When interviewers ask me, "How did you write your novel?" I usually cut them short and reply: "From left to right." But here I have enough space for a more complex reply.

The fact is that I believe (or at least I now understand better, after four attempts at fiction) that a novel is not just a linguistic phenomenon. A novel (like the narratives we construct every day, explaining why we arrived late that morning, or how we got rid of someone annoying) uses a plane of expression (words that are very difficult to translate into poetry because what also counts there is their sound) to convey a plane of content, namely, the narrated facts. But on the level of content itself we can identify two more sides, story and plot.

The story of Little Red Riding-Hood is a pure sequence of actions that are chronologically ordered: the mother sends the little girl into the woods, the girl meets the wolf, the wolf goes to wait for her at her grandmother's house, eats the grandmother, dresses up as her, etc. The plot can organize these elements differently: for instance, the story could begin with the girl seeing the grandmother, being astonished at how she looks, and then go back to the moment she left home; or with the child returning home safely, thanking the woodsman, and telling her mother the preceding phases of the story. . . .

The tale of Little Red Riding-Hood is so centered on its story (and, through it, on the plot) that it can be rendered in satisfying terms in any discourse, that is to say, using any form of representation: through cinematic images, or in French, German, or in comic strips (all of which has happened).

I have considered the relationships between expression and content in the contrast between prose and poetry on several occasions. Why in the Italian nursery rhyme did *"la vispa Teresa avea tra l'erbetta / al volo sorpresa gentil farfalletta"* (sparky Theresa catch amid the grass / a gentle little butterfly)? Why did she not catch it in a bush, or among climbing flowers, where it would have found it easier to suck the pollen that inebriates it? Naturally it is because *"erbetta"* (grass) rhymes with *"farfalletta"* (butterfly), whereas *"cespuglio"* (bush) would have rhymed with *"guazzabuglio"* (a mess). This is not a game. Let us leave sprightly Theresa and move to Montale: *"Spesso il male di vivere ho incontrato: / era il rivo strozzato che gorgoglia, / era l'incartocciarsi della foglia / riarsa, era il cavallo stramazzzato . . ."* (I have often met the evil of living: / it was the strangled stream gurgling, / it was the crumpling of a leaf / totally parched, it was the horse that had collapsed to the ground. . .). Why among all the symbols or epiphanies of the ills of living has the poet identified the leaf totally parched, and not some other phenomenon of withering and death? Why the strangled stream "gurgling"? Or perhaps the stream gurgles ("*gorgoglia*"), and it is a stream precisely because it had to prepare for the appearance of that leaf ("*foglia*")? In any case, the need for that rhyme encouraged the splendid enjambment of "*riarsa*" (totally parched), which prolongs onto the next line the agony of a life that is already vegetal and which is now gasping out its last breath in a final spasm that pulverizes it.

For if (and here we really are playing, luckily for the history of poetry) a stream that "*borbotta*" (murmurs) had come along first, then the ills of life would have had to be revealed in the darkness and stench of a "*grotta*" (cave).

On the other hand, although Verga's novel begins with *"Un tempo i Malavoglia erano stati numerosi come i sassi della strada vecchia di Trezza . . ."* (At one stage the Malavoglia had been as numerous as the stones on the old road to Trezza . . .) and *"ce n'erano persino ad Ognina, ad Aci Castello"* (there were even some at Ognina and Aci Castello), he certainly could have chosen some other name for his town or village (and perhaps he might have liked Montepulciano or Viserba), but his choice was limited by the decision to make his story happen in Sicily, and even the simile of the stones was determined by the nature of that place, which did not allow stretches of pastoral, almost Irish, *"erbetta."*

Thus in poetry it is the choice of expression that determines the content, whereas in prose it is the opposite; it is the world the author chooses, the events that happen in it, that dictate its rhythm, style, and even verbal choices.

However, it would be a mistake to say that in poetry the content (and along with it the relationship between story and plot) is irrelevant. To give just one example, in Leopardi's *"A Silvia"* there is a story (there was a young girl just like that, the poet was in love with her, she died, the poet remembers her), and there is a plot (the poet appears first, when the girl is now dead, and brings her alive again in his memory). It is not enough to say that in a translation of this poem the change of expression means giving up on so many phonic and symbolic values (the play on "Silvia" and "*salivi*" [you were crossing]), on rhyme and meter. The fact is that no adequate translation would fail to respect both story and plot. It would be the translation of another poem.

This may seem a banal observation, but even in a poetic text the author is speaking to us about a world (there are two houses, one opposite the other, there is a young girl *"all'opre femminili intenta"* [busy with her girl's work]). All the more reason then that this should happen in narrative. Manzoni writes quite well (we might say), but what would his novel be if it did not have the Lombardy of the seventeenth century, Lake Como, two young lovers from a humble social background, an arrogant local aristocrat, and a cowardly curate? What would the *Promessi sposi* (*The Betrothed*) be if it were set in Naples while Eleonora Pimentel Fonseca was being hanged? Come on.

This is why, when I wrote *The Name of the Rose,* I spent a full year, if I remember correctly, without writing a line (and for *Foucault's Pendulum* I spent at least two, and the same for *The Island of the Day Before*). Instead I read, did drawings and diagrams, invented a world. This world had to be as precise as possible, so that I could move around in it with total confidence. For *The Name of the Rose* I drew hundreds of labyrinths and plans of abbeys, basing mine on other drawings and on places I visited, because I needed everything to work well, I needed to know how long it would take two characters in conversation to go from one place to another. And this also dictated the length of the dialogues.

If in a novel I had to write "while the train stopped at Modena station, he quickly got out and bought the newspaper," I could not do so unless I had been to Modena and had checked whether the train stops there long enough, and how far the newsstand is from the platform (and this would be true even if the train had to stop at Innisfree). All this may have little to do with the development of the story (I imagine), but if I did not do this, I could not tell the tale.

In *Foucault's Pendulum* I say that the two publishing houses of Manuzio and Garamond are in two different but adjoining buildings, between which a passage had been built, with a frosted-glass door and three steps. I spent a long time drawing several plans and working out how a passage could be built between the two buildings, and whether there had to be a difference of level between them. The reader takes those three steps without realizing it (I believe), but for me they were crucial.

Sometimes I have wondered whether it was necessary to design my world with such precision, seeing that those details were not prominent in the tale. But it was certainly useful for me in gaining confidence with that environment. Moreover, I have been told that if in one of Luchino Visconti's films two characters had to talk about a box full of jewels, even though the box was never opened, the director would insist that there were real jewels in it, otherwise the characters would not have been credible—that is to say, the actors would have performed with less conviction.

So for *The Name of the Rose* I drew all the monks of the abbey. I drew almost all of them (though not every single one) with a beard, even though I was not at all sure that the Benedictines wore beards at that time—and this was later a scholarly problem that Jean-Jacques Annaud, when he made the film, had to solve with the help of his learned consultants. It is worth noting that in the novel it is never said whether they were bearded or not. But I needed to recognize my characters as I was making them speak or act, otherwise I would not have known what to make them say.

For *Foucault's Pendulum* I spent evening after evening, right through to closing time, in the Conservatoire des Arts et Métiers, where some of the main events of the story took place. In order to write of the Templars I went to visit the Forêt d'Orient in France, where there are traces of their commanderies (which are referred to in the novel in a few vague allusions). To describe Casaubon's night walk through Paris, from the Conservatoire to Place des Vosges and then to the Eiffel Tower, I spent various nights between 2 A.M. and 3 A.M. walking, dictating into a pocket tape recorder everything I could see, so as not to get the street names and intersections wrong. For *The Island of the Day Before* I naturally went to the South Seas, to the precise geographical location where the book is set, to see the color of the sea, the sky, the fishes, and the corals—and at various hours of the day. But I also worked for two or three years on drawings and small models of ships of the period, to find out how big a cabin or cubbyhole was, and how one could move from one to the other.

When a foreign publisher asked me recently if it was not worthwhile including a plan of the ship with the novel, as had been done for all editions of *The Name of the Rose* with the plan of the abbey, I threatened to call a lawyer. In *The Name of the Rose* I wanted the reader to understand perfectly what the place was like, but in *The Island* I wanted the reader to be confused, and not be able to find his bearings in the little labyrinth of that ship, which held surprise after surprise in store. But to be able to talk about a dark, uncertain environment, experienced amid dreams, waking, and alcoholic stimulation, to confuse the reader's ideas, I needed my own ideas to be very clear, and to write constantly referring to a ship's structure that was calculated down to the last millimeter.

FROM THE WORLD TO THE STYLE

Once this world has been designed, the words will follow, and they will be (if all goes well) those that that world and all the events that take place in it require. For this reason the style in *The Name of the Rose* is—throughout—that of the medieval chronicler, precise, faithful, naive, and amazed, flat when necessary (a humble fourteenth-century monk does not write like

Gadda, nor remember things like Proust). In *Foucault's Pendulum,* on the other hand, a plurality of languages had to come into play: Aglié's educated and archaizing language, Ardenti's Pseudo-Dannunzian, the disenchanted and ironically literary language of Belbo's secret files, which is both deliberate and tortuous, Garamond's mercantile kitsch style, and the ribald dialogues of the three editors during their irresponsible fantasies, who are able to mix erudite references with double entendres of dubious taste. But what Maria Corti defined as "leaps of register"* (and I am grateful to her for pointing this out) did not depend on a simple decision about style: they were determined by the nature of the world in which the events took place, which was culturally uneven.

Then for *The Island of the Day Before* it was the very nature of the world it took off from that determined not just the style but the very structure of dialogue and the constant conflict between narrator and character, with the subsequent participation of the reader who is continually appealed to as a witness and accomplice in that conflict. In fact, in *Foucault's Pendulum* the story takes place in our time, so there was no problem of recovering a language that was no longer used. In *The Name of the Rose* the story is set in fairly remote centuries, but at a time when people spoke a different language, the ecclesiastical Latin that appears so often (according to some, too often) in the book to remind us that the story took place in a distant time. For this reason the stylistic model was indirectly the Latin of the chroniclers of the time, but directly it was the modern translations that are commonly read (and in any case I had taken the precaution of warning the reader that I was transcribing from a nineteenth-century translation of a medieval chronicle). In *The Island,* however, my character could not but talk in a baroque way, though I myself could not do so, except by parodying the manuscript that Manzoni

---

*Maria Corti, "I giochi del Piano," in *L'Indice dei Libri del Mese* 10 (1988), 14–15.

rejects at the beginning of his transcription of it in *The Betrothed*. So then I had to have a narrator who at times gets irritated with the verbal excesses of his character, at times indulges in them himself, and at times tempers them with appeals to the reader.

Thus three different worlds imposed three different *"exercices de style"* on me, which then, in the course of writing, became three ways of thinking and seeing, and I was almost led to translate my own daily experiences at that time into those terms.

BAUDOLINO THE EXCEPTION

Up to this point I have said that (i) one starts with a seminal idea, and that (ii) the construction of the narrative world determines the style. My latest experience in fiction, *Baudolino,* seems to contradict these two principles. As for the seminal idea, for at least two years I had many, and if there are too many seminal ideas it is a sign that they are not seminal. In fact, each one of them gave rise not to the general structure of the book but only to situations that were limited to just a few chapters.

I won't say what my first idea was, because I abandoned it— for a variety of reasons, but first and foremost because I was unable to develop it—and perhaps I will keep it in reserve, who knows, for a fifth novel. This idea was accompanied by a secondary idea, which can be connected in a banal way with the topos of a murder in a closed room, and as you will see if you read the novel, I took up the topos only in the chapter on Frederick's death.

The second idea was that the final scene should take place among the mummified corpses in the Capuchin church in Palermo (in fact, I had been there several times and had collected many photographs of the place and of the individual mummies). Whoever has read the book knows that this idea is exploited in the final confrontation between Baudolino and the Poet, but in the economy of the novel it has only a marginal, or, rather, purely scene-setting, function.

The third was that the novel was to be about a group of characters who made forgeries. I had dealt with the semiotics of the fake on several occasions, of course.* Initially the characters were to have been contemporaries who decided to found a daily paper and who experimented, in a series of dummy numbers, with how they could create scoops. In fact, I thought of entitling the novel *Numero Zero* (*Dummy Run*). But even then there was something that did not convince me, and I was afraid I would find myself dealing with the same set of characters as in *Foucault's Pendulum*.

Until I thought of what was one of the most successful fakes of Western history, namely, the Letter of Prester John. This idea fructified a series of memories and reading experiences. In 1960 I edited the Italian edition (*Le terre leggendarie*) of *Lands Beyond* by Ley and Sprague du Camp for Bompiani. There was a chapter on Prester John's kingdom and another on the lost tribes of Israel. On the cover they had put a skiapod, or shadow-footed monster (from a fifteenth-century engraving, I think, with fake coloring and done with a stencil). Years later I bought a colored map from an Ortelius atlas that had been cut up, the very map representing the lands of Prester John, and I hung it in my study. In the 1980s I read various versions of the letter.[†] In short, Prester John had always intrigued me, and I was attracted by the idea of making the monsters that populated his Kingdom come alive again, as well as those spoken of in the various Alexander Romances, Mandeville's travels, and a whole series of bestiaries. And finally it was a good opportunity to return to my beloved Middle Ages. So my seminal idea was that of Prester John. But I had not started with this idea, I had simply arrived at it.

---

*See "Fakes and Forgeries," in *The Limits of Interpretation* (Bloomington: Indiana University Press, 1990), 174–202. See also in this volume my inaugural lecture on forgeries (pp. 272–301), which perhaps, given its date (1994), constitutes the first nucleus of *Baudolino*.

[†]Especially Gioia Zaganelli, ed., *La lettera del Prete Gianni* (Parma: Pratiche, 1990).

Perhaps all this would not have been enough for me had the letter not been attributed (it is one possible hypothesis) to the Imperial Chancery of Frederick Barbarossa. Now Frederick Barbarossa was another magical name for me, because I was born in Alessandria, the city that was founded in order to oppose the emperor. That led to a series of instinctive decisions, like a chain reaction: to discover a Frederick that went beyond the traditional clichés, seen by a son rather than by his enemies and courtiers (and off I went with further reading on Barbarossa), to tell the origins of my city and its legends, including that of Gagliaudo and his cow. Years earlier I had written an essay on the foundation and history of Alessandria (entitled, as it happens, "The Miracle of San Baudolino"),* and from there came the idea to have this history lived through by a character called after the patron saint of the city, Baudolino, to make Baudolino the son of Gagliaudo, and to give the story a popular, picaresque thrust—thus creating a sort of counterpoint to *The Name of the Rose*, since the latter was a story of intellectuals talking in the high style, whereas this was a tale about the people and military men who were on the whole rather crude, talking in a style that was almost like dialect.

But here too, what was I to do? Make Baudolino talk in his Po Valley twelfth-century pseudodialect, when we have very few vernacular documents from that period, and none of them from the Piedmont area? Make a narrator talk, and have his modern style spoil Baudolino's spontaneity? However, suddenly at this point another obsession came to my rescue, one that had been going through my head for some time, without my ever thinking that it would be of use to me on that occasion: narrate a story set in Byzantium. Why? Because I knew very little about Byzantine civilization, and I had never been to Constantinople. To many

---

*In *How to Travel with a Salmon and Other Essays,* trans. William Weaver (New York: Harcourt Brace, 1994), 234–278.

this might seem a rather weak motive for deciding to narrate something that happened in Constantinople, all the more so since Constantinople had only a tangential link with Frederick Barbarossa's story. But sometimes one decides to tell a story only to get to know it better.

No sooner said than done. Off I went to Constantinople. I read many things about ancient Byzantium, mastered its topography, and came across Nicetas Choniates and his *Chronicle*. I had found the key, the way to articulate the "voices" of my story: an almost transparent narrator recounts the discussion between Nicetas and Baudolino, alternating Nicetas's learned, high-flown reflections with Baudolino's picaresque tales, without Nicetas, or the reader, ever being able to tell if and when Baudolino is lying, the only fixed point being that he maintains he is a liar (the paradox of the liar and the Cretan Epimenides).

I had this play of "voices," but not Baudolino's voice. Here I contradicted the second of my two principles. When I was still reading the chronicles of the Crusaders' capture of Constantinople (and I decided that I would have to narrate the story of that event which already appears so novelistic in the texts of Villehardouin, Robert de Clary, and Nicetas), just to pass the time I wrote out in pen, in the country, a sort of diary by Baudolino, in a hypothetical twelfth-century Po Valley pidgin, which then became the opening of the novel. It is true that I rewrote those pages several times in subsequent years, after consulting historical and dialect dictionaries, and all the documents I could lay my hands on, but already in that first draft, through its linguistic style, it became clear to me how Baudolino would think and speak. Thus, in the end, Baudolino's language was not born from the construction of a world, but a world was created from the stimulus of that language.

I do not know how to solve this dilemma in theoretical terms. All I can do is quote Walt Whitman: "Do I contradict myself?

Very well then I contradict myself." Except that this use of dialect probably took me back to my childhood and my native area, and therefore to a preconstructed world, at least in memory.

CONSTRAINTS, AND TIME

And yet (world versus language or language versus world) it is not that you spend two or three years constructing a world as though that world existed on its own, independently of the story you want to set in it. This "cosmogonical" phase goes hand in hand with (and in a way that I really could not reduce to a formula or program) a hypothesis about the supporting structure of the novel—and of the world you are creating. This structure consists essentially of constraints and temporal rhythms.

Constraints are fundamental in every artistic operation. A painter who decides to use oil rather than tempera, or a canvas rather than a wall, is choosing a constraint; likewise the composer who opts for one tonality at the outset (he may then modulate it all he likes, but he has to return to that opening tonality), and the poet who builds what is a cage of rhyming couplets or of hendecasyllables. And do not think that avant-garde painters, composers, and poets—who seem to avoid *those* constraints—do not construct others. They do, but you may not be obliged to notice them.

Choosing the seven trumpets of the Apocalypse as a scheme for the succession of events can be a constraint. But also setting the story at a precise date: you can make some things happen then, but not others. It can be a constraint deciding that, to indulge the magic obsessions of your characters, the number of chapters in *Foucault's Pendulum* has to be 120, not one more or one less, and it has to be divided into ten parts, like the Sephiroth in the Kabbalah.

Constraints then gradually determine a temporal sequence. In *The Name of the Rose,* if the story had to follow a sequence based on the Apocalypse, plot time could coincide (except for substantial digressions) with the time of the story: the story begins with the arrival of William and Adso at the abbey, and ends with their departure. Easy (and easy to read).

With *Foucault's Pendulum* the very pendular movement of the eponymous device forced me to adopt a different temporal structure. Casaubon arrives at the Conservatoire one evening, hides there, and conjures up past events, then the story returns to its starting point, etc. If for *The Name of the Rose* I had gradually built up a kind of sequential timetable or calendar, trying to work out what was to happen each day for a week, for *Foucault's Pendulum* I created a sort of serpentine structure, which registered the shifts back to the past and the anticipations of the future. Like a measuring scale, or orthogonal Cartesian axes. The character is here now, but remembers what happened at time X in the past.

The beauty is that these schemes are rigid when you think of them at the time, but I have drawers full of schemes I constantly redid as the novel progressed. I mean, the beauty of the story is that you have to create constraints, but you must feel free to change them in the course of writing. Except that at that point you have to change everything and start again from scratch.

Besides, one of the constraints in the *Pendulum* was that the characters had to have lived through 1968, but since Belbo then writes his files on computer—which also plays a formal role in the whole story, since it in part inspires its aleatory and combinatory nature—the final events absolutely had to take place between 1983 and 1984 and not before. The reason is very simple: the first personal computers with word-processing programs went on sale in Italy in 1983 (or perhaps 1982). And this is worth bearing in mind by all those who try to explain the success of *The Name of the Rose* by insisting that it was written by computer. In 1978–79 you could scarcely find in America those cheap little computers called Tandy, and no one would ever have dared write more than one letter on them.

In order to make all that time elapse from 1968 to 1983, I was forced to send Casaubon somewhere else. Where? Memories of some magic rituals I had witnessed there led me to Brazil (there I knew what I was talking about and what the shape of that world was). And this was the reason and the auspicious origin of what many found too long a digression, and which for me (and for some benevolent readers) was essential, because it allowed me to make happen in Brazil to Amparo, in shortened form, what would happen to the other characters in the course of the book. If IBM, Apple, or Olivetti had started selling word processors six or seven years earlier, my novel would have been different; there would have been no Brazil, to the relief of many superficial readers, but from my point of view it would have been a great loss.

The Island of the Day Before was based on a series of historical constraints and rigid novelistic restrictions. The historical constraints evolved from the fact that I needed Roberto to participate as a young man in the siege of Casale, to be there at Richelieu's death, and then to arrive at his island after December 1642, but not later than 1643, the year in which Tasman went there, even though this was some months earlier than the time in which my story was set. But I could set the story only between July and August because that was the period when I saw the Fiji islands, and a ship took several months to get there: this explains the mischievous novelistic insinuations that I made in the final chapter, to persuade myself and the reader that perhaps Tasman had come back later to that archipelago without saying anything to anybody. Here one sees the heuristic usefulness of constraints that force you to invent silences, conspiracies, ambiguities.

You will ask me: why all these constraints? Was it really necessary for Roberto to be present at Richelieu's death? Not at all. But it was necessary for me to set myself constraints. Otherwise the story could not have gone along under its own steam.

As for the novelistic constraints, Roberto had to be on the ship, not be able to get off it, and try in vain to learn to swim in order to reach the island. In the meantime, as he reflected on life and death, he would have to invent bit by bit, and then reject, through lack of intelligence, all the philosophical thought of that century. For the benevolent reader this would be more than just a constraint, placed just to receive stimuli: it would be the very essence of Desire. I would be the last to deny it. But since I am speaking about *how* I wrote and not *what* the reader could or should find in what I wrote (because, to say the latter, either the novel is enough on its own, or I have been wasting my time writing it and you reading it—which is not impossible), what I mean to say is that, on the one hand, it is the constraint that allows the novel to develop according to a particular Sense, and on the other it is the still-unclear idea of this Sense that suggests the constraints. Since one of these cannot function without the other, we talk of constraints rather than Sense, which is not something an author should pronounce on a posteriori.

A parenthesis. A rude hack—who wanted to mock Eco the novelist in order to punish Eco the politically committed polemicist—defined the novel as one long act of masturbation. In his crudeness, which was also lexical, the unwitting hack was dead right: the condition of a shipwreck separated forever from the object of desire is certainly, and by definition, onanistic. Except that the scribbler I am talking of, anchored in his own obtuse carnality, saw manna falling from heaven and read it as excreta from foul birds of prey. Nor did he catch the nature of "something mental"—and in the end metaphysical—in that solitary virtue, in that attempt to generate Being by spilling in disordered fashion the seed of a soul exasperated by solitude, until it reaches the point of vision.

But let us get back to the point. The point is that Roberto could not leave the ship (except at the end, but for uncertain objectives and outcomes). Consequently everything that had to be narrated but that did not happen on the ship had to come about via memory, unless the plot was to be flattened into just being the story, and end up relating in every detail how a young man, who went to Paris after his adventures at Casale, found himself on a ship, etc. Try if you like, but I can assure you that however vain my labors have been, yours will be even more so.

This imposed on me not a serpentine temporal sequence, as in the *Pendulum,* but more one step forward and three back, one step forward and two back, one step forward and one back. Roberto remembers something, and meanwhile something happens on the ship. Something happens on the ship, and Roberto remembers something. Gradually, as Roberto's memories move from 1630 to 1643, events on the ship happen hour by hour. All this up to the arrival of Father Caspar. At that point the story stops, as it were, in the present, for some time. Then Father Caspar disappears in the sea, and Roberto is on his own again.

What was I to make him do? The novelistic constraints meant I had to make him try various ways of getting ashore. But these had to be slow, recorded day after day, repetitive and monotonous. In the end I still had to write a novel, whose aim—let it be said in the face of every aesthete, and in full respect for the laws of the genre as they have come down to us from the Hellenistic romance to our own time, not to mention Aristotle's *Poetics*—had to be that of providing narrative pleasure.

Fortunately I was the victim of another constraint. To conform to the spirit of the seventeenth-century novel, I had to introduce a Double, and I really did not know what to do with him. Suddenly this Double came good: while he tries to reach the island, learning each day to swim better (but never well enough), Roberto imagines the novel about his Double, and thus the one-step-forward-three-back structure could be reproduced, since Roberto cannot reach the island but makes his Double reach it, making him start from the point where he himself started. How nice to see a novel writing itself! I did not know where I would get to, because the novelistic constraint dictated that Roberto should not get anywhere. The novel ends because it heads directly toward its conclusion on its own. This is what I would like my Model Reader to notice. That the novel writes itself, since that is how it happened, and how it always happens, really.

Speaking of constraints, the finale of *Baudolino* had to take place in 1204, because I wanted to narrate the conquest of Constantinople. But Baudolino had to be born around the middle of the century (I fixed on 1142 as a point of reference, so as to have my character at the age of reason and consent at the time of many events I wanted to relate). The first mention of Prester John's letter is around 1165, and I already make it circulate a few years later, but why then does Baudolino, after persuading Frederick to give him permission, not set off immediately for Prester John's Kingdom? Because I had to have him coming back from the Kingdom only in 1204, so he could tell the tale to Nicetas during the burning of Constantinople. And what did I have to make Baudolino do in that interval of almost four decades? It was a bit like the business of the computer in *Foucault's Pendulum*.

I make him do many things, and I constantly make him delay his departure. At the time it seemed like a waste to me, it was like inserting a series of temporal stopgaps into the story in order to arrive finally at that damned date of 1204. And yet, when you look at it closely (and I hope, or rather I know, that many readers did realize this), I created the Spasm of Desire (or, rather, the novel created it without my realizing it there and then). Baudolino wants the Kingdom but constantly has to postpone his search. Thus Prester John's Kingdom grows in Baudolino's desire, and in the reader's eyes (I hope). Once more the advantages of constraints.

How I write

At this point one can understand how useless are questions like "Do you begin with notes, immediately write the first or last chapter, write with pen, pencil, typewriter, or computer?" If one has to construct a world, day by day, and try out endless temporal structures, if the actions the characters perform and have to perform according to the logic of common sense or of narrative convention (or against narrative convention) have to fit with the logic of the constraints (involving constant rethinks, cancellations, and rewrites), there is no uniform way of writing a novel.

At least for me. I know of writers who wake up at 8:00 A.M., work at their keyboard from 8:30 to 12:00 (*"nulla dies sine linea; no day without at least a line"*), and then stop and go out and enjoy themselves until evening. Not me. First of all, when I write a novel, the act of writing comes later. First I read, make notes, draw portraits of the characters, maps of the places, and plans for the time sequences. And these are done with a felt pen, or computer, depending on when and where one does this, or on the kind of narrative idea or detail one wants to record: on the back of a train ticket, if the idea comes to you on a train, in a notebook, on an index card, using ballpoint, tape recorder, or blackberry juice if really necessary.

Then what happens is that I chuck out, tear up, tear into pieces, forget things in different places, but I have boxes full of notebooks, with blocks of pages in different colors, bits of card, even sheets of foolscap. And this chaotic variety of props helps my memory, because I remember that I jotted down that particular note on the letterhead paper of a London hotel, and the first page of that chapter was scribbled down in my study, on an index card with pale blue lines, and using a Mont Blanc pen, whereas the following chapter was initially written down in the country, on the back of a recycled piece of draft paper.

I do not have any special method, days, hours, or seasons. But between the second and third novels I established a habit. I would collect ideas, write notes, make provisional drafts wherever I was, but then, when I could spend at least a week in my house in the country, that was where I would type out the chapters on the computer. When I left, I printed them out, corrected them, and left them to mature in a drawer, until the next time I returned to the country. The definitive versions of my first three novels were done there, usually in two or three weeks over the Christmas holidays. The result was that I started to cultivate a superstition (I who am the least superstitious person in the world: I go under ladders, greet affectionately any black cats crossing my path, and, to punish superstitious students, I always fix my university exams for a Friday, so long as it is a thirteenth): the almost definitive version, apart from minor corrections, had to be completed by 5 January, my birthday. If I was not ready for that year, I would wait for the next year (and once, when I was almost ready in November, I put everything away so I could finish in January).

Here too, *Baudolino* was the exception. Or rather, it was written with the same rhythm, out in the country as usual, but about halfway through the writing, during the Christmas holidays of 1999, I got stuck. I thought it was due to the Millennium Bug. I was on the chapter with Barbarossa's death, and what was to happen in that chapter dictated the final chapters, and the very way in which I would recount the journey toward Prester John's Kingdom. I was blocked for several months, I could not imagine how to get over that hurdle, or around that cape. I could not do it, and I secretly yearned for those chapters (still to be written) that I had been most passionate about right from the start, the encounters with monsters and especially the meeting with Hypatia. I dreamed of being able to start on those chapters, but I did not want to do so until I had solved the problem that was obsessing me.

When I got back to the country, in the summer of 2000, I "rounded the cape" in the middle of June. I had begun to think about the novel in 1995, it had taken me five years to get halfway, and therefore—I said to myself—I still needed five more years to finish.

But obviously I had thought out the second half of the book so intensely in those five years that it had all sorted itself out in my head (or heart, or stomach, I don't know). In short, between mid-June and the beginning of August the book was completed almost on its own, in a spurt (afterward there were a few months of checking and rewriting, but by then it was done, the story was finished). At that point another of my principles crumbled, because even a superstition is also a principle, however irrational it is. I had not finished the book for the 5th of January.

There was something that was not quite right, I thought for a few days. Then, on 8 August my first grandchild was born. It all became clear, for this fourth occasion I had to finish the novel not on the day of my birthday but on *his* birth day. I dedicated the book to him and felt reassured.

The computer and writing

How much has the computer influenced my writing? A huge amount, in my experience, but I don't know how much from the point of view of results.

By the way, seeing that *Foucault's Pendulum* spoke of a computer that created poetry and connected events in an aleatory way, many interviewers wanted me at all costs to confess that the entire novel had been written by giving a program to the computer, which then invented everything. Note that these were all journalists who by now worked in editorial offices where articles are written on computer and then go directly to press—so they knew how much one can expect from this servile machine. But they also knew they were writing for a public that still had a magical idea of what the computer was, and we know that often we write to tell readers not the truth but what they want to hear.

In any case, at a certain point I got annoyed and gave one of them the magic formula:

First of all you need a computer, obviously, which is an intelligent machine that thinks for you—and this would be an advantage for many people. All you need is a program of a few lines, even a child could do it. Then one feeds into the computer the content of a few hundred novels, scientific works, the Bible, the Koran, and many telephone directories (very useful for characters' names). Say, something like 120,000 pages. After this, using another program, you randomize, in other words, you mix all those texts together, making some adjustment, for instance eliminating all the *a*'s. Thus as well as a novel you would have a lipogram. At this point you press "print" and it prints out. Having eliminated all the *a*'s, what comes out is something less than 120,000 pages. After you have read them carefully, several times, underlining the most significant passages, you load them onto an articulated truck and take them to an incinerator. Then you simply sit under a tree, with a piece of charcoal and good-quality drawing paper in hand, and allowing your mind to wander you write down a couple of lines. For instance: "The moon is high in the sky / the wood rustles." Maybe what emerges initially is not a novel but, rather, a Japanese haiku; nevertheless, the important thing is to get started.

No one had the courage to report my secret recipe. But someone said, "one can feel that the novel was written directly on the computer, apart from the scene of the trumpet in the cemetery; that scene is heartfelt, and he must have rewritten it several times, and in pen." I am ashamed to say so, but in this novel that underwent so many phases of drafting, in which the ballpoint, the fountain pen, the felt-tip, and many revisions played a part, the *only* chapter written directly on the computer, and in a spurt, without many corrections, was precisely that trumpet chapter. The reason is quite simple: I had that tale so present in my mind, I had told it to myself or others so many times that by then it was as if it had already been written. I had nothing to add. I moved my hands over the keyboard as if it were a piano on which I was playing a melody I knew by heart, and if there is felicitous writing in that scene, it is due to the fact that it started as a jam session. You play, letting yourself go with the flow, record it, and what's there is there.

In fact, the beauty of the computer is that it encourages spontaneity: you dash down, in a hurry, whatever comes to mind. Meanwhile you know that later you can always correct and vary it.

The use of the computer concerns, in fact, the problem of corrections, and therefore of variants.

The Name of the Rose, in its definitive versions, was written on a typewriter. Then I would correct, retype, sometimes cut and paste, and in the end I gave it all to a typist, and then again I had to correct, replace, and cut and paste. With the typewriter you can correct only up to a certain point. Then you get tired of retyping, cutting, pasting, and then having it retyped again. The rest of it you correct at proof stage, and off it goes.

With the use of the computer (*Foucault's Pendulum* was written in Wordstar 2000, *The Island of the Day Before* in Word5, *Baudolino* in Winword in its various versions over the years), things change. You are tempted to correct ad infinitum. You write, then print out, and you reread. You correct. Then you retype according to your corrections and printouts. I have kept the various drafts (with the odd gap). But it would be a mistake to think that a fanatic of textual variants could ever reconstruct your process of writing. In fact, you write (on the computer), print out, correct (by hand), and make the corrections on the computer, but as you do so you choose other variants, in other words you do not rewrite exactly what you have corrected by hand. The critic who studies variants would find further variants between your final correction in ink on the printout and the new version produced by the printer. If you really wanted to encourage pointless theses, you have all of posterity at your disposal. The fact is that the existence of the computer means that the very logic of variants has changed. They are neither a rethinking nor your final choice. Since you know that your choice can be changed at any time, you make many changes, and often you go back to your original option.

I really do believe that the existence of electronic means of writing will profoundly alter criticism of variants, with all due respect to the spirit of Contini. I once worked on the variants in Manzoni's *Inni sacri* (*Sacred Hymns*).* At that time the substitution of a word was crucial. Nowadays it is not: tomorrow you can go back to the word you rejected yesterday. At most what will count is the difference between the first handwritten draft and the last one out of the printer. The rest is all coming and going, often dictated by the amount of potassium in your blood.

JOY AND SADNESS

I do not have anything else to say about the way I write my novels. Except that they have to take many years. I do not understand those who write a novel a year; they might be wonderful, and I do admire them, but I don't envy them. The beauty of writing a novel is not the beauty of the live match, it is the beauty of the delayed transmission.

I am always annoyed when I realize that one of my novels is coming to the end, that is to say, that according to its internal logic it is time that it (he/she) stopped, and that I stopped too; when I notice that if I were to go any further it would only make it worse. The beauty, the real joy, is living for six, seven, eight years (ideally forever) in a world that you are creating bit by bit, and which becomes your own.

Sadness begins when the novel is over.

This is the only reason you would instantly want to write another one. But if it is not there waiting for you, it is pointless trying to rush it.

---

*"Il segno della poesia e il segno della prosa," in *Sugli specchi* (Milan: Bompiani, 1985).

The writer and the reader

However, I would not like these last statements to generate automatically another view common to bad writers—namely, that one writes only for oneself. Do not trust those who say so: they are dishonest and lying narcissists.

There is only one thing that you write for yourself, and that is a shopping list. It helps to remember what you have to buy, and when you have bought everything you can destroy it, because it is no use to anyone else. Every other thing that you write, you write to say something to someone.

I have often asked myself: would I still write today if they told me that tomorrow a cosmic catastrophe would destroy the universe, so that no one could read tomorrow what I wrote today?

My first instinct is to reply no. Why write if no one will read me? My second instinct is to say yes, but only because I cherish the desperate hope that, amid the galactic catastrophe, some star might survive, and in the future someone might decipher my signs. In that case writing, even on the eve of the Apocalypse, would still make sense.

One writes only for a reader. Whoever says he writes only for himself is not necessarily lying. It is just that he is frighteningly atheistic. Even from a rigorously secular point of view.

Unhappy and desperate the writer who cannot address a future reader.

A first version of this piece was written for Maria Teresa Serafini, ed., *Come si scrive un romanzo* (Milan: Strumenti Bompiani, 1996). The editor had asked a number of writers a series of questions, which correspond to the sections of this essay. In the meantime I also published my fourth novel, *Baudolino,* and consequently I have inserted into the present version some passages dedicated to this, my latest experience with writing fiction.

The translator is very grateful, for assistance with particular problems, to Tim Farrant, Ann Jefferson, Cathy McLaughlin, Giuseppe Stellardi.